Batchography

The Art of Batch Files Programming

Batchography

The Art of Batch Files Programming

PassingTheKnowledge series

By Elias Bachaalany

PassingTheKnowledge Publishing

First Edition: April, 2016
Printed in the United States of America
ISBN: 978-0-692-68131-2

Artwork by WenzCreative.com

About the Author

Elias Bachaalany has been a computer programmer and a software reverse engineer for more than 14 years. Elias is also the co-author of two books published by Wiley: "Practical Reverse engineering" and "The Antivirus Hacker's Handbook".

Elias worked with various technologies and programming languages such as: web programming, database programming, Windows device drivers programing (boot loaders and minimal operating systems), writing .NET and managed code, writing scripts, assessing software protections, and writing reverse engineering and desktop security tools. Elias has also presented twice (in 2012 and 2013) at the reverse engineering conference (REcon) in Montreal.

In his free time, Elias enjoys writing, learning new things, maintaining his personal blog, reading about metaphysics, mysticism and self-improvement.

May all beings be well and safe, may they be at ease.
Whatever living beings there may be, whether moving or standing still,
without exception, whether large, great, middling, or small, whether tiny or substantial,
Whether seen or unseen, whether living near or far,
Born or unborn; may all beings be happy.
Let none deceive or despise another anywhere. Let none wish harm to another, in anger or in hate.

–Metta Prayer

Table of Contents

Acknowledgement

This book was a result of an idea and an exercise in patience, hard work and self-publishing. That idea would have not been possible without the contribution, help and influence of my family and friends.

Thank you to the following individuals who without their contributions and support this book could not have been written:

My dad Nassif Bachaalany: thanks for buying me my first computer when computers were costing an arm and a leg back in 1993, in Lebanon. Thanks for being an example of patience and hard work.

My dear friend Camil Shamoun: thank you for always giving me an advice when I needed one and for encouraging me to follow my dreams.

To all others who were a source of inspiration, I say thank you to: Roland S., Swamy S.N, Bruce Dang, Sydney Argenta, Carol Long, Bill Pollock, Thomas K, Tommy T, and all the generous people on the Internet who constantly contribute knowledge and help others.

To all the pirates who do what they are best at: pirate the creative work of others. Earn the knowledge, don't steal it.

Introduction

This book is part of the *PassingTheKnowledge Series* educational books. These series are aimed at teaching in an efficient and practical manner. I personally do not believe that a lot is better therefore, in this book I have carefully chosen the material so that your learning experience will be very enjoyable.

This Batch file programming book is a result of extensive research and efforts put together to unravel the undocumented or sparsely documented Batch file programming syntax and commands usage. Even if you have programmed using the Batch files scripting language before, you might be surprised to find new tricks that you never had the chance to encounter before.

I wrote my first program as a Batch file script when I was 13 years old while living in Beirut, Lebanon. Back then, I had no Internet access, minimal to non-existent English language knowledge and no understanding about what a computer program is. I learned how to write Batch file scripts by imitating other scripts found on my hard drive. The operating system I was using was MS-DOS 5.0. I am grateful to my dad who taught me how to run my favorite MS-DOS games (Supaplex, Stunts, Soccer Kid, The Incredible Machine, Leisure Suit Larry, Cannon Fodder, etc.) by typing the MS-DOS commands in a specific sequence.

Back then, the Batch files scripting language was also not as advanced as it is today in more modern operating systems. In fact, this book is written with Windows 10 in mind and all the scripts and language features presented therein have been developed and tested to work with Windows 10.

Perhaps you are wondering why I wrote this book? Why Batch files? Is this not an obsolete language? Why not a PowerShell book instead?

Having already co-authored two other successful books with Wiley publishing prior to taking this endeavor, I chose to write this Batch file scripting book as a commemoration to the first programming language I learned. This book is also my first self-published book, which is a new learning experience for me. This is also an opportunity to jump-start the *PassingTheKnowledge* books series.

I also wrote this book because I feel there is a need for it. Batch files scripting is far from obsolete and the need for this skill will stay around as long as the command interpreter (**`CMD.exe`**) still ships with MS Windows. As you shall discover in this book, Batch file scripts are simple to write and everybody can pick up the language very fast. On the other hand, the

PowerShell scripting language is not very simple, has a steep learning curve and requires knowledge (to some extent) of the .NET Framework. One can say the same about the learning curve when talking about other scripting languages such as Python, Perl, Bash under Cygwin or the Linux Subsystem in MS Windows 10.

In short: Batch file scripting is rewarding, fun, very useful and easy to master.

I hope this book will boost your knowledge and help you with your career as you solve automation problems easier with the Batch files scripting language.

What are Batch files?

Batch files are text files that contain a set of commands that get executed by the command interpreter. By default, the interpreter is the **CMD.EXE** program that ships with Windows XP and Windows Server 2000 and up.

If you have used a UNIX based operating system before, then you can compare Batch files to Bash scripts, only that the latter are definitely much more powerful.

Batch files have the ".BAT" or ".CMD" extensions and contains a set of commands that you would normally execute individually from the command prompt. As an example, imagine that you normally type the following commands on a daily basis to customize your command prompt window:

```
C:\>set language=C++
C:\>title Game Programming Environment
C:\>cd c:\projects\mygames\
```

To automate the commands above, you can paste them in a text file, save it with the ".BAT" (or ".CMD") extension and then run it to achieve the same results.

Batch files are used a lot in build systems, with scheduled tasks, for writing home-made backup/restore/sync scripts, or to automate repetitive tasks.

To give you a real life example, the *Visual Studio IDE (integrated development environment)* from Microsoft comes with a Batch file script called *vcvars.bat* that prepares the build environment for a given platform (X86, AMD64 or ARM) and adjusts the path, the C++ headers include path, the linker's libraries path, etc.

Who is this book for?

This book is for beginner to advanced computer users. It is assumed that you have basic understanding of the following:

- The command prompt.
- Files and folders concepts.
- Some knowledge of the built-in command line utilities.
- Minimal programming language concepts such as: conditional statements and repetition control structures.

If you don't have any programming experience, then don't worry because I will be covering basic concepts as the need arises. I will then slowly transition to more advanced Batch file scripting concepts to ensure that you get the most of this scripting language.

Having said that, this book is best suited for the following audience:

- System administrators can use Batch file scripts to automate system configuration commands, install programs, enforce policies, and write deployment scripts, etc.
- Software developers can use Batch file scripts in a build system to prepare the environment, update the build tools chain or do post/pre build operations.
- Power users can use Batch file scripts to automate mundane tasks such as backing up files, running commands or to quickly prototype a simple logic.

After you read Chapter 1, you might be surprised to learn that Batch file scripts are also a good candidate to teach young kids about programming concepts using just the built-in software on your computer: a text editor (like Notepad) and the command interpreter (**`CMD.exe`**).

How to best read this book?

It is advised that you read this book twice because the material is all interconnected and sometimes a concept will be briefly explained before another prerequisite concept is. Due to that intertwining, you might feel that you are missing out. I address this issue by clearly mentioning where to read more about certain topics that are introduced ahead of their times.

In the first reading round of this book, you will get a sense of the material. It is okay if there are concepts that are not very clear as you read the book from beginning to end. The second time you read this book, everything will fall into perspective. Actually, a second time reading is helpful when you're looking up a specific Batch file recipe or how to use a certain syntax.

Conventions used in this book

The keywords or commands will be displayed in bold like this: **ECHO**, **TIMEOUT**, **CD**.

In facsimile, variable names, script names and environment variables will either be enclosed in quotations or displayed using a smaller font and in italic like this: *MyEnvVarName, TheScript.bat,* or like this: "VariableName", "FileName.bat", etc.

Code listings are displayed using the monospace font and indented, like this:

```
ECHO Welcome to the Batch file scripting world!
```

Annotated code listing has a similar style to the regular code listing, except that circled numeric markers are present in the script next to the code lines. These annotations are not part of the script and should be ignored.

The code markers or annotations are used later on when explaining the script code:

```
@echo off
:main
      if exist log.txt del log.txt ①

      pushd compiler ②
      if not exist cl.exe ( ③
            echo The compiler was not found!
            goto :end
      )

      cl.exe hello.c ④

      if %ERRORLEVEL% EQU 0 ( ⑤
            echo Compilation successful!
      ) ELSE (
            echo Compilation failed!
      )

:end
      popd
```

The explanation of the numbered annotations or code markers usually follow the script code. The explanation may be laid out in the form of numbered lists where each numbered item match the code marker number. For example:

1. Check for the existence of the log file and delete it.

2. First remember the current directory, then go to the compiler directory.
3. Check if the compiler executable is found.
4. Etc.

The code annotations/markers may also be explained in free text form and are usually referred to with the term “marker” or “code marker” followed by the circled number.

For example: in the snippet above, the code at marker ① checks if the *log.txt* file exists. At marker ②, the script remembers the current directory before going inside the *compiler* directory. Etc.

Optional parameters for keywords or commands are usually surrounded with the square brackets like this:

```
IF [DEFINED] varName DoSomething
```

Notice how the “**DEFINED**” keyword above is surrounded with the square brackets (“[“ and “]”).

> *Note: It is conventional to use the square brackets to surround optional parameters. Do not include the square brackets when copying the example code from this book.*

Finally, this book exhibits various example scripts and since there is not one single method to solve a particular problem, the methods I use to solve problems are oriented towards illustrating the syntax and exercising the commands that I am explaining throughout the example script in question. Sometimes, I use a longer logic to solve a problem because it makes the script less cryptic and easy to understand. Feel free to adopt my solutions as they are or just re-write the script in a more optimal manner.

What does the book cover?

This book is written in a very structured manner. You won’t have to scavenge and hunt down information from all over the Internet or Web forums. It covers all the important aspects and syntax of the Batch files scripting language. It progresses slowly from introductory topics to more advanced topics. This book aims to be a complete reference for the Batch files scripting language.

Here's a quick rundown of all the chapters in this book:

- Chapter 1 serves as an introduction to the Batch files scripting language. It covers very basic topics such as how to start and customize the command line environment, how to create and run scripts, how to write compound and conditional statements, how to work with labels and comments. It also covers the concept of environment variables and the standard input/output redirection along with various examples explaining what pipes are all about.

- Chapter 2 approaches the Batch files scripting language as if it was a more apt programming or scripting language such as C++ or Python. Conditional statements and repetition control structures are explained in details. This chapter also covers how to do string operations such as sub-string, string search and replace, string tokenization and sorting. It concludes by showing you how to build data structures such as arrays, dictionaries, stacks and sets.

- Chapter 3 presents you with coding conventions, programming techniques, debugging and troubleshooting tips, methods to write Batch file libraries and how to test them. It brings to light various obscure tricks that the two previous chapters did not cover.

- Chapter 4 is full of scripts (also referred to as recipes). Those scripts aim at solving real technical problems that may be encountered by professionals. All the scripts in this chapter are heavily documented. This chapter cements all the things you learned throughout the book by using all the techniques in unison to build useful scripts.

After reading this book, I hope that you feel comfortable writing new scripts or maintaining and updating scripts that were written by your colleagues or peers.

More Batch files scripting material

This book is a result of extensive research and experimentation. Most of the resources I used came from the help and usage information screens of the built-in keywords and commands themselves.

In order to read about a certain keyword or external command's usage information, it is customary that those keywords or commands display a help page when they are invoked with the "/?" switch.

For instance, if you want to learn more about the **`IF`** keyword, then you may type:

```
IF /?
```

Similarly, to learn more about the command interpreter itself, type:

```
cmd /?
```

Or:

```
%COMSPEC% /?
```

In a similar fashion, the usage information of an external command (one that is not built into **`CMD.EXE`**), such as **`FINDSTR.EXE`** can be retrieved like this:

```
C:\>findstr /?
Searches for strings in files.
…
```

If the help information/reference of the Batch keywords or commands were enough or even presented in a structured and progressive manner, then I would have not written this book. For that reason, I had to resort to other online resources to learn more about certain Batch file scripting syntax.

The following sites were very helpful and I encourage you to refer to them as well if you need to:

1. http://ss64.com/nt/ – An A-Z index of the Windows CMD command line.
2. http://www.stackoverflow.com – A community of 4.7 million programmers. Lots of Batch file scripting questions and answers are found there.
3. http://www.dostips.com – "The DOS Batch Guide". This website is very resourceful and contains lots of useful scripts, tutorials and command reference.

You may get all the source code of the scripts used in this book from the PassingTheKnowledge.net website or its GitHub repository at: https://github.com/PassingTheKnowledge.

CHAPTER 1

Batch Files Scripting Language Basics

In this chapter, I will cover the most essential Batch files scripting language syntax so you can better understand the more advanced topics in Chapter 2 and the Batch file scripting recipes in Chapter 4.

The Batch file syntax is very simple yet very powerful for solving basic to intermediate automation tasks.

The Batch file scripting keywords are case insensitive: **`ECHO`**, **`eCHO`**, **`echo`**, or **`Echo`** all mean the same thing. However, just make sure you adopt a single coding style throughout your Batch file script. More ideas and explanation about the style and coding conventions will be covered in Chapter 3.

The external command line tools names are also case insensitive. This is because the file systems (exFAT, NTFS, FAT) on the MS Windows operating system are case insensitive. The same goes for file names and file paths.

In this chapter, I will cover fundamental topics such as compound statements, conditional statements, the environment variables, standard input/output redirection and pipes, etc.

Getting started

To get started with Batch files programming, all you need is a text editor and the command interpreter.

As far as text editor choices go, you can use the built-in Notepad or WordPad applications. However, I personally prefer to use a text editor with syntax highlighting and code completion support.

If I may, let me propose two of my favorite editors:

- EditPlus - from http://www.editplus.com/
- Sublime Text - from http://www.sublimetext.com/

The second step is to create a work folder where you will be writing the scripts and experimenting. Throughout this book, I will be using the *C:\BatchProgramming* folder to develop and test the scripts. Please create that folder in the "C:" drive accordingly.

The final step is to run an instance of the command interpreter (**`CMD.EXE`**):

1. On Windows XP and above: Press the **`Win+R`** key or click the "Start Menu" and choose "Run" then type: "cmd.exe"
2. On Windows 7 and up, simply press the **`Win`** key on your keyboard or press on the "Start Menu" icon and start typing: "Command Prompt" and then press ENTER to run the command prompt.

After you launch the command prompt, simply type:

```
CD /D C:\BatchProgramming
```

Optionally, also type:

```
TITLE Batchography: The Art of Batch files programming
```

Now you are ready to start typing commands and start experimenting.

As I mentioned in the introduction of this book, you may also download the source code used throughout this book from:

- The PassingTheKnowledge website at: http://www.passingtheknowledge.net/ under the "Books" section.
- GitHub online source code repository at: https://github.com/PassingTheKnowledge.

CMD keyboard shortcuts and other tips

In this section, I will share with you various **`CMD.exe`** keyboard shortcuts and tips that you can use while typing commands and working in the command prompt in general.

All of the tips and keyboard shortcuts I will be introducing are tested to work on Windows 10. Nonetheless, the majority of them still work on older operating systems.

Customizing the command prompt

You can customize the command prompt by clicking on its icon on the top left window, then choosing the "Properties" menu.

You will be presented with a dialog containing four tabs:

1. Options tab: allows you to configure things like command history buffer size (how many maximum commands to recall), the cursor size, edit options, etc.
2. Font tab: allows you to choose the font and its size.
3. Layout tab: allows you to specify the command window size (width and height), its buffer size (how many lines to retain before it starts to purge older lines), default window position, etc.
4. Colors tab: allows you to choose the default colors, opacity, etc.

You may also change the layout of the command prompt using the **MODE** command. For example, use the following syntax to change the columns to 80 and the lines to 25:

```
C:\BatchProgramming>mode con: COLS=80 LINES=25
```

Recalling commands with keyboard shortcuts

When you type a command in the prompt, you can press the **UP** or **DOWN** arrows on your keyboard to recall the commands. If you press the **ESC** key, then you may cancel the recall which will clear the proposed command recall text.

You may also start typing one or more letters then press **F8** repeatedly to recall commands that start with the letters you typed.

If you press **F7**, then a list with the command history will pop up on the screen. Each command in that history list will be prefixed by a command number. You may then use the arrow keys to choose a command to recall. Press ENTER to recall a command or ESC to dismiss the history window.

Press **F9** to recall a command by entering its command number (one of the values you saw in the F7 screen). When you press ENTER then the command will be pasted-in but not executed. This gives you a chance to edit and modify the command before running it.

Press **F3** to recall the last command (this is equivalent to pressing the **UP** key). Invoking this command repeatedly does not do anything.

Press **F1** to recall just a single letter at the current cursor position. The letter that is recalled is from the last command that you entered.

Finally, press **Alt-F7** to clear the command history.

Creating commands aliases with the DOSKEY utility

The **DOSKEY** utility allows you to create and manage macros and work with the command line history. To work with the command history, I suggest you use the keyboard shortcuts I mentioned above because they are more efficient and faster to invoke.

On the other hand, I encourage you to use the **DOSKEY** command to create and work with macros.

So what are macros?

Macros allow you to create command aliases. For instance, you can alias the **ECHO** keyword to be just the letter "e" for instance:

```
DOSKEY e=ECHO $*
```

Which means that the "e" command is now an alias of the **ECHO** keyword. The "$*" designates that all the arguments that are passed to the alias "e" should also be passed to the aliased keyword **ECHO**:

```
C:\BatchProgramming>e hello world
hello world
```

Instead of using the "$*" to capture all the arguments and pass them along, you can use any combination of the "$1" to "$9" special identifiers. They will get substituted with the corresponding argument that are passed to the macro/alias:

```
C:\BatchProgramming>doskey e=echo $1

C:\BatchProgramming>e hello world
hello

C:\BatchProgramming>
```

Notice how we are just passing the first argument ("$1") to the **ECHO** keyword. The remaining arguments that were passed to the alias are not passed to the **ECHO** keyword.

The "*$1*" to "*$9*", and "*$**" correspond to the "*%1*" to "*%9*", and the "*%**" which denote the command line arguments in the Batch files scripting language. The topic of "Command line arguments" will be explained in details later in this chapter.

When aliasing a command, that does not mean that one macro equals one alias. You can actually have one alias carry multiple commands. The secret to that is to join commands using the ampersand ("&") as we shall explain later in this chapter.

For now, to quickly illustrate this, we will create a macro called *echopause* that **ECHO**s a message on the screen and then **PAUSE**s:

```
C:\BatchProgramming>doskey echopause=echo $* ^&pause


C:\BatchProgramming>echopause hello world
hello world
Press any key to continue . . .
```

Note: I had to escape the ampersand character with ("&)" the caret ("^") sign. This will be explained later on.

If you don't want to escape the ampersand character, the **DOSKEY** command provides a special identifier named "*$T*" that allows you to join commands. Therefore, we can create an equivalent alias to the above using a slightly simpler syntax:

```
C:\BatchProgramming>doskey echopause2=echo $* $T pause
```

With **DOSKEY**, it is possible to load a predefined set of macros directly from a file instead of inserting them one at a time.

Let's assume we have a macro file called *linux.macro* that contains aliases with names similar to commands found in a Linux- like environment:

```
ls=dir $*
pwd=echo %cd%
cp=copy $*
mv=move $*
traceroute=tracert $*
```

We can insert those macros directly with a single command using the "/MACROFILE" switch like this:

```
C:\BatchProgramming>doskey /MACROFILE=linux.macro
```

Note: You don't have to escape special characters (like the percent "%" or the ampersand "&") when they are present in a macro file.

To list all the installed macros, you can use the following command:

```
C:\BatchProgramming>doskey /macros
```

Which outputs:

```
traceroute=tracert $*
mv=move $*
cp=copy $*
pwd=echo ^%cd^%
ls=dir $*
```

To delete all the macros, press the **Alt+F10** hotkey.

To delete a single macro, just assign the macro to an empty alias like this:

```
C:\BatchProgramming>doskey mv=
```

To verify that the *mv* alias is gone, we can list the macros again:

```
C:\BatchProgramming>doskey /macros
traceroute=tracert $*
cp=copy $*
pwd=echo ^%cd^%
ls=dir $*

C:\BatchProgramming>
```

Since I mentioned that **DOSKEY** also allows you to work with the command history, you can use the "/HISTORY" switch to list all the commands in the history buffer.

To illustrate this use case, let's start with a fresh command prompt that has no prior command history (or by simply clearing the current command prompt's history using the **Alt+F7** hotkey). Let's run some commands to populate the command history:

```
C:\BatchProgramming>echo 1
1

C:\BatchProgramming>echo 2
2

C:\BatchProgramming>echo 3
3
```

And now, let's list the command history:

```
C:\BatchProgramming>doskey /history
echo 1
echo 2
echo 3
doskey /history

C:\BatchProgramming>
```

Automatically running a script when the command prompt starts

In the previous section, I explained the use of the **DOSKEY** command to create aliases. The aliases are useful as long as they are loaded in the current command prompt session.

You don't want to load them manually each time, and most certainly you don't want to be bothered to run a Batch file script each time you open a command prompt in order to set up the aliases.

In this section, I will explain how to set up a Batch file script that gets executed automatically each time you start a new command prompt.

To do that, we have to tweak the registry and specify which Batch file script should be executed automatically.

The following are the registry modifications we need to do:

```
REGEDIT4

[HKEY_CURRENT_USER\SOFTWARE\Microsoft\Command Processor]
"AutoRun"="c:\\Path-To-Your-Auto-Script\\ScriptName.bat"
```

You just need to create a new **REG_SZ** value called *AutoRun* in either the **HKEY_CURRENT_USER** (to make changes for your user profile only) or the **HKEY_LOCAL_MACHINE** (to make changes for all users on the computer) registry hives. In that registry string value, we set the full path and name of the script that will be executed automatically.

Run RegEdit.exe, navigate to the registry key path specified above and apply the modifications using RegEdit's user interface. It is much easier like that.

In most cases, the auto start script might contain the appropriate commands to load the macros using the **DOSKEY** command and perhaps do a few extra things (like changing the command prompt color and title).

> *Very important security tip:* *When working with the* ***HKEY_CURRENT_USER*** *registry hive, it is preferable that you store the auto start script in your profile data directory so no other users can tamper with it. The same applies when working with* ***HKEY_LOCAL_MACHINE****: you want to make sure you properly set the permissions of the auto start script file or folder and allow authorized users to write to it and the "Everyone" group to read from it. For instance, make the script "Read only" to all users except yourself or the admin.*

On my current machine for instance, the auto start script is called "*CmdInit.bat*" and is located in my profile folder along with a macro file that gets loaded with the **DOSKEY** command.

Here's how my auto start script looks like:

```
@echo off
doskey /macrofile=%~dp0CmdInit.macro
```

I use the "*%~dp0*" modifier to instruct **DOSKEY** to load the macro file (*CmdInit.macro*) from the same path as the script. The modifier syntax will become clear in the section entitled "Command line arguments and FOR loop variables modifiers".

Path completion shortcuts

You may press the **TAB** key (the default completion hotkey) to enumerate the files or folders while you type.

For instance, if you typed "Notepad my" then pressed **TAB**, then the command will auto-complete with the first file name that starts with "my", then if you keep pressing **TAB**, then the remaining files that start with "my" will cycle forward and show up as completion options. You may keep pressing TAB until no more files are found with the following criteria. In facsimile, if you press **Shift-TAB** then the completion suggestions will cycle backwards.

> *Note: The path completion hotkey is configurable. Please refer to the MSDN website under the following topic: "Command Processor CompletionChar".*

Editing tips

It is possible to select, copy, paste and find text in the command window.

In order to select text, simply press and hold the **SHIFT** key and then use one of the direction or page scrolling keys (**UP**, **DOWN**, **LEFT**, **RIGHT**, **HOME**, **END**, **PgDn** or **PgUp**). By doing this, the selection mode will start. Similarly, you can press **Ctrl-M** to start the selection mode (aka "Mark Mode").

Whether you are already in text selection mode or not, press **Ctrl+A** to select the whole console window text.

Press **ENTER**, **Ctrl-Shift-C** or **Ctrl-Insert** to copy the selection to the clipboard. Press **ESC** to cancel the selection.

If the "Quick Edit" mode is enabled, then you can directly start text selection by clicking with the mouse on the text inside the command prompt. If "Quick Edit" mode was disabled, then you can **Right-Click** anywhere inside the console window and then choose the "Select" menu item. After a selection is made, **Right-click** again with the mouse, or press **Ctrl-V** or **Shift-Insert** to paste text from the clipboard.

To edit the text and do corrections, use the **LEFT** or **RIGHT** keys to move the cursor one letter at a time. Use **Ctrl-Left** or **Ctrl-Right** to move the cursor one word at a time to the left or to the right. Use the **HOME** key to take the cursor to the beginning of the line and the **END** key to go to the end of the typed text.

Press the **Ctrl-Up** or the **Ctrl-Down** keys to scroll the console window up or down by a single line.

Press the **BackSpace** key to delete the character before the cursor and press the **DEL** key to delete the character at the cursor.

Use the **Ctrl-End** key to delete all the text to the right of the cursor, and use the **Ctrl-Home** key to delete all the letters to the left of the cursor.

Press **Ctrl-F** to bring up the "Find text" dialog. Start typing any text to search for in the console window text then press ENTER. Keep pressing ENTER to cycle between the matches. Press ESC to close the dialog.

Press **F11** to toggle the full screen mode.

Press **Ctrl+Z** or **F6** to emit the EOF (end of file) character (^Z). This is handy when the standard input is redirected to the console and you want to signal the end of editing/end of file. More about the input redirection later in the book.

Useful commands

In this section, I will briefly mention a list of useful commands that you can start using already. To learn more about each command usage, simply type the command name followed by the "/?" switch.

Later in the book, when you learn the Batch files scripting language basics and proceed to more advanced scripting topics (such as conditional statements, repetition control structure, and string tokenization), you will find that using those commands in conjunction with a script logic can help you achieve more complicated and useful tasks.

COLOR

The **COLOR** command allows you to change the foreground and background color of the command prompt. It takes a single argument composed of two hexadecimal digits describing the background and foreground color numbers.

For example, to have a white background with a red text, issue the following command:

```
C:\BatchProgramming>color 74

C:\BatchProgramming>
```

Type "COLOR /?" to get a list of color codes.

ASSOC/FTYPE

The **ASSOC** command lets you see or change which file extension is associated with which program. For example:

```
C:\BatchProgramming>ASSOC .pl
.pl=Perl

C:\BatchProgramming>assoc .py
.py=Python.File

C:\BatchProgramming>
```

Notice that what is returned is not the program path that handles the extension, but just an identifier. The second step is to resolve that file type identifier to the actual program path with the **FTYPE** command:

```
C:\BatchProgramming>ftype Python.File
Python.File="C:\Python27\python.exe" "%1" %*

C:\BatchProgramming>ftype Perl
Perl="C:\Perl64\bin\perl.exe" "%1" %*

C:\BatchProgramming>
```

When the **ASSOC** and **FTYPE** commands are used in a script together, you can programmatically compute where (and if) a given program is installed. Using these two commands combination can be very handy when writing polyglot scripts (please refer to Chapter 4).

TYPE

The **TYPE** command allows you to display the contents of a file. It is very handy when you want to take a peek into the contents of a file without having to launch a full blown text editor.

CLIP

The **CLIP** command allows you to redirect the output of a command or the contents of a file to the Windows clipboard.

For example, the following command will redirect the output of the **DIR** command to the clipboard:

```
DIR /W | CLIP
```

And the following command allows you to copy the contents of a file to the clipboard:

```
CLIP < C:\PathToMyFile\myfile.txt
```

Equally, you can use the syntax:

```
TYPE C:\PathToMyFile\myfile.txt | CLIP
```

You can easily copy a long command from the command history by pressing **HOME** and typing **ECHO**, then pressing **END** and typing " **| CLIP**":

```
ECHO A very long command | CLIP
```

Press ENTER to execute the command and have the command copied to the clipboard. More about output redirection and pipes in later sections in this book.

RUNAS

The RUNAS command lets you run a command as another user. It is commonly used to let you run a program as an administrator like this:

```
C:\BatchProgramming>runas /user:Administrator cmd.exe
Enter the password for administrator:
Attempting to start cmd.exe as user "PC001\Administrator" ...
```

DIR/COPY/XCOPY/MOVE/RENAME/DEL

These are useful commands to list, copy, rename, move or delete files and directories. Their use is very prevalent in Batch file scripting.

- DIR → Lists the directory contents. It allows you to explore what files and folders are on your system from the command prompt.
- COPY/XCOPY → Allows you to copy files and folders.
- MOVE → Moves files or folders to new locations.
- RENAME → Renames files or folders.

PUSHD/POPD/CD/CHDIR/MD/MKDIR

The **PUSHD/POPD** commands are very useful when you want to navigate away from the current directory to a new one while at the same time saving the current directory (before the navigation takes place) in a directory navigation stack. Later, you can return to the saved directory by issuing the counter command: **POPD**.

> *Note: SETLOCAL and ENDLOCAL also save and restore the working directories.*

PUSHD and **POPD** come in handy if you had your command prompt's prompt value set to include the "$+" modifier.

Try typing the following command first:

```
C:\Temp>prompt $+%PROMPT%
```

Then use:

```
C:\Temp>pushd c:\windows\system32

+c:\Windows\System32>pushd %APPDATA%

++C:\Users\Ashmole\AppData\Roaming>popd

+c:\Windows\System32>popd

C:\Temp>
```

Did you notice the "+" sign prior to the directory name (in the prompt text)?

Each time the pushed directory stack has a new entry then another plus sign will indicate so in the prompt.

The **CHDIR** and the **CD** commands are equivalent. They are used to change the current directory. The **MKDIR** or **MD** commands are used to create new directories.

Using the WMIC tool

The WMIC tool is a command line utility that allows you to do various WMI (Windows Management Instrumentation) operations from the command line or your Batch file script.

You can do many powerful things with the **WMIC** command:

- Query running processes and extract information: process id, path, command line, etc. You can also terminate a process with WMI.
- Query and manage the registry.
- Query system information: process names, available physical memory, computer name, joined domain information, etc.
- Manage users and groups in the machine.
- Query installed programs and uninstall them if needed.
- Etc.

There are so many things to list that you can do with **WMIC**. Discussing those topics are beyond the scope of this book.

Using the REG command to work with the registry

It is possible to manipulate the registry keys and values and/or query them using the **REG.EXE** command:

```
C:\BatchProgramming>reg /?

REG Operation [Parameter List]

  Operation  [ QUERY   | ADD    | DELETE  | COPY    |
               SAVE    | LOAD   | UNLOAD  | RESTORE |
               COMPARE | EXPORT | IMPORT  | FLAGS ]

Return Code: (Except for REG COMPARE)

  0 - Successful
  1 - Failed

For help on a specific operation type:

  REG Operation /?
```

As you can see from the usage output above, there a lot of operations, including operations such as QUERY, ADD, DELETE and SAVE/RESTORE.

Here are some ideas on why you may want to use the **REG** command from your script:

- Create registry keys as part of an environment setup prior to running a certain program.
- Clean up the registry keys after a program is removed. This is useful if programs leave a mess behind them even when they are uninstalled.
- Check if a program is installed by looking for its registry keys existence.
- Affect system changes by applying various registry keys and values modifications from your script. This is useful when you are writing a system lock-down script for instance.
- Apply registry settings policies to a machine.
- Etc.

Process management commands

There are at least two commands that ship with MS Windows that can be used to work with processes.

The **TASKKILL** utility allows you to find one or more processes that match your search criteria (by name, by process id or another filter) and then killing them:

```
C:\BatchProgramming>taskkill /?

TASKKILL [/S system [/U username [/P [password]]]]
         { [/FI filter] [/PID processid | /IM imagename] } [/T] [/F]

Description:
    This tool is used to terminate tasks by process id (PID) or image
name.
```

On the other hand, the **TASKLIST** utility allows you to list running processes and display information about them (process id, window title, status, etc.):

```
C:\BatchProgramming>tasklist /?

TASKLIST [/S system [/U username [/P [password]]]]
         [/M [module] | /SVC | /V] [/FI filter] [/FO format] [/NH]

Description:
    This tool displays a list of currently running processes on
    either a local or remote machine.
```

Often times, **TASKLIST** and **TASKKILL** are used together in order to first search for a process with a given criteria and then kill it if needed.

Here are some ideas on why you may want to use those utilities:

- Find and kill a group of stuck or unwanted processes. For example, find and terminate all instances of "iexplore.exe".
- Find and kill a process by name prior to compiling it from sources again.
- Find information about services ("TASKLIST /SVC") or Windows Store apps ("TASKLIST /APPS").
- Etc.

Command echo

Commands and keywords on each line in the Batch file script are normally echoed to the standard output or let's call it "the console" (for simplicity). That means, every line in the Batch file script will be displayed and then executed. By default, the command echo is turned on. Having the command echo on is very useful for debugging Batch file scripts, more on that topic will be presented in Chapter 3.

When you are done programming or troubleshooting the script you may want to turn off the command echo. There are two methods to turn off the command echo.

The first method is to turn off the command echo for individual commands by preceding each command with the at-sign ("@"), like this:

```
@dir /w
```

This will execute the directory listing command and the only output you will see is the directory listing and not the command being executed.

The other method is to turn off the command echo at the start of your script and keep it off. You can use the **ECHO** keyword and pass it the "*OFF*" or "*ON*" parameter:

```
@echo OFF
dir/w
cd c:\Tools
```

Notice that we prefixed the first command (**ECHO OFF**) with the "@" sign so that this command itself is not echoed before it has a chance to turn off the echo for the rest of the script!

Note: You can, at any time in your script, change the command echo value.

If you just issue the **ECHO** command without any parameters, then **ECHO** will print the current status of the command echo:

```
@ECHO
```

Outputs:

```
ECHO is on.
```

The ECHO keyword is also used to print text to the screen. Its syntax is very simple:

```
ECHO This is the message I want to display
```

Each time you echo a string, a new line will follow automatically. So for instance, if you wanted to echo the numbers 1 to 5 all next to each other, then doing something like this:

```
Echo 1
Echo 2
Echo 3
Echo 4
Echo 5
```

Will not give the correct result, instead each number will be displayed on its own line:

```
1
2
3
4
5
```

In order to display a string to the console without emitting a new line after each text, you can use the “SET /P” trick like this:

```
set /p "=1"<nul
set /p "=2"<nul
set /p "=3"<nul
set /p "=4"<nul
set /p "=5"<nul
```

And this:

```
set /p "=hello "<nul
set /p "=world"<nul
```

The syntax above can also be re-written like this:

```
<nul set /p "=hello "
<nul set /p "=world"
```

To display an empty line (or a new line), use the following syntax:

```
ECHO.
```

Do not put spaces between the ECHO and the dot (“.”), otherwise the dot will be displayed.

To summarize, let’s illustrate everything using this script (*echo-test.bat*):

```
:: Basic echo
echo This line is echoed
@echo This line is not echoed
@echo off
echo I am under echo off
ECHO.
echo me too
@echo on
echo Hello, echo is back on!


:: Echo 2
@echo off
set /p "=hello "<nul
<nul set /p "=world"
```

When executed, it outputs:

```
C:\BatchProgramming>echo-test.bat

C:\BatchProgramming>echo This line is echoed
This line is echoed
This line is not echoed
I am under echo off

me too

C:\BatchProgramming>echo Hello, echo is back on!
Hello, echo is back on
hello world
C:\BatchProgramming>
```

Lastly, to **ECHO** the strings "ON" or "OFF", use the following syntax:

```
ECHO.ON
ECHO.OFF
```

The "Errorlevel"

The **ERRORLEVEL** designates a number (or error code) that is set as a result of executing a Batch file keyword or an external command. It designates the exit code from the last executed statement.

In Batch files, it is possible to return an **ERRORLEVEL** so another Batch file picks it up. This is accomplished by using the **EXIT** keyword like this:

```
EXIT /B errorcode
```

The "/B" switch designates that only the currently executing Batch file should exit. This is handy to return from a Batch file (or function, as it will be explained later) a numeric value back to the caller.

In addition to using the "EXIT /B" syntax, you may influence and indirectly set the **ERRORLEVEL** value by calling commands that are known to change its value. For example, a common trick to reset the **ERRORLEVEL** back to zero, is to call the **VERIFY** command like this:

```
VERIFY >nul
```

Let's check this behavior with *err-clr.bat* and *err.exe*:

```
@echo off
err 35
verify > nul
echo ERRORLEVEL= %ERRORLEVEL%
```

Note: err.exe is a simple utility that returns the same exit code that was passed as its argument.

Which yields the following output when executed:

```
C:\BatchProgramming>err-clr
returning 35
ERRORLEVEL= 0

C:\BatchProgramming>
```

There are plenty of commands that change the **ERRORLEVEL** value when they are executed. The **SET** command is one of them, but the **ECHO** command is not.

To exit all the executing Batch files, type:

```
EXIT [errorcode]
```

Later in this book, I will cover how the error codes returned by executing programs can be used to influence the logic of a Batch file script.

Command extensions

The Batch files scripting language can be enhanced when the *Command Extensions* are enabled. The command extensions provide additional language features such as new dynamic environment variables, existing keywords enhancement, etc.

In the subsequent sections, I will be mentioning which syntax or feature is only available when the *Command extensions* are enabled.

Command extensions are enabled by default; however, it is possible to enable the *command extensions* on demand using the **SETLOCAL** keyword like this:

```
SETLOCAL ENABLEEXTENSIONS
```

Or to disable them like this:

```
SETLOCAL DISABLEEXTENSIONS
```

Breaking long commands into multiple lines

It is possible to break a long command into multiple lines for clarity purposes. The caret symbol (^), if present at the end of a line, signifies that the next line is a continuation of the current line.

Here's the *long-command.bat* script:

```
echo Hello!
echo This ^
is ^
a ^
very ^
long ^
command
echo Goodbye!
```

This Batch file, when executed, will display three lines only:

```
Hello!
This is a very long command
Goodbye!
```

Executing multiple commands on the same line

It is possible to execute multiple commands on the same line by joining them using the ampersand character ("&"):

```
Echo This is a line & Echo This is another line
```

You can join as many commands as you want on the same line:

```
Command1 & Command2 & Command3 & ...
```

Compound statements

Compound statements are treated as a single block of commands when they are enclosed inside the opening and closing parenthesis. With compound statements, you are not obliged to have all the commands on the same line, instead you can use a new line for each command.

First example:

```
C:\BatchProgramming>( echo 1
More? echo 2
More? echo 3
More? )
1
2
3
```

As you can see from the above output, the command interpreter will ask for more commands if you press ENTER while a compound statement is not closed yet with a ")".

Of course, in a Batch file script, you will not see the "More?" prompt (*compound-1.bat*):

```
@echo off
(
	echo 1
	echo 2
	echo 3
)
```

When executed, that script outputs the following:

```
C:\BatchProgramming>compound-1.bat
1
2
3

C:\BatchProgramming>
```

You can also combine joined and long commands inside compound statements (*compound-2.bat*):

```
@echo off
(
	echo 1 & echo 2
	echo this ^
is ^
a ^
long ^
line
	echo 3
)
```

When executed, it produces the following output:

```
C:\BatchProgramming>compound-2.bat
1
2
this is a long line
3

C:\BatchProgramming>
```

Last but not least, you can use compound statements within compound statements ad infinitum (*compound-3.bat*):

```
@echo off
(
        (
                echo 1 & echo 2
                (
                echo this ^
is ^
a ^
long ^
line
                )
        echo 3
        )
)
```

Beware of unnecessarily creating compound statements lest you forget to properly close them properly (leaving the opening and closing parenthesis imbalanced).

Conditionally executing multiple commands on the same line

It is possible to execute multiple commands on the same line conditionally depending on whether the previous command succeeds or fails.

For instance, you may want to execute one command but only execute the subsequent commands if the first one failed.

Before I proceed with the explanation, I will need a dummy program that returns an exit code of my choice. This program has been briefly introduced earlier when we spoke about the *ERRORLEVEL* topic. We will use the *err.exe* utility to simulate success or failure situations.

Let *err.c* be this simple C test program:

```
#include <stdio.h>

int main(int argc, char *argv[])
{
      int err = argc < 2 ? -1 : atoi(argv[1]);
      printf("returning %d\n", err);
      return err;
}
```

This test program prints the number we passed to it (as the first argument) and then exits and sets the exit code to that passed number.

Please do not concern yourself whether you understand the C programming language or not. What is important to know is that in your day to day job when you execute commands they normally return an error code to designate whether they succeed or failed. The script can retrieve the exit codes via the *%ERRORLEVEL%* pseudo-environment variable.

> *Note: For convenience purposes, the compiled err.exe (along with the source code are available for you to download).*

Let us test *err.exe* with those commands (*err-test.bat*):

```
err 1
echo ERRORLEVEL = %ERRORLEVEL%
err 33
echo ERRORLEVEL= %ERRORLEVEL%
```

We observe the following output:

```
C:\BatchProgramming>err-test
returning 1
ERRORLEVEL = 1
returning 33
ERRORLEVEL= 33

C:\BatchProgramming>
```

Okay, now that we can control the *ERRORLEVEL* value, let me explain to you how to conditionally chain commands together.

There are two special operators we can use to conditionally join commands: the double ampersand characters ("&&") and the double pipe characters ("||"). In the C language, those operators stand for the logical-AND and the logical-OR respectively.

> *<u>Note:</u> Do not confuse the single pipe character ("|") with the double pipes. They have totally different purposes in Batch files scripting.*

Those operators treat an error code with value of 0 as success and any other error code as failure.

In simple terms, if a program succeeds it should return 0 and if it fails it should return anything else.

The logical-AND operator will execute the second command only if the previous command succeeds (that means the return code was 0).

To illustrate this, let us use this example:

```
err 0 && echo I am the second command
```

This will execute the second command (**ECHO**) because *err.exe* returns success. Therefore, we observe the following output:

```
returning 0
I am the second command
```

Now let us see what happens if the first command fails (returns non-zero value):

```
C:\BatchProgramming>err 33 && echo I am the second command
returning 33
```

As you observed, the **ECHO** command (which is the second command) did not get executed because 33 is not equal to 0 (which is not the success error code). This is how we conditionally join two commands with the logical-AND operator.

Conversely, the logical-OR operator ("||") will execute the second command only if the first command fails.

In the following example, the first command returns a failure error code, thus the **ECHO** command will execute:

```
C:\BatchProgramming>err 33 || echo I am the second command
returning 33
I am the second command
```

In the following example, the first command returns a success error code, thus the **ECHO** command will not execute:

```
C:\BatchProgramming>err 0 || echo I am the second command
returning 0
```

It is also possible to chain multiple logical operators together on the same command line, for example:

```
C:\BatchProgramming>err 0 && err 0 && echo Hello
returning 0
returning 0
Hello
```

In a compound statement, the exit code value is the value of the last command executed in the block. Therefore, when we surround the commands with parenthesis then a single return value is produced, which is then used when applying the logical operators that are used to join other statements:

```
C:\BatchProgramming>(err 0 || err 1) && echo Second command
returning 0
Second command
```

Or:

```
C:\BatchProgramming>(err 1 && err 0) && echo Second command
returning 1
```

The last example was composed of two commands: the first command is a compound command (which is in itself composed of two commands), then the second command is the **ECHO** command. Remember that when two commands are joined with the logical-AND operator, the second command gets executed only if the first command succeeds. The first command, "err 1 && err 0", does not succeed because the "err 1" does not succeed.

Note: I advise you to read a bit about the logical AND/OR operators and the Boolean truth table (https://en.wikipedia.org/wiki/Truth_table).

Similarly, if we try to conditionally execute two compound statements, then the result of each compound statement determines how the conditional execution of commands happens. Consider the following:

```
C:\BatchProgramming>(err 0 || err 1) && (err 0 && err 0)
returning 0 ← output from the fist compound statement
returning 0 ← output from the second compound statement
returning 0 ← second command's output from the second compound statement
```

The first compound statement short-circuited after getting its first true (or success) result from the "err 0" command without having to also test for "err 1". Because the first compound statement is joined with a logical-AND, the second compound statement has a chance to execute. The second compound statement uses the logical-AND to conditionally execute its inner commands. Since the logical AND operator requires that all commands return true, then for the sake of demonstration, we have no choice but to call the "err 0". This is why we got three times the output "returning 0".

Note: Short-circuit evaluation simply means to stop the evaluation of conditions in a statement when what has been evaluated so far is sufficient to evaluate the whole statement. The OR operator will short-circuit when the first success code is found, while the AND operator will short-circuit when the first failure code is found.

To summarize:

- The logical-AND operator ("&&") executes the second command only if the first (compound or not) command succeeds. It continues executing all the subsequent commands as long as they keep succeeding and it will stop at the first sight of a failure condition.
- The logical-OR operator ("||") executes the second command only if the first command fails. If any command (evaluated from left to right) succeeds first, then the logical OR-operator is said to short-circuit and will stop evaluating all the subsequent right hand statements.

- You can use compound statements (commands surrounded with parenthesis) and form more complex expressions before applying the logical-OR/logical-AND operators while joining commands.

Can you guess what the output of the following commands is?

1. err 0 && err 0 && err 1 && err 0 && err 0
2. (err 1 || (err 0 || err 1)) && echo Second command

What about guessing the output of this command?

```
C:\>(err 11 || err 26 || err 1941 || err 0 || err 961) && (
   (err 1 && err 0) || (err 2 || err 0))
```

Comments

Comments or remarks allow you to type text that will be ignored by the interpreter. There are various ways to add comments in a Batch file script as we shall explain in the following subsections.

Comments at the beginning of the line

Comments are declared in two ways. The first way is using the **REM** (short for "remark") keyword:

```
REM this is a comment
REM this is another comment
```

The second method to define comments is to use the labels trick. Since defining labels does not really execute any command, you may use the colon (":") label prefix to set comments. Many script writers also use the double-colon ("::") prefix to designate comments:

```
: This is a comment
:: This is another comment
```

Comments at the end of the line

It is possible to add comments at the end of a command, like you would do in C++ using the double forward slash ("//").

Do you remember how to unconditionally join commands on the same line? Yep, you can use the ampersand character "&".

We will use this trick to join the first command with another command which is a comment. This will give us the effect of adding a comment at the end of the line:

```
C:\BatchProgramming>ECHO This is a command & :: This is a comment
This is a command

C:\BatchProgramming>
```

Multi-line comments

It is possible to have multi-line comments using the **GOTO** keyword. The trick here is to use **GOTO** keyword to jump to a label past the multiple lines you want the interpreter to ignore:

```
ECHO Multiple line comments
GOTO after_comment
Hello
This is really free text!
The interpreter will not execute those lines
:after_comment
ECHO End of multiple line comments
```

Please check the *comments.bat* example for the complete example.

Escaping special symbols

As we have previously seen, there are certain characters that have special meaning:

- I/O redirection characters: "<" and ">".
- The pipe character: "|".
- The escape character (the caret): "^".
- The command concatenation character: "&".
- Environment variable expansion letters: "%" and "!" (only when delayed environment variables expansion is enabled).

Those special symbols have to be escaped in order to be used. To escape them, you can prefix them with the caret character "^".

For example, you cannot simply **ECHO** the following:

```
ECHO 4 < 5, 2 > 1, 8 likes to smoke a |, and 9 loves to wear a ^
```

because we have the input redirection (“<”), output redirection (“>”), a caret symbol (“^”) and the pipe (“|”) symbols. To correct the situation, we will prefix each of those special characters with the caret symbol (“^”):

```
ECHO 4 ^< 5, 2 ^> 1, 8 likes to smoke a ^|, and 9 loves to wear a ^^
```

As you can see, we have to prefix those special characters with the caret symbol in order to be able to print them. Another option is to surround the whole string with quotes.

Similarly, if you wanted to print the percent sign (that usually surrounds an environment variable), you can prefix it with another percent sign like this:

```
SET name=Hiram
ECHO The %%name%% environment variable value is %name%
```

This will output:

```
The %name% environment variable value is Hiram
```

Please note that the first time we wanted to display “%name%” literally (note the double “%” sign), and the second time we wanted to display the value of the environment variable “*name*” (just a single percent sign was used).

When the delayed environment variables expansion syntax is enabled, then the exclamation character (“!”) need to be escaped with a double caret like this:

```
echo The end is nigh^^!
```

Outputs:

```
The end is nigh!
```

Passing command line arguments

Like executable programs, Batch file scripts can also receive command line arguments.

If you ever programmed in C before, you may recognize how a C program receives its command line arguments:

```
#include <stdio.h>

int main(int argc, char *argv[])
{
       printf("arg0=%s, arg1=%s, arg2=%s", argv[0], argv[1], argv[2]);
       return 0;
}
```

And when executed, it will output:

```
C:\BatchProgramming>test.exe "argument 1" and "argument 2"
arg0=test.exe, arg1=argument 1, arg2=and
C:\BatchProgramming>
```

In the same fashion as the C programs can read the command line arguments using the *argv* array, so can Batch file scripts read the command line arguments by prefixing the argument number with a percent sign ("%").

Argument number zero, like in C, stands for the current executing script name. Argument number one is the first argument, argument number two is the second argument, and so on.

Let's illustrate this with *args-1.bat*:

```
@echo arg0=%0, arg1=%1, arg2=%2
```

And when executed, it will output:

```
C:\BatchProgramming>args-1.bat "argument 1" "argument 2"
arg0=args-1.bat, arg1="argument 1", arg2="argument 2"

C:\BatchProgramming>
```

The command line arguments are separated by the space character unless they are surrounded by the double quotes.

Instead of getting one argument at a time, it is possible to get all of the passed arguments using the "%*" (*args-all.bat*):

```
@echo All arguments: %*
```

When executed, it outputs:

```
C:\BatchProgramming>args-all the arguments that are passed
All arguments: the arguments that are passed

C:\BatchProgramming>
```

Using the SHIFT keyword

The **SHIFT** keyword shifts all the arguments to the left by one. When it is passed three arguments for instance, then the original %1 disappears, %2 becomes %1 and %3 becomes %2, etc.

One practical example of using **SHIFT** is when you want to dynamically enumerate all the passed arguments (*args-enum1.bat*):

```
@echo off

:repeat
    if "%1"=="" goto end
    echo Arg: %1

    SHIFT

    goto repeat

:end
```

When executed with four parameters, it outputs:

```
C:\BatchProgramming>args-enum1.bat 1 2 3 4
Arg: 1
Arg: 2
Arg: 3
Arg: 4

C:\BatchProgramming>
```

Note: In Chapter 2, you will learn how to enumerate all the command line arguments using the "FOR /L" syntax.

You can also shift arguments at a given position rather than just starting at the first argument using the following syntax:

```
SHIFT [/n]
```

Let's call "**SHIFT** /3" as demonstrated in the *args-enum2.bat* script below:

```
@echo off

echo Args 1 to 6 are: %1 %2 %3 %4 %5 %6

shift /3

echo New args 1 to 6 are: %1 %2 %3 %4 %5 %6
```

The script above is supposed to start shifting starting at the 3rd argument. Therefore, in the output below at marker ①, we can see that "3" is missing:

```
C:\BatchProgramming>args-enum2.bat 1 2 3 4 5 6
Args 1 to 6 are: 1 2 3 4 5 6
New args 1 to 6 are: 1 2 4 5 6 ①

C:\BatchProgramming>
```

As a side note, when the **SHIFT** keyword is used in a compound statement, then the shifted arguments are not reflected properly but the shift operation does take place. Let's take the *shift-compound.bat* script as an example to illustrate that:

```
@echo off

setlocal enabledelayedexpansion

echo a^) 1=%1 2=%2 3=%3

if 1==1 (
      shift
      echo 1'=%1 2'=%2 ①
) ②

shift
echo b^) 1=%1 2=%2 3=%3
```

And run it with four parameters:

```
C:\BatchProgramming>shift-compound.bat a b c d
a) 1=a 2=b 3=c
1'=a 2'=b ①
b) 1=c 2=d 3=

C:\BatchProgramming>
```

Notice how inside the **IF** compound statement, the output at marker ① did not reflect the shifting side effects immediately. This is because we were inside the compound statement block. After the block's end, at marker ②, we could see that the **SHIFT** did indeed take place twice.

Command line arguments and FOR loop variables modifiers

The command line arguments and the **FOR** loop variables can be expanded differently by using certain modifiers. Even though we have not explained the **FOR** keyword syntax yet, the modifiers concept is the same.

The general syntax is as follows:

```
%~{Modifier}{ArgumentNumber or VariableName}
```

The list below uses the first argument (%1) to illustrate all the supported modifiers:

- %~1 - Expands %1 and removes any surrounding quotation marks ("").
- %~**f**1 - Expands %1 to a fully qualified path name.
- %~**d**1 - Expands %1 to a drive letter.
- %~**p**1 - Expands %1 to a path.
- %~**n**1 - Expands %1 to a file name.
- %~**x**1 - Expands %1 to a file extension.
- %~**s**1 – Expands %1 to a path that contains short names only.
- %~**a**1 - Expands %1 to file attributes.
- %~**t**1 - Expands %1 to date and time of file.
- %~**z**1 - Expands %1 to size of file.

- %~**$PATH**:1 - Searches the directories listed in the *PATH* environment variable and expands %1 to the fully qualified name of the first one found. If the environment variable name is not defined or the file is not found, this modifier expands to the empty string.
- %~**dp**1 - Expands %1 to a drive letter and path.
- %~**nx**1 - Expands %1 to a file name and extension.
- %~**dp$PATH**:1 - Searches the directories listed in the PATH environment variable for %1 and expands to the drive letter and path of the first one found.
- %~**ftza**1 - Expands %1 to an output similar to that of the **`dir`** command.

It is possible to combine various single letter modifiers to get a compound effect. In the example below, the modifier at ⑫ is a combination of the modifiers at ⑤ and ⑥. The same goes for the modifier at ⑪ which is made of the modifiers at ③ and ④.

The script *args-modifiers.bat* is a comprehensive example that illustrates how the modifiers work:

```
@echo off

echo The first argument as is: %1

:: Start modifiers example
echo 1. without quotes: %~1
echo 2. fully qualified path name: %~f1
echo 3. drive letter: %~d1
echo 4. path part: %~p1
echo 5. just the file name part: %~n1
echo 6. just the extension part: %~x1
echo 7. file's attributes: %~a1
echo 8. file's date and time: %~t1
echo 9. file's size: %~z1
echo 10. file path in the PATH environment variable search: %~$PATH:1
echo 11. file's full path: %~dp1
echo 12. file's name and extension part: %~nx1
echo 13. 'dir' like modifier: %~ftza1
echo 14. fully qualified script path: %~dpnx0
```

Assuming that we have a *"test.txt"* file in the current directory, then when the script above is executed with the first parameter as *test.txt*, then the modifiers applied to *%1* will cause the following output:

```
C:\BatchProgramming>args-modifiers.bat "test.txt"
The first argument as is: "test.txt"
1. without quotes: test.txt
2. fully qualified path name: C:\BatchProgramming\test.txt
3. drive letter: T:
4. path part: \BatchProgramming\
5. just the file name part: test
6. just the extension part: .txt
7. file's attributes: --a--------
8. file's date and time: 08/14/2021 01:23 PM
9. file's size: 1264
10. file path in the PATH environment variable search:
11. file's full path: C:\BatchProgramming\
12. file's name and extension part: test.txt
13. 'dir' like modifier: --a-------- 08/14/2021 01:23 PM 1264
C:\BatchProgramming\test.txt
14. fully qualified script path: C:\BatchProgramming\args-modifiers.bat

C:\BatchProgramming>
```

Later in Chapter 2, when the **FOR** keyword is explained, I will illustrate how the same modifiers can be equally applied on the **FOR** loop's variables and not just the numbered arguments (%0 to %9).

Environment variables

Every program has its own environment block and the command interpreter (**cmd.exe**) is not exception to the rule. An environment block is just a memory store where programs can store a set of strings of the form: "variableName=variableValue". There is a 32kb size limit per environment block.

In the Batch files scripting language, the **SET** keyword is used to create, modify, query or delete environment variables.

Environment variables are evaluated (also said to be "expanded") by wrapping their names from both sides with the percentage symbol "%" like this:

```
%VariableName%
```

The environment variable names are case insensitive.

Environment variables can be expanded and used anywhere in the Batch file script. They can even be used as dynamic **GOTO** targets, for example:

```
GOTO MyLabel%ChoiceNumber%
```

The above code snippet will jump to a variable-named label that starts with *MyLabel* and ends with whatever the *ChoiceNumber* environment variable expands to.

They can also be expanded as the command to be executed, for example:

```
SET theCommand=dir /w
%theCommand%
```

Manipulating environment variables

You can introduce new environment variables using the **SET** keyword. To add a new environment variable, use any syntax from below:

Create a variable:

```
SET playerName=The Big Lebowski
```

Optionally use the quotes to surround the value:

```
SET "playerName=The Big Lebowski"
```

Create another numeric variable:

```
SET PlayerLevel=17
```

Create a variable that uses other variables:

```
SET variableName2=Hello %PlayerName%, your level is %PlayerLevel%
```

To delete an environment variable, use the **SET** keyword but do not pass any value after the equal sign ("="):

```
SET variableName=
```

To display the values of environment variables or the value of a single environment variable, you can either use the **ECHO** keyword to display the values or just use the "**SET** EnvVarName" (without the equal or the percentage signs) syntax.

By using the **ECHO** keyword, you can display the expanded value like this:

```
ECHO %variableName%
```

Or equally use the **SET** keyword followed by the environment variable name or part of its name.

If part of the name is passed, then all variables starting with the passed prefix will be displayed:

```
SET var ← displays any environment variable matching the wildcard "var*"
SET variableName ← displays the exact matching environment variable
value
```

When assigning a string that contains any reserved symbol to an environment variable, remember that you have to escape any special symbols with the caret (^).

For example:

```
set "variableName=I 3^> you"
echo value=%variableName%
```

Yields the following output:

```
value=I 3> you
```

Please refer to the section entitled "Escaping special symbols" for more information.

Useful environment variables

In this section, I will mention some useful and predefined environment variables. Some of the variables are dynamic (also called as pseudo-environment variables) and are present when the *Command extensions* are enabled.

Some of those dynamic environment variables might evaluate to different values each time you try to expand them (for example the *%CD%*, *%TIME%*, *%RANDOM%*, etc.).

Current Directory

Use the special *%CD%* environment variable to retrieve the current directory. Each time the current working directory is changed, then this environment variable is automatically updated by the interpreter (*cmd.exe*).

Error level

The *%ERRORLEVEL%* expands to the exit code from a command, keyword or other Batch file execution. Please refer to the "The Errorlevel" section above.

User profile

Some user profile related environment variables:

- *%USERDOMAIN%*: The domain name of the currently logged in user
- *%USERNAME%*: The current username
- *%USERPROFILE%*: The user profile directory. Under that directory, you may also find the *Downloads*, *Desktop* and other folders.
- *%APPDATA%*: The user's app data folder
- *%LOCALAPPDATA%*: The user's local application data folder

System variables

These are some useful system related environment variables:

1. *%windir%* / *%SystemRoot%*: The current installation folder of MS Windows.
2. *%SystemDrive%*: The drive letter of where MS Windows is installed.
3. *%TMP%* / *%Temp%*: Writable temporary folder location. Use this path to generate intermediate / work files to be used while your script is executing.
4. *%ProgramFiles%* / *%ProgramFiles(x86)%*: The program files location. The former is for 64bits operating systems and the latter is the 32bits path.

Path

There are two important environment variables relevant to the search path of programs and how they get executed.

The first is the *%PATH%* variable that contains semicolon separated values containing a list of folders. When you type a command name, the command interpreter will first look in the current directory for that command, and if the command is not found then it will start looking in the *%PATH%* list until it finds the command name you typed.

Here's an example that sets the *PATH* environment variable by using other environment variables:

```
SET PATH=%windir%;%ProgramFiles%\WinRar;
```

Many times you may want to add a new search path to point to your utility folder. In that case, you can re-use the *%PATH%* variable as an input and then append or prepend the new path:

```
SET PATH=%PATH%;c:\tools\utils ← append to the path
SET PATH=c:\tools\utils;%PATH% ← prepend to the path
```

The second path-related environment variable is the *%PATHEXT%*. This variable contains a set of semicolon separated extensions that are used when resolving the full command path and extension of the command that you typed and want to run.

By default, the *PATHEXT* environment variable may contain something like the following values:

```
PATHEXT=.COM;.EXE;.BAT;.CMD;.VBS;.VBE;.JS;.JSE;.WSF;.WSH;.MSC
```

This means that if you try to execute any program or script without specifying its extension then each of the values of *PATHEXT* will be appended one at a time until the full command name (including its extension) is found. For example, if you have a program called *MyCopy.exe*, then it is sufficient to type "*MyCopy*" and the *.EXE* extension will be automatically deduced.

The order of the extensions in the *PATHEXT* environment variable dictates which program name will be picked and executed first. That means, if you have both a Batch file script and an executable with the same name (*MyTest.bat* and *MyTest.exe)*, then the executable will be executed first. In that case, you need to specify the program name and its extension to avoid confusion.

Other environment variables

1. *%PROCESSOR_ARCHITECTURE%*: The current processor architecture. Typical values are *x86* (for 32bits OSes) and *AMD64* (for 64bits OSes).
2. *%NUMBER_OF_PROCESSORS%*: The number of virtual processors.

3. *%ComSpec%*: It is a special environment variable that points to the current command interpreter. In MS Windows NT, this usually points to **CMD.EXE**. On the old MS-DOS or Win 9x/ME, it used to point to the **COMMAND.COM** program.
4. *%PROMPT%*: The current value of the prompt prefix. Please run "**PROMPT** /?" for more information.
5. *%DATE%*: This dynamic environment variable will expand to the current date string.
6. *%TIME%*: This dynamic environment variable will expand to the current time string.
7. *%RANDOM%*: This dynamic environment variable expands to a random decimal number between 0 and 32767.

Localizing the environment variables block

By default, any changes (creation, deletion or edition) to the environment variables taking place in Batch file scripts are exported to the parent command interpreter or the parent Batch file script.

For example, suppose we have a Batch file script (*t.bat*) with just the following contents:

```
@set TheVar=1
```

Now, let us call it and see its effect on the command interpreter's environment block:

```
C:\BatchProgramming>t.bat

C:\BatchProgramming>set TheVar
TheVar=1

C:\BatchProgramming>
```

As you can see, *TheVar* variable which was set in the script was exported to the environment block of the interpreter even after the script has terminated.

In simple terms, this means that the environment variables changes that took place in the Batch file were not local to the Batch file only.

To localize the environment variables and keep the changes bound within the executing Batch file script only, you can use the **SETLOCAL** and **ENDLOCAL** keywords. Any changes that are between those two keywords will not outlive the scope in which they are currently executing and are not exported to the caller's environment variables.

Let us illustrate those keywords with the *localvars.bat* script:

```
@echo off

setlocal

set Name=Mr. Anderson ①

echo The %%Name%% variable will not be exported to the interpreter...

endlocal

set Age=33 ②
echo The %%Age%% variable will be exported to the parent's environment
variable space.
```

Which will output:

```
C:\BatchProgramming>localvars
The %Name% variable will not be exported to the interpreter or calling
script
The %Age% variable will be exported to the parent's environment variable
space.

C:\BatchProgramming>set Name ①
Environment variable Name not defined

C:\BatchProgramming>set Age ②
Age=33

C:\BatchProgramming>
```

Having established that environment variables localization will revert all the changes to the environment block after **ENDLOCAL** is called, you may wonder if there is a way to persist some variables if needed. This topic will be addressed in details in the section entitled "Persisting changes beyond the ENDLOCAL call" in Chapter 3.

Delayed environment variables expansion

To understand what delayed environment variables expansion (DEVE) means, it is important to understand that by default, environment variables are expanded only once and that is when the statement/command referring to the variable is read.

This rule equally applies to compound commands like a multi-line **IF/ELSE** statement or the **FOR** loop statement. This is because the **IF**'s condition and the **FOR** body are all read at once and thus considered a single command.

Let me give you an example (*eve-test1.bat*) to illustrate how environment variables expansion happen when the statement is read rather than when the statement is executed (please refer to the “Conditional statements” and “Repetition Control Structures” sections to understand the **IF/FOR** keywords syntax):

```
@echo off

set value=1 ①

if "%value%"=="1" ( ②
      set value=2 ③
      echo The value inside the IF block is '%value%' ④
) ⑤

echo The value after the IF block is '%value%' ⑥
```

When executed, the script will give the following output:

```
C:\BatchProgramming>eve-test1.bat
The value inside the IF block is '1'
The value after the IF block is '2'
```

In the code above, the variable *value* is set to “1" at marker ①, then at marker ② the variable is read and expanded. The variable will retain its value as long as it is inside the scope of the **IF** statement which spawns a couple of lines (until the closing parenthesis at marker ⑤). At marker ③, a new value is assigned (inside the compound statement) and at marker ④ the variable is read again. This time it won't reflect the new value that was assigned to it at marker ③ because its value was previously read at marker ②. After marker ⑤, the command at marker ⑥ will have a chance to read the variable *value* again, but this time it will output the new and correct value.

Let me illustrate this using another example (*eve-test2.bat*), but this time without using compound statements, just to make it clear how the environment variables expansion plays out without the DEVE mechanism:

```
@echo off

      set value=1 ①

:repeat ②
      echo value is '%value%' ③

      if "%value%"=="1" set value=2 ④
      if "%value%"=="2" set value=3 ⑤
      if "%value%"=="3" goto end ⑥

      goto repeat ⑦
:end ⑧

      echo Done!
```

When executed, the script will give the following output:

```
C:\BatchProgramming>eve-test2.bat
value is '1'
Done!
```

If you were expecting a different, longer output, then let me chime in once more:

1. Set the *value* variable to 1.
2. Declare a label called *repeat*.
3. This is the first evaluation of the variable when the **ECHO** command is read and executed. It will be evaluated as 1.
4. The variable value is read again, and since this line does not belong to a compound statement, it will evaluate correctly and it will be updated to 2.
5. Similarly, for the same reasons as above, the value will be read and interpreted correctly as 3.
6. The variable "*value*" was previously set to 3 and will be expanded as such. This **IF** statement will evaluate to true and the **GOTO** will jump to the *end* label (at marker ⑧).
7. This line won't have a chance to execute!
8. Define the *end* label and terminate the script.

Another problematic example is illustrated using the following script (*eve-test3.bat*):

```
@echo off

SET C=-1 ①
FOR /L %%a IN (1, 1, 4) DO (
        set C=%%a ②
        echo a=%%a, C=%C% ③
) ④

ECHO after the loop, C=%C% ⑤
```

The script above displays the following when executed:

```
C:\BatchProgramming>eve-test3.bat
a=1, C=-1
a=2, C=-1
a=3, C=-1
a=4, C=-1
after the loop, C=4
```

As you noticed, the variable *C* is correctly updated after each **FOR** loop iteration (at marker ②), but it kept being incorrectly evaluated (at marker ③) until the **FOR** loop's body end at marker ④. However, the statement at marker ⑤ correctly evaluated the value of *C*.

With the delayed environment variables expansion (DEVE) syntax, it is possible to force the interpreter to evaluate the environment variables on statement execution rather than on statement reading.

By default, DEVE is turned off. There are two methods to enable DEVE.

Using the command:

```
SETLOCAL ENABLEDELAYEDEXPANSION
```

Or launching the command interpreter (*CMD.EXE*) with the "*/V:ON*" switch:

```
C:\BatchProgramming>cmd /?
Starts a new instance of the Windows command interpreter

CMD [/A | /U] [/Q] [/D] [/E:ON | /E:OFF] [/F:ON | /F:OFF] [/V:ON |
/V:OFF]
    [[/S] [/C | /K] string]
...
/V:ON   Enable delayed environment variable expansion using ! as the
        delimiter. For example, /V:ON would allow !var! to expand the
        variable var at execution time.  The var syntax expands variables
        at input time, which is quite a different thing when inside of a
FOR
        loop.
```

It is more common for Batch file scripts writers to enable DEVE dynamically from the script with the **SETLOCAL** keyword, rather than asking their users to re-run the command interpreter (*CMD.EXE*) with the "*/V:ON*" switch.

> *Note: it is possible to permanently enable or disable DEVE using the registry as well. Please run the "CMD.EXE /?" command for more information.*

When DEVE is enabled, you can expand the environment variables using two methods:

1. `%`*VarName*`%`: Expand on read. This is the regular mode.
2. `!`*VarName*`!`: Expand on execute. This mode is enabled only when DEVE is enabled.

The first method is the regular, non-delayed, expansion method. It happens when the command is read, as previously explained.

The second method is only available when DEVE is enabled. It tells the interpreter to expand the variable on execute. This expansion method is suitable when you are updating the variables inside compound **IF** statements or repetition control structures such as the **FOR** loop.

Let us now go over both the *eve-test1.bat* and *eve-test3.bat* and fix them so they work as intended. I will be applying two changes:

1. Enabling DEVE dynamically with "**SETLOCAL** ENABLEDELAYEDEXPANSION"
2. Replacing the environment variable expansion indicator character "**%**" (percent) with the "**!**" (exclamation mark).

The script *deve-test1.bat* illustrates all the required modifications:

```
@echo off

SETLOCAL ENABLEDELAYEDEXPANSION
set value=1

if "%value%"=="1" (
        set value=2
        echo The value inside the IF block is '!value!'
)

echo The value after the IF block is '%value%'
```

The second example is corrected as illustrated in the *deve-test3.bat* script below:

```
@echo off

setlocal ENABLEDELAYEDEXPANSION ①
SET C=-1
FOR /L %%a IN (1, 1, 4) DO (
  set C=%%a ②
echo a=%%a,regular expansion of C=%C% ③ and delayed expansion of ④C=!C!
)

ECHO After the loop, C=%C% ⑤
```

Please check the output of the script when it is executed, and observe how *C* is evaluated differently (marker ③ versus marker ④) based on the variable expansion syntax used:

```
C:\BatchProgramming>deve-test3.bat
a=1, regular expansion of C=-1 and delayed expansion of C=1
a=2, regular expansion of C=-1 and delayed expansion of C=2
a=3, regular expansion of C=-1 and delayed expansion of C=3
a=4, regular expansion of C=-1 and delayed expansion of C=4
After the loop, C=4
```

What changed is that I enabled DEVE as indicated by marker ① and used the exclamation mark ("!") at marker ④ to expand the variable on execution.

The last example in this section, *join-tokens.bat*, illustrates how to write a script that joins all the passed arguments and return them as a single string:

```
@echo off
setlocal enabledelayedexpansion

set RESULT=
for %%i in (%*) do set RESULT=!RESULT!%%i
echo %RESULT%

endlocal
```

Note the use of "%*" that returns all the arguments that were passed (separated by the space character), which are then passed to the **FOR** statement's "**set**" argument. The **FOR**'s body will use the delayed environment variable expansion syntax to append each argument to the *RESULT* variable. This script will become much more easy to understand when the **FOR** keyword syntax is explained in Chapter 2.

Two-level environment variables expansion

Often times, you may need to do double environment variables expansion. The first expansion resolves to a value (usually another environment variable name) and then the second expansion will return the actual value. In mathematical terms, it is like computing the result of a composite function *g(f(x))*. In pointer arithmetic terms, it is like dereferencing pointers.

Suppose that for instance, you have the following two environment variables:

```
set VARNAME=Name
set Name=Albert
```

The *VARNAME* variable contains the name of an environment variable, and in this case the value is "Name". Now the variable "Name" contains the actual value.

Effectively, if you managed to expand the variable *VARNAME* twice, then you should get the value "Albert".

Intuitively, you may attempt to write the following syntax to solve this scenario:

```
echo The variable value designated by VARNAME is: '%%%VARNAME%%%'
```

The double percent characters ("%%") surrounding the variable are used to escape the percent character itself. Effectively, after the first level of variable expansion, we would have the following output:

```
The variable value designated by VARNAME is: '%Name%'
```

Almost there! We need to run this output once more so that we get the "*%Name%*" properly expanded.

Thus, to achieve two-level expansions, we rely on using the **CALL** keyword.

By preceding a statement with the **CALL** keyword, we will get two-level expansion as intended:

```
call echo Two-level: The variable value designated by VARNAME is:
'%%%VARNAME%%%'
```

Which outputs the following:

```
The variable value designated by VARNAME is: 'Albert'
```

The source code of the snippet above can be found in the *env-expand-2.bat* script file.

In Chapter 2, in the section entitled "Using variable parameters with string operations", we will revisit this topic in more details and provide additional examples.

Using the SETX command

The **SETX** command allows you to create or modify environment variables system-wide or in the context of a given user on a local or remote machine. It has three major modes of operations which allow you to set an environment variable's value from:

1. A string
2. A value from registry
3. A string or line value from a file on disk

This command is beyond the scope of this book. Please run "SETX /?" to get the complete usage syntax.

Labels

In the Batch files scripting language, labels act like anchors or bookmarks: they are used to create a logical association between a script line number and a label name. When they are present in the script, they don't produce any output or execute anything.

Labels are defined in Batch file scripts by preceding the label name with the colon (":") character. For example:

```
:MyLabel
```

In order to go to a label, use the **GOTO** keyword:

```
echo Hello world
goto label1
echo Skipped
:label1
echo This is label 1
goto label2
echo Skipped
:label2
Echo This is Label 2
```

Unless the **GOTO** keyword is linked with another conditional command, then attempting to go to an invalid or non-existent label will cause your script to abort with an error.

Take a look at the *goto-label.bat* test script:

```
@echo off

goto %1 ①

echo Unreachable code ②

:ValidLabel ③
      echo yes!
      goto :eof
```

The script above takes the label name from the command line arguments and attempts to go to the label (marker ①). However, in the script there's only one valid label, defined at marker ③, and it is called "*ValidLabel*". In all cases though, the code at marker ② is unreachable no matter what the label value is!

Let's run this script with a few invalid label arguments and observe what happens:

```
C:\BatchProgramming>goto-label InvalidLabel
The system cannot find the batch label specified - InvalidLabel

C:\BatchProgramming>goto-label AnotherInvalidLabel
The system cannot find the batch label specified - AnotherInvalidLabel

C:\BatchProgramming>
```

Both of the errors that were displayed come from the interpreter who complained and aborted the script.

Now let us run the script again with a valid label argument:

```
C:\BatchProgramming>goto-label ValidLabel
yes

C:\BatchProgramming>
```

We can make our script more resilient to errors stemming from jumping to invalid or non-existent labels by joining the **GOTO** keyword with the logical-OR ("||") as illustrated in the *goto-label-resilient.bat* script:

```
@echo off

goto %1 || (
      echo Failed to go to that label!
      goto :eof
)

echo Unreachable code

:ValidLabel
      echo ValidLabel reached!
      goto :eof
```

This script does not differ too much from the *goto-label.bat* script, except that it is coupled with the logical-OR and a compound statement that will be executed if the **GOTO** fails:

```
C:\BatchProgramming>goto-label-resilient.bat invalidlabel
The system cannot find the batch label specified - invalidlabel ①
Failed to go to that label!

C:\BatchProgramming>
```

As we have seen in the previous script, when the **GOTO** keyword fails it will display an error and abruptly terminate the script unless it is coupled with a conditional statement.

When it is coupled with another statement, the **GOTO** will return a non-zero return value if it fails, thus giving a chance to the conditional statement (joined with the logical-OR operator in our case) to execute the second statement.

Even though the conditional statement got a chance to execute, we still got an error message on the screen (marker ①). We can mask that error by redirecting the standard error output of the **GOTO** keyword to the **NUL** device (*goto-label-resilient-2.bat*):

```
@echo off

goto %1 >nul 2>&1 || (
	echo Failed to go to that label!
	goto :eof
)

echo Unreachable code

:ValidLabel
	echo ValidLabel!
	goto :eof
```

Let's execute the script and observe how we won't get the error message as before:

```
C:\BatchProgramming>goto-label-resilient-2.bat invalidvalidlabel
Failed to go to that label!

C:\BatchProgramming>
```

More about that masking command errors in the section entitled "Standard Input/Output redirection".

The EOF label

The "*:eof*" label is a special label and is available for use only when the *Command Extensions* are enabled. Depending on the context, if you jump to that label (with the **GOTO** keyword) then the Batch file script will either terminate or return back to the caller.

Unlike the previous **GOTO** examples, you have to explicitly prefix the destination label name with ":" like this:

```
GOTO :eof
```

Therefore, the above is not equivalent to the following:

```
 GOTO EOF
```

Let's test this special label using the following example (*goto-eof.bat*):

```
@echo off

goto eof ①

echo Unreachable, due to jumping to a label in the file.

:eof ②

echo a real label is here

goto :eof ③


echo Unreached code, due to "GOTO :EOF"
```

The code at marker ① goes to the actual label called "*eof*" that is defined at marker ②. However, at marker ③, we simply terminate the Batch file script.

```
C:\BatchProgramming>goto-eof.bat
a real label is here

C:\BatchProgramming>
```

Note: Using "GOTO :EOF" is equivalent to using "EXIT /B" except that the former does not change the %ERRORLEVEL% pseudo-environment variable value.

Function calls

You can call a label using the **CALL** keyword by preceding the label name with the colon (":"). When a label is called, then it is possible to return back from the call to the caller. This is akin to the "function calls" concepts in high-level programming languages.

To return from a "function call" just issue a "**GOTO** :eof" as explained in the previous section.

Let's take a look at the script *func-call.bat*:

```
@echo off

      call :function1
      call :function2 arg1 arg2

      goto :eof

:function1
      echo This is function 1
      rem Return from the function
      goto :eof

:function2
      echo Inside function 2
      echo The arguments are: %*
      goto :eof
```

When executed, we observe the following output:

```
C:\BatchProgramming>func-call.bat
This is function 1
Inside function 2
The arguments are: arg1 arg2
```

You may also use the "EXIT /B [optionalReturnCode]" syntax to return from a function call.

> *Note: Remember that if "EXIT /B" is used outside the scope of a function call then the script will terminate!*

It is also possible to call labels inside other files. This can be achieved with a little bit of trickery and creativity. Please refer to the section entitled "Building, testing and using a utility Batch file script library" in Chapter 3.

Now the following question arises: how to have a function terminate the Batch file script knowing that the "**EXIT /B**" syntax will not do that when executing from the scope of a function?

To address that, we need to introduce a syntax error inside the function call and have the interpreter terminate the Batch file script execution for us:

```
@echo off

call :L1

echo after L1 ①

goto :eof

:L1

  echo Fatal error in L1. Terminating the script! ②

  call :TermScript 2>nul
  goto :eof


:TermScript
if ③
```

Let us execute the script and see if the code a marker ① gets executed or not:

```
Fatal error in L1. Terminating the script!
```

Nope, it did not. Only the code at marker ② gets executed and the code at marker ① never gets a chance because the script called the "*TermScript*" label which introduced a syntax error at marker ③, thus forcing the interpreter to terminate the script.

Calling invalid or non-existent labels

As it is the case with labels, there is a possibility of making the mistake of calling a non-existent label. When that happens, unlike the **GOTO** keyword, the **CALL** keyword will complain but will not fatally terminate the script (*func-call-invalid.bat*):

```
@echo off

echo -- Calling invalid function
call :function-not-there ①
echo After invalid function call -- ②

echo.

echo -- Calling function1
call :function1
echo After function 1 --

goto :eof

:function1
      echo This is function 1
      rem Return from the function
      goto :eof
```

*Note: it is on purpose that the code at marker ① calls the label "*function-not-there*" which is invalid. This is just to have the interpreter complain and display an error message.*

Let's execute the script and observe the output:

```
C:\BatchProgramming>func-call-invalid.bat
-- Calling invalid function
The system cannot find the batch label specified - function-not-there
After invalid function call --

-- Calling function1
This is function 1
After function 1 --

C:\BatchProgramming>
```

We got an error (at marker ①) that clearly explains what the problem was. Instead of aborting, the script continued to execute at marker ② and onwards.

We can suppress the error and fail silently using the standard error redirection (as we did previously with the **GOTO**):

```
call :function-not-there 2>nul
```

Additionally, we can join the **CALL** with a conditional statement and display a custom error message instead (and opt to resume or abort):

```
echo -- Calling invalid function
call :function-not-there 2>nul || (
      echo The CALL failed...opting to resume...
      :: You may decide to just "EXIT /B"
)
echo After invalid function call --
```

The full function source of the previous snippet is found in *func-call-resilient.bat*.

> *Note: It is very important to only redirect the standard error and not also the standard output. This is especially important if the CALL succeeds and the called function returns output to the standard output (with ECHO or any other means). We do not want that output to be masked out.*

Make sure you clear the *ERRORLEVEL* value after successfully returning from the called label, otherwise the caller that is using the conditional-OR will still execute the next statement if the return value was non-zero. Therefore use "EXIT /B 0" specifically.

Defining function prototypes

If you have a lot of functions in your Batch file script, for clarity purposes, you may want to define the "prototype" of the called labels using any style you wish. You may, for example, add descriptive text after the label declaration on the same line.

For example:

```
@echo off
setlocal
call :add 1 5 ①
echo The result is %result%
goto :eof

:: Add two numbers
:add (num1, num2) ②
      SET /A result=%1+%2
      GOTO :eof

endlocal
```

Note how at marker ①, we called the function called *add* and at marker ②, the function body is defined along with its prototype (in freestyle form).

When returning numbers from a Batch file script function, you can use the "**EXIT** /B [optionalExitCode]" trick to return the numeric value as the exit code and then pick it up from the caller's site with the *%ERRORLEVEL%* pseudo-environment variable (*func-add.bat*):

```
@echo off
:main
      setlocal
      call :add 1 5
      echo The result is %errorlevel%
      goto :eof

:: Add two numbers
:add (num1, num2)
      SET /A result=%1+%2
      exit /b %result%
```

Checking the existence of a label

There's another method that we can use to check if a **CALL** or **GOTO** target label exists in the executing script. This method involves invoking the **FINDSTR** to scan for the label in the script that is currently executing. The script *goto-label-resilient-findstr.bat* illustrates this case:

```
@echo off

if "%1"=="" (
      echo  No label passed, please pass a label name
      goto :eof
)

findstr /B /X /C:":%~1" "%~f0">nul && goto %~1 || ( ①
      echo The label "%~1" does not exist!
      exit /b -1
)

goto :eof

:mylabel1
      echo this is mylabel1
      goto :eof

:mylabel2
      echo this is mylabel2
      goto :eof
```

We are invoking the **FINDSTR** command with the "/X" switch for an exact match, with the "/B" to match the label name at the beginning of the line and with the "/C:" to specify the string to look for. The **FINDSTR** and the **GOTO** are joined conditionally with the "&&" (which will let the **GOTO** execute if the **FINDSTR** succeeds).

Those two AND-joined commands are then joined with an OR compound statement which only gets executed if the former command fails (the last two joined commands). When the label is not found, **FINDSTR** will return non-zero and the AND will short-circuit, thus giving a turn to the OR ("||") statement to execute and display the error message explaining that the label does not exist.

Let's run the script twice, one time with an existing label and another with a non-existing label:

```
C:\BatchProgramming>goto-label-resilient-findstr.bat mylabel1
this is mylabel1

C:\BatchProgramming>goto-label-resilient-findstr.bat mylabel313
The label "mylabel313" does not exist!

C:\BatchProgramming>
```

Taking input from the user

Taking input from the user is very useful because it makes your script interactive. One way to take a string input from the user is accomplished by using the **SET /P** syntax (*ask-user.bat*):

```
set /P Name="Please enter your name: "
echo Welcome %Name%
```

The "/P" switch has the following syntax:

```
SET /P EnvironmentVariableName="The prompt you want to display"
```

Let's execute this script:

```
C:\BatchProgramming>ask-user.bat
Please enter your name: Ashmole
Welcome Ashmole

C:\BatchProgramming>
```

Let us suppose that you want to keep taking input from the user until the user enters nothing by just pressing the ENTER key. You would normally write a script like this:

```
@echo off
setlocal
:repeat
       set /p input=enter value:
       if "%input%"=="" goto :eof
       echo -^> %input%
       goto repeat
```

Which is correct expect for the case when the user really just presses ENTER without entering anything: the loop will not terminate!

If you press ENTER as a response to a "**SET /P**" prompt without entering anything, then the environment variable will not be updated and its previous value is kept unchanged. For this reason, you have to make sure you clear the input environment variable before you pass it to "**SET /P**".

The new script (*ask-user-2.bat*) becomes:

```
@echo off
setlocal

:repeat
       set input= ①
       set /p input=enter value:
       if "%input%"=="" goto :eof
       echo -^> %input%
       goto repeat
```

Note how at marker ①, we clear the input environment variable value prior to each prompt.

Let's run this script and observe the input when we enter two non-empty lines and a third empty line (which causes to loop to break):

```
C:\BatchProgramming>ask-user-2.bat
enter value: hello
-> hello
enter value: world
-> world
enter value:

C:\BatchProgramming>
```

Standard Input/Output redirection

The standard input and output are predefined channels for consuming input or output. If they are not redirected, then the standard input and output are associated with the console input and output.

Other channels for consuming input or output are: files, devices, printers, COM ports, serial and parallel ports, etc.

There is another output channel called the standard error. It is a separate output channel used to output error messages.

Each one of those three predefined channels have a pre-assigned file handle (or number) associated with them:

- Standard input (*stdin*) has the file number 0
- Standard output (*stdout*) has the file number 1
- Standard error (*stderr*) has the file number 2

This knowledge will be handy in the cases where we want to explicitly specify which channel we intend to redirect by specifying its number.

Special files and devices

There are special files and devices defined in MS Windows that you can use as candidates for I/O consumption (redirection, reading and/or writing):

- **CON**: This special device is associated with the console. Anything written to it goes to the screen buffer, and anything read from it is interactively retrieved by waiting for user input.
- **NUL**: This special device, as its name implies writes to nowhere when it is used for output redirection and returns the EOF when used for input redirection.
- **COM1** to **COM9**: These devices are connected with the serial COM ports.
- **PRN**: This device is usually associated with the printer port.

Please note that you cannot directly create a file named "CON" or any of those special device names. Instead, you have to use the "\\?\" prefix like this:

```
C:\BatchProgramming>notepad c:\temp\con       ← Does not work!
C:\BatchProgramming>notepad \\?\c:\temp\con   ← Works!
```

Using output redirection in Batch file scripts

Let me now explain how to use the output redirection in Batch file scripts. When you run a command that outputs something to the standard output (*stdout*), you can choose to redirect the output somewhere else: to another file or device.

A typical use of output redirection in Batch file scripts is to either redirect the output to the **NUL** device or to a new or existing file (in that case, appending takes place).

Redirecting to the **NUL** device means that you don't care about the output of certain commands and you want to mask the output.

On the other hand, redirecting to a file usually means that you want to log the execution of certain commands for later processing.

To redirect the output, the command you type should terminate with one of the following redirection symbols/syntax:

- Use the ">" sign to redirect to a new file.
- Use the double ">" sign like this ">>" to append to an existing file or create a new file (if the file did not exist before) and start appending to it.
- Prefix the ">" sign with the output file number in case you want to be explicit. By default, the ">" sign alone (without any output file number prefix) indicates that *stdout* is being redirected. This is equivalent to using "*1>*". To redirect the *stderr*, use "*2>*".
- Use the "2>&1" syntax to have the *stderr* redirect to the same output as *stdout*. If *stdout* was redirected to the **NUL** device for instance, so will *stderr*.

Here are some examples from *io-redir.bat*:

```
(1) ECHO This will be written to a file>newfile.txt
(2) ECHO This will be appended or written to file2.txt >>file2.txt
(3) ECHO This will also be written to file2.txt >>file2.txt
(4) ECHO This will overwrite newfile.txt>newfile.txt
(5) ECHO This will redirect the stdout and stderr to two separate text
    files>stdout-file.txt 2>stderr-file.txt
(6) ECHO This will redirect the stdout to a file and stderr to the same
    output >stdout-file.txt 2>&1
(7) ECHO Nothing will be displayed!>NUL
```

Notice that we appended the ">" at the end of the command. Now, the explanation of the above examples is as follows:

(1) Outputs a message, not to the console, but to a new file.
(2) Creates or appends the output to *file2.txt*.
(3) It will append to *file2.txt* (because the file was created already in the previous line).
(4) Because a single redirection symbol (">") is used, then the file created in line 1 is overwritten.
(5) Here we redirect both the standard output and standard error to two separate files (*stdout-file.txt* and *stderr-file.txt*).
(6) Redirect *stdout* to a file and then redirect *stderr* to the same (without repeating the redirection output target name).
(7) Here we display a string but only to end up redirecting it to the *NUL* device.

There is another syntax that you can use to redirect the output. The command starts with the redirection symbol, followed by the redirection destination and then the command to execute:

```
>out.txt echo hello world!
```

Or:

```
>nul dir /w
```

Etc.

Redirecting output of multiple commands

You can redirect the output of several commands like this:

```
dir /w >out.txt & echo hello>msg.txt
```

The example above will redirect the two commands into two different files.

To redirect the output of various commands into the same file, we should group the commands with parenthesis like this (*io-redir-compound.bat*):

```
REM Single line compound commands
(dir /w & echo Some output & echo Some more output) >out.txt ①

REM Multiple lines compound commands
( ②
      dir /w
      echo Some output
      echo Some more output
) >out2.txt ③
```

1. At the first marker, we use the ampersand "&" to unconditionally join commands on a single line.
2. Here we used the compound statements syntax by surrounding the commands to group with "(" and ")".
3. We closed the commands group with ")" and then redirected the output of the whole compound statement to a file.

> *Note: The output will be emitted serially: first command's output goes first, second command's output goes after and so on.*

Using input redirection in Batch file scripts

Having explained the output redirection in the previous section, it is now easier to understand how the input redirection works.

When you run a command that requires input, usually from the console (typed with the keyboard, interactively), you can redirect the input to another file or device (such as **CON**, **COMx** and the like).

A typical use of input redirection is when you want to answer a set of input questions in a scripted manner. A text file that contains a set of responses to be passed as input to a program is usually called a "response file".

To redirect the input, the command you type should terminate with the "<" symbol followed by the input file or device name.

For instance, the **FTP.EXE** utility is an interactive command line tool. Let us assume that it cannot be scripted (in reality, it is scriptable when the "*-s*" switch is passed).

The first thing the **FTP** utility prompts for is the login user name and then the password. We can prepare a response file (*ftp-resp.txt*) like this:

```
anonymous
ebooks@passingtheknowledge.net
ls
quit
```

And then we run **FTP** like this:

```
C:\BatchProgramming>ftp ftp.mozilla.org<ftp-resp.txt
```

And the output we expect is:

```
User (ftp.mozilla.org:(none)): Password:
README
index.html
pub

C:\BatchProgramming>
```

Essentially, all we did is simply provide the user name on the first line, the password (as an email address) on the second line, a command to run on the third line (the **ls** command) and then the "**quit**" command.

Redirecting the input to the CON device

When redirecting the input to the **CON** device, the program will start to take the input interactively (from the console). To terminate the input, press *Ctrl+Z* (or *F6*) on your keyboard then press ENTER. This key combination has the ASCII code value of 26 which designates the end of file (EOF). This is equivalent to pressing *Ctrl+D* under UNIX based operating systems.

Mixing input and output redirection

It is possible to mix the input and output redirection by using the input and output syntax simultaneously in the same command. For instance, suppose that you have a utility called *makeupper.exe*. This utility takes input from **stdin** (the console) and writes back to the standard output all the lines in upper case letters. This utility is designed to work interactively and it does not have command line switches that lets the user pass input or output file names to be used.

Can we make this utility work from our Batch file script without requiring interactive input?

Yes. Luckily, with I/O redirection, we can automate this utility so it takes all the input needed from a file and have it write the result to a file instead of the console:

```
C:\BatchProgramming>makeupper <inputfile.txt >outputfile.txt
```

Here's what we did: first redirect the input of this utility to a file called *inputfile.txt* and then redirect its output to a new file called *outputfile.txt*.

Voila! We automated a third party utility.

Pipes

The concept of pipes is very similar to that of the I/O redirection concept but they are not the same thing. As the name suggest, a pipe is used to connect two programs together: the output of one program is piped to and used as input in another program.

By now you know what the following command does:

```
ECHO My name is agent Smith
```

And what the following does:

```
SET /P Name="What is your name?"
```

Those two separate commands can be piped together. The first one produces an output and the second one prompts for an input. That's a perfect example to illustrate the general syntax of how to use pipes (*pipe-1.bat*):

```
ECHO My name is agent Smith | SET /P Name="What is your name?"
ECHO Result is %Name%
```

Traditionally, we cannot talk about pipes without talking about the **MORE** utility. This utility displays the input it receives one screen at a time. It useful when you run a command that produces a long output or when you are dumping the contents of a text file (using the **TYPE** keyword) and you want to read the output one page at a time.

For example, type the following command:

```
DIR %WINDIR%
```

You may get a long listing, therefore forcing you to scroll up and down in your console window to read the output. This is where piping to the **MORE** command comes into play:

```
DIR | MORE
```

In this case, the whole output is captured (because of the pipe "|") and then it is passed to **MORE** which will display the output one page at a time.

Chaining pipes

It is possible to chain multiple pipes together and then also use I/O redirection if needed.

Let's suppose we have a text file with the following contents (*more-lines.txt*):

```
line 1
line 2
line 3
line 4
line 5
line 6
```

The **MORE** command has various command line arguments. If it is passed the "+*N*" argument, then **MORE** will skip *N* lines and starts displaying the output after *N* lines:

```
TYPE more-lines.txt | MORE +1
```

We should get the file content except the first line because we instructed **MORE** to skip it:

```
C:\BatchProgramming>type more-lines.txt | more +1
line 2
line 3
line 4
line 5
line 6
```

Now let us chain a few **MORE** commands together:

```
C:\BatchProgramming>type more-lines.txt | more +1 | more +1
line 3
line 4
line 5
line 6
```

Pipes will be very handy especially when we want to pipe the output to the **FINDSTR** command for further filtering.

In the following simple example, we will use the **FINDSTR** command with the "/V" switch to display all lines except for the lines containing the string "line 3":

```
C:\BatchProgramming>type more-lines.txt | findstr /V /C:"line 3"
line 1
line 2
line 4
line 5
line 6
```

In Chapter 4 of this book there will be more examples involving pipes and external commands like the **FINDSTR** command.

Arithmetic operations

It is possible to do arithmetic operation in Batch file scripts. The **SET** keyword with the "/A" switch can be used for that purpose:

```
SET /A VariableName=(Expression1 Operator Expression2)
SET /A Var1=Expression2,Var2=Expression2, …
```

Similar to the C programming language or other high-level languages, it is possible to do various computations. Some of the operators coincide/conflict with the reserved Batch files scripting operators such as the I/O redirection symbols, etc. Therefore, we have to escape conflicting symbols.

These are some of the possible operations:

1. Group expressions to override the operators' precedence using the parenthesis symbols (")" and "(").
2. Bitwise operations:
   - >> and << for shifting right or left
   - | (OR), & (AND), ^ (XOR)
3. Arithmetic operations:
   - +, -, *, / (division) and "%" (modulus)
4. Unary operators:
   - "!" logical not
   - "~" bitwise not

        - "-" negation
5. Assignment operators:
    - The equal sign is used for assignment
    - An operator preceding the assignment character can be used as well (>>=, <<=, *=, +=, etc.)
6. Multiple expressions:
    - Separate multiple expressions using the comma character (",").

<u>Some important things to consider:</u>

1. As you may have noticed, there are operators that also coincide with the special symbols. In that case, you either have to escape those operators with the caret symbol or just encapsulate the expression inside quotes instead.
2. If you want to refer to previously defined variables, you don't have to enclose them with the percent sign, instead just write the variable name directly.
3. If you try to refer to a variable that is not defined then it will resolve to 0.
4. It is possible to use other number bases as you would in C-like high-level programming languages:
    - Prefix numbers with "0x" to designate hexadecimal numbers.
    - Prefix numbers with "0" to designate octal numbers.

Here's a comprehensive example, *expr-1.bat*, to illustrate most of the operations:

```
@echo off

:: Do not expose all the environment variables used in this script
SETLOCAL

:: Simple expression

SET /A var1="1+(2*4)"

:: Referring to another variable w/o enclosing with the % character
SET /A var2=var1 + 2

:: Bitwise AND
SET /A var3="var1 & 1"

:: Modulus
SET /A var4="var1 %% 2"

:: Shift to the left
SET /A var5="1<<7"

:: Bitwise negation
```

```
SET /A var6="~var1"

:: Defining hexadecimal number
SET /A var7="0x1234"

:: Shift left assignment
SET /A var8=1
SET /A var8^<^<=2

:: Display all the variables
SET var

IF %var3% EQU 1 echo var1 is odd

ENDLOCAL
```

Let's execute this script and observe the output:

```
C:\BatchProgramming>expr-1
var1=9
var2=11
var3=1
var4=1
var5=128
var6=-10
var7=4660
var8=4
var1 is odd

C:\BatchProgramming>
```

Summary

This chapter laid down the foundations of the Batch files scripting language by showing you how to get started with the command prompt from customization tips, keyboard shortcuts, editing tips, command recalling and path completion, to briefly introducing you to a bunch of useful commands.

Subsequently, the chapter continued by introducing the remaining of the foundational topics:

- The "command echo" which is the most basic command and concept.
- The *ERRORLEVEL* concept and how it is used and why.
- Command extensions and what more value they bring along.
- Long, multi-line, compound and conditional statements.
- Batch file scripting comments and their various styles.
- Special characters and how to escape them.
- Brief introduction to parsing command line arguments and using the **`SHIFT`** keyword.
- Environment variables, pseudo/dynamic environment variables, environment variables localization and finally how to work with the delayed variables expansion.
- Labels and function calls.
- Standard input/output redirection and pipes.
- Arithmetic operations and how to take input form the user.

In the next chapter, I will introduce more advanced Batch files scripting language topics that allow you build more complex program logic.

CHAPTER 2

Batch Files Programming

This chapter brings you one more step further to understanding more of the advanced features in the Batch files scripting language. I will cover various important programming concepts such as conditional statements, repetition control structures and string operations.

After those topics are covered, I will cover data structures such as single dimensional arrays, multi-dimensional arrays, associative arrays (dictionaries), stacks and sets.

Along the way, there will be lots of examples that explain each topic.

Conditional statements

No language is complete without allowing conditional statements and the Batch files scripting language is no exception: it also has support for **IF** statements.

Here's the basic syntax of the **IF** keyword:

```
IF [NOT] ERRORLEVEL number command
IF [NOT] string1==string2 command
IF [NOT] EXIST filename command
```

The square brackets around the **NOT** keyword indicate that this keyword is optional. If the **NOT** keyword is present right after the **IF** keyword, then the condition will be negated.

This is the explanation of the three previous different syntaxes of the **IF** keyword:

1. Checks if the **ERRORLEVEL** equals or not equals a given numeric value.
2. Checks if two strings or anything that resolves to strings (environment variables for example) are equal or not.
3. Checks if a file exists or not.

After each **IF** condition, you have to pass a command. For example, to check if a given file exists and then carry an action afterwards:

```
IF EXIST myfile.bat ECHO The file exists!
IF EXIST logfile.txt DEL logfile.txt
IF NOT EXIST utility.exe ECHO The utility was not found! & GOTO end
```

In facsimile, to check if the exit code of a previously executed command is 1, we can do:

```
IF ERRORLEVEL 1 command
```

And to see if the exit code is not 1, then we simply invert the condition like this:

```
IF NOT ERRORLEVEL 1 command
```

The **IF** keyword can be paired with the **ELSE** keyword that is used to logically complement the condition:

```
IF Condition (Command) ELSE Command
```

Notice how we surrounded the **IF**'s command inside parenthesis (we can optionally surround the ELSE's command in parenthesis as well).

Let's illustrate this with an example:

```
IF EXIST file.txt (ECHO The file exists) ELSE ECHO The file does not
exist!
```

For clarity purposes, it is preferable that you use multiline commands whenever you plan to use the **ELSE** keyword.

Multiline commands

It is possible to execute multiple commands (aka compound statements) inside an **IF**'s or **ELSE**'s body clause. You need to open the parenthesis just after the condition on the same line as the **IF** or the **ELSE** keywords:

```
IF Condition ( ←open parenthesis
Command1
Command2
…
) ←Close the parenthesis
```

Similarly, if you intend to have an **ELSE** clause, then the syntax should look like this:

```
IF Condition ( ← open
   Commands go here
   ...
   ...
) ELSE ( ← Close the IF's parenthesis, then open new ones for the ELSE
   ...
   Else commands go here
   ...
) ← Close the ELSE's parenthesis
```

You may nest as many **IF** and **ELSE** statements you want inside each other:

```
IF Condition (
       IF Condition (
              ...
       )
) ELSE (
       IF Condition (
       ) ELSE (
              ...
       )
)
```

Note that the parenthesis should be present on the same line as the **IF** or the **ELSE** keyword. Thus, the following syntax is incorrect:

```
IF Condition
(
)
ELSE
(
)
```

Checking the command line arguments

You can use the **IF** statement to check if certain command line arguments were passed or not. In this section, I will focus on explaining just the basics but in the next chapter I will explain this topic in more detail.

The *args-check1.bat* script will give you an idea of what can be done:

```
@echo off

:main
      if "%1"=="" goto Usage ①
      if "%1"=="compress" goto compress
      if "%1"=="uncompress" goto uncompress

      rem Unknown command passed, display the usage!
      echo Unknown command '%1'!!
      goto usage

:Usage ①
      ECHO %0 compress^|uncompress archive.zip ③
      goto end

:compress
      if "%2"=="" (
            echo No archive name was passed!
            goto Usage
      )

      echo Compressing current folder into archive '%2'
      REM invoke the compression utility
      goto end

:uncompress
      if "%2"=="" goto Usage ②
      if "%2"=="" ( ②
            echo No archive name was passed!
            goto Usage
      )

      if not exist %2 ( ④
            ECHO The archive '%2' is not found!
            goto end
      )
      echo Uncompressing the archive '%2' into the current folder
      REM invoke the decompression utility
      goto end
```

```
:end
```

And when executed with various arguments or the lack of them, it outputs the following:

```
C:\BatchProgramming>args-check1 ← no arguments passed!
args-check1 compress|uncompress archive.zip

C:\BatchProgramming>args-check1 cmd ← one arg. passed
Unknown command 'cmd'!!
args-check1 compress|uncompress archive.zip

C:\BatchProgramming>args-check1 compress
No archive name was passed!
args-check1 compress|uncompress archive.zip

C:\BatchProgramming>args-check1 compress file.zip ← two args passed
Compressing current folder into archive 'file.zip'

C:\BatchProgramming>args-check1 uncompress nofile.zip
The archive 'nofile.zip' is not found!

C:\BatchProgramming>args-check1 uncompress file.zip
Uncompressing the archive 'file.zip' into the current folder

C:\BatchProgramming>
```

Some important code annotations to observe:

1. To handle each **IF** statement and execute code when the condition is met, I could have used function calls instead of using **GOTO** statements.
2. I mix and match single-line **IF** statements and multi-line **IF** statements.
3. The caret character was used to escape the pipe character before displaying it.
4. File existence checks were used.

The reason the argument variables (%1, %2, etc.) are wrapped on both sides with quotes is because if those variables are missing (or if they expand to nothing), then we won't get an **IF** syntax error.

Here's an illustrative example:

```
IF %1==help ECHO Showing help screen
```

Let me run this script twice, once with a command line argument passed and once without:

```
C:\BatchProgramming>check-vars-quotes.bat ← no argument passed
ECHO was unexpected at this time.

C:\BatchProgramming>IF ==help ECHO Showing help screen
```

Notice how the **IF** syntax became "IF ==help" because "%1" expanded to an empty value, hence the syntax error!

On the other hand, if an argument was passed:

```
C:\BatchProgramming>check-vars-quotes.bat compress

C:\BatchProgramming>IF compress == help ECHO Showing help screen
```

Then the expansion yields a correct syntax: "IF compress == help".

You are not limited to using just the quotes character to wrap the variables inside an **IF** statement. You can use any other character. The goal is to prevent empty expansions from causing syntax errors.

Consider the following example:

```
IF .%1.==.help. ECHO Showing help screen
```

Notice how I wrapped the *%1* with the dot character this time (it could be any other suitable character).

When this script is executed, even if no arguments were passed, then the statement would expand to:

```
IF .. == .help. ECHO Showing help screen
```

Which is still a correct syntax. In facsimile, if we pass command line arguments:

```
C:\BatchProgramming>check-vars-quotes.bat help

C:\BatchProgramming>IF .help. == .help. ECHO Showing help screen
Showing help screen
```

Then the condition still works properly as intended. Please refer to the *check-vars-quotes.bat* sample snippet.

Extended syntax

The **IF** statement has an extended syntax when the command extensions are enabled.

The new syntax of the **IF** statement becomes:

1. IF **[/I]** Value1 comparison-operator Value2 Command
2. IF [NOT] **DEFINED** variableName Command

The optional "/I" switch will turn the case-insensitive comparison on; this is useful when you are comparing strings.

The **DEFINED** keyword can be used to check if an environment variable is defined or not.

Additionally, the following comparison operators can be used:

1. **EQU** and **NEQ** for equality and inequality respectively.
2. **LSS** and **LEQ** for less-than and less-than-or-equal respectively.
3. **GTR** and **GEQ** for greater-than and greater-than-or-equal respectively.

The values to be compared on the left and right side of the comparison operators do not have to be just strings: if they can be interpreted as numbers then numerical comparison will take place.

Here's a simple example, *if-ex.bat*, illustrating the extending **IF** syntax:

```
@echo off

setlocal ENABLEEXTENSIONS

set GodMode=

SET /P Name="Please enter your name: "
IF /I "%Name%" EQU "iddqd" ( ①
      ECHO God mode enabled!
      SET GodMode=1 ②
)

SET /P Age="Please enter your age: "
IF %Age% LSS 18 ( ③
      ECHO Sorry, you're under age...terminating.
      GOTO :EOF
)
```

```
if %Age% GEQ 90 ( ④
        if NOT DEFINED GodMode ( ⑤
                ECHO Whooa, you still have the spirit mortal!
        )
)

echo Let the party begin...
if DEFINED GodMode ( ⑥
        ECHO !! God mode ON. You earned unlimited free drinks!!
)
endlocal
```

Let me explain the annotated code:

1. Use case-insensitive string comparison to compare the entered name against a special magic string value.
2. If the special name value is entered, then "God mode" is enabled by setting the *GodMode* environment variable.
3. Use the **LSS** (less than) operator to see if the user is under age or not. The script will terminate if so.
4. Use the **GEQ** (greater or equal) operator to check if the user is too old.
5. If so, then greet him/her with an awesome message, only if *GodMode* is not defined.
6. Check if *GodMode* is defined and give unlimited free drinks.

Switch/Case syntax

There is no built-in "switch/case" syntax in the Batch files scripting language, however we can achieve that with environment variables and the **GOTO** or the **CALL** syntax.

Let's assume we have the following set of **IF** statements which check the values of the variable "*N*" and act accordingly:

```
set /P N=Enter number:
call :nested-if
goto :eof

:nested-if

        echo Nested IFs...

        if %N%==1 (
                echo One
        ) ELSE (
```

```
        if %N%==2 (
                echo Two
        ) ELSE (
                if %N%==3 (
                        echo Three
                ) ELSE (
                        echo Something else
                )
        )
)

echo After IFs
goto :eof
```

In short, the code above converts numbers 1 to 3 to their textual representations, and for any other number the text "Something else" is printed. Due to the lack of the **`ELSE IF`** keyword, we ended up having lots of nested **`IF`** statements.

Now, let's see how we can convert those **`IF`** statements into a similar logic but using the "switch/case" syntax:

```
:switch-case
echo Switch/case

:: Call and mask out invalid call targets
call :switch-case-N-%N% 2>nul || ( ①
        :: Default case ②
        echo Something else
)
goto :switch-case-end ③

:switch-case-N-1 ④
        echo One
        goto :eof ⑤

:switch-case-N-2 ④
        echo Two
        goto :eof ⑤

:switch-case-N-3 ④
        echo Three
        goto :eof ⑤

:switch-case-end ⑥
⑦
echo After Switch/case
```

```
        goto :eof
```

At marker ①, we used the **CALL** keyword to call a variable label name of the form "switch-case-N-<*number value*>". We also redirect the standard error output of the **CALL** to the **NUL** device and conditionally execute the default case (marker ②) if the called label was not found.

If the called label exists, then the appropriate label will be called. The code markers ④ designate the beginning of each case handler. The code markers ⑤ terminate the handler and return back to the next statement after the caller (which is at marker ③). If the called label (at marker ①) did not exist, the conditional statement (the default case, at marker ②) will be executed and thereafter marker ③ will also be reached again. Therefore, the "*GOTO :switch-case-end*" statement (at marker ③) is very important because it plays an important role of skipping past all the handlers, all the way down to the rest of the statements that have nothing to do with the "switch/case" logic (markers ⑥ and ⑦).

If you are familiar with the C programming language, the code above is similar to the following:

```
switch (n)
{
        default:
                printf("Something else\n");
                break;
        case 1:
                printf("One\n");
                break;
        case 2:
                printf("One\n");
                break;
        case 3:
                printf("One\n");
                break;
}
printf("After Switch/case");
```

We can clearly see that each "*GOTO :eof*" statement (at the code markers ⑤) leads back to marker ③, which in turn jumps past the handlers. Such syntax usage is similar to using the "*break*" keyword in the C code above.

The advantage of using the "switch/case" logic is that we can combine multiple cases under the same code handlers. If we wanted to express that with **IF** statements, then the code would become a mess. Let me illustrate with an example:

```
:switch-case-combined

      echo Switch/case

      :: Call and mask out invalid call targets
      call :switch-case-N-%N% 2>nul || (
            :: Default case
            echo Something else
      )
      goto :switch-case-end

      :switch-case-N-1 ①
      :switch-case-N-2 ①
            echo One or two
            goto :eof


      :switch-case-N-3 ②
      :switch-case-N-4 ②
            echo Three or Four
            goto :eof

      :switch-case-end
          echo After Switch/case
          goto :eof
```

In the code snippet above, we combined the case handler for "N==1" and "N==2" (at marker ①) and we also combined the case handler for "N==3" and "N==4" (at marker ②).

The last benefit of using a "switch/case" syntax is that we can leverage the "fall-through" mechanism. A case handler falls through to the next case handler when the former does not issue a "goto :eof" after handling the case. In this manner, when the first handler finishes, the execution continues from the case handler just beneath it.

Let me illustrate the "fall-through" mechanism with a simple example:

```
:switch-case-fallthrough

    echo Switch/case

    :: Call and mask out invalid call targets
    call :switch-case-N-%N% 2>nul || (
        :: Default case
        echo Something else
    )
    goto :switch-case-end

    :switch-case-N-1 ①
        echo One
        :: Fallsthrough
        ②

    :switch-case-N-2 ③
        echo Two
        goto :eof


    :switch-case-end
    echo After Switch/case

    goto :eof
```

So what happens in the code snippet above, is that when *N* equals to "1", we get two lines of output:

```
One
Two
```

This is because the handler for "N==1" (at marker ①) does not "*goto :eof*" instead, it falls-through (at marker ②) to the "N==2" handler (at marker ③).

The source code of the snippets used in this section can be found in the script *"switch-case.bat"*. Let us execute the script and observe the output when *N* is 1:

```
C:\BatchProgramming>switch-case.bat
Enter number:1
Nested IFs...
One
After IFs

Switch/case
One
After Switch/case

Switch/case combined
One or two
After Switch/case combined

Switch/case fallthrough
One
Two
After Switch/case fallthrough

C:\BatchProgramming>
```

Repetition control structures

Repetition control structures are used to iterate (loop) in order to repeat the execution of parts of the code in the Batch file script or the command line.

In the coming sections, I will be explaining how the Batch files scripting language provides multiple ways to introduce loops in your script.

The FOR keyword

The **FOR** keyword allows you to repeat the execution of a single or multiple commands for each item in its "set" parameter.

Let me illustrate the basic syntax for the **FOR** keyword:

1. When used from the command interpreter directly:

```
FOR %variable IN (set) DO command [command-parameters]
```

2. When used in a Batch file script, you must prefix the variable with the double-percent character ("%%"):

```
FOR %%variable IN (set) DO command [command-parameters]
```

The variable parameter should be a single letter character and it is case sensitive.

Examples of valid FOR loop variable names

Here are some examples of valid variable names that can be used with the **FOR** loop inside your script:

- "%%a" to "%%z" and their uppercase counterparts ("%%A" to "%%Z").

The following are not documented but they are also supported:

- "%%#", "%%@", etc. are also valid variable names.
- "%%1" to "%%9" are also valid variable names.

Please note that **FOR** loop variables are not the same as environment variables (which are surrounded from both sides by "%"). The **FOR** loop variables cannot be used with the DEVE syntax and in fact, there is no need to.

File names and wildcards in the "set" parameter

When the command extensions are disabled, then the "set" parameter represents a set of file names separated by the *space*, *new line*, *comma* or the *semi-colon* characters.

The file names in the set parameter can contain the usual DOS wildcard characters:

- The "?" to match any single character.
- The "*" to match any character with zero or more occurrences.

If the file names to be matched contain the space character, then make sure you enclose the file names with quotes (").

Let me illustrate this basic syntax using a simple example (*for-files-set.bat*):

```
@echo off

setlocal

set /a c=0
for %%a in (t*.bat,*.exe, "my *.txt") do (
        echo found: %%a
        set /a c=c+1
)

echo.
echo Listed in %c% file(s)
endlocal
```

The same example may be re-written with the "set" items each on a separate line (*for-files-set-2.bat*):

```
for %%a in (
t*.bat
*.exe
"my *.txt"
Myfile.txt

Readme.txt

) do (
        echo found: %%a
)
```

Before moving on to explain the extended **FOR** keyword syntax, let me mention that the **FOR** loop variables can also be prefixed with special modifiers as explained in the previous section entitled "Command line arguments and FOR loop variables modifiers".

It is also worthwhile noting that in theory, the "set" parameter is supposed to contain a list of file names, but effectively you put any value there. In this fashion, you can put a series of strings to be processed in a loop (*for-files-set-3.bat*):

```
@echo off

setlocal
for %%a in (
       "command 1"
       "command 2"
       "command 3"
       "string 1"
       "string 2") DO (
       ECHO item=%%~a
)

endlocal
```

When executed, it yields the following output:

```
C:\BatchProgramming>for-files-set-3.bat
item=command 1
item=command 2
item=command 3
item=string 1
item=string 2

C:\BatchProgramming>
```

Extended FOR keyword syntax

When the command extensions are enabled, which they are by default, the **FOR** keyword can take an extra switch which modifies how the "set" parameter is interpreted.

Depending on the switch passed to the **FOR** keyword, the "set" parameter can be used for any of the following tasks:

- Number counting.
- Enumerating directories only.
- Enumerating directories and files recursively.
- Enumerating lines from files contents and optionally tokenize each line.
- Enumerating the lines from the output of an executed commands and optionally tokenize each line.

In the following sub-sections, I will explain all the supported parameters.

Number counting

Use the "/L" switch with the **FOR** keyword to start a counter from the command line:

```
FOR /L %variable IN (start, step, end) DO command [command-parameters]
```

Use a slightly different syntax inside Batch file scripts:

```
FOR /L %%variable IN (start, step, end) DO command [command-parameters]
```

Notice how the "set" parameter now describes how to count:

- start → the starting count number.
- step → the number of steps taken after each iteration. The steps can be a negative or a positive number.
- end → at which number should the counting stop (the ending number is included in the counting).

Let's take the *for-count.bat* script as an example:

```
@echo off
if "%3"=="" (
        echo Usage: %~n0 start end step ①
        goto :eof
)
FOR /L %%i IN (%1, %3, %2) DO (
        ECHO i=%%i
)
```

This simple script takes three arguments as we can see from marker ①, then it starts counting using the **FOR /L** syntax.

Let's run this script with different arguments and observe the output:

```
C:\BatchProgramming>for-count.bat ← no arguments passed
Usage: for-count start end step

C:\BatchProgramming>for-count 1 10 2 ← count from 1 to 10, step by 2
i=1
i=3
i=5
i=7
i=9
```

```
C:\BatchProgramming>for-count 10 1 -1 ← count backwards from 10 to 1
i=10
i=9
i=8
i=7
i=6
i=5
i=4
i=3
i=2
i=1
```

*Note: There seems to be a bug or it is by design that it is not always possible to break out of the counting loop by using the **GOTO** to jump to a label outside the compound body of the loop. Please test your script and decided how you want to iterate (using GOTOs or a FOR /L).*

Enumerating directories only

Use the "/D" switch with the **FOR** keyword to enumerate directories from the command line:

```
FOR /D %variable IN (set) DO command [command-parameters]
```

Use a slightly different syntax inside Batch file scripts:

```
FOR /D %%variable IN (set) DO command [command-parameters]
```

The "set" parameter may contain anything in it, however if it contains wildcards, then only the matching directory names will be returned (and not file names).

The following example will return the names of all the sub-directories in the current directory:

```
FOR /D %%P IN (*.*) DO (ECHO %%P)
```

The above code snippet is similar to issuing the command "**DIR /B /AD**" and capturing the output.

However, because we can apply modifiers to the **FOR** loop variables, we have more control on how to display the matched directories. For instance, applying the "f" modifier will yield the fully qualified path name instead of just the base name:

```
FOR /D %%P IN (*.*) DO (ECHO %%~fP)
```

In the following example (*for-enum-dirs.bat*), the "set" parameter contains regular strings along with wildcards (which will be used to match directory names only):

```
@echo off

FOR /D %%f IN ( ①
                      item1 ②
                      item2
        *.* ③
) DO (
        ECHO %%f
)
```

1. For readability, notice how the "set" items are each on a separate line.
2. Arbitrary file names. They don't have to be file names nor they have to exist on the file system, however they will be served in the "%%f" variable during the **FOR** loop's iterations.
3. Here we used wildcards. They will only match directory names.

Recursively walking the directory tree

Use the "/R" switch to recursively walk the directory tree and enumerate all files and folder names.

When used from the command line, the general syntax is:

```
FOR /R [[drive:]path] %variable IN (set) DO command [command-parameters]
```

When used from inside a script, use a slightly modified syntax:

```
FOR /R [[drive:]path] %%variable IN (set) DO command [command-parameters]
```

If the "path" parameter is not passed, then the current directory will be used. In that case, it is equivalent to the following:

```
FOR /R %CD% %variable IN (set) DO command [command-parameters]
```

> *Note: the "%CD%" pseudo-environment variable denotes the current directory. The dot character (".") may also be used to denote the current directory.*

The "set" parameter is used as a file names filter that is used to decide what to match and what not while recursively visiting the directory tree.

Here's a simple example (*for-enum-recursive.bat*) that looks for *.bat files recursively in the current directory (donated by "."):

```
@echo off

for /r . %%a IN (*.bat) DO (
        ECHO matched file: %%a
)
```

This syntax is very similar to running the command "DIR /B /S *.bat" then capturing and processing its output.

Enumerating and tokenizing lines from a file

The "/F" switch has various uses. In this section, I will describe the syntax that allows you to open each file in the specified file set, read each line and optionally tokenize the line items. Additionally, we will explain the advanced syntax (or options) that go along with the "/F" switch.

The explanation methodology in this section will be very important for later when I explain in other sections the other ways we can use the "/F" switch (to tokenize output from commands or literal strings for example).

Use the following syntax from the command prompt:

```
FOR /F ["options"] %variable IN (file-set) DO command
```

And the following syntax inside Batch file scripts:

```
FOR /F ["options"] %%variable IN (file-set) DO command
```

The basic syntax

Let's start with a simple example. Assume the following sample text file (*text1.txt*):

```
Line1
Line2
Line3
Line4

Line5
Line 6
Line7
```

Now, let's use the most basic "FOR /F" syntax to list the contents of this file line by line (*for-file-lines-no-options.bat*):

```
@echo off

setlocal enabledelayedexpansion ①

set /a linecount=0 ②

for /F %%a IN (text1.txt) DO ( ③
        set /a linecount=linecount+1
        ECHO Line #!linecount!: %%a ④
)

endlocal
```

Important code markers to note in this example:

1. Enable delayed environment variables expansion.
2. Create a line counter variable and initialize it to zero.
3. Use the "FOR /F" syntax, don't pass any options at all, parse each line in *text1.txt* into the variable *%%a.*
4. Display all the read lines and the current line count. Note the use of the delayed variable expansion syntax (*!linecount!*).

When executed, the following output is produced:

```
C:\BatchProgramming>for-file-lines-no-options.bat
Line #1: Line1
Line #2: Line2
Line #3: Line3
Line #4: Line4
Line #5: Line5
Line #6: Line
Line #7: Line7
```

This was the simplest example because no options were passed. Empty lines will always be skipped no matter what. That's why we don't see the empty line between lines 4 and line 5.

In facsimile, when no options are specified then the first token returned is the token separated by a blank character (the space or the tab characters). This explains why "Line 6" was returned as the token "Line" only.

The variable "*%%a*" was specified explicitly as the variable that should contain the retrieved tokens. This syntax will be explained more in the subsequent examples below.

In the next section, I will explain more about all the possible options that allow you to control the end of line delimiter, the tokens delimiter and other options.

The "file-set" parameter, as its name suggests, allows you to specify a set of file names. The files will be opened and their lines will be read and tokenized in order. As far as the **FOR** loop's body is concerned, it will receive all the lines from all the files combined.

The advanced syntax

Let us explain the relevant options that can be specified to customize the tokenizer.

- eol=c → This allows you to specify the end of line character ("c").
- skip=n → Specifies how many lines ("n") to skip from the beginning of the file.
- delims=cccc → Specifies various delimiter characters that are used to break the line into tokens.
- tokens=x,y, m-n, k* → Specifies which token numbers are to be passed to the FOR loop body's variables.
    - The "x, y, ..." syntax represent the token numbers to be passed to the FOR loop variables. You can specify one or more variable names separated by commas (and not just a single pair).
    - The "m-n" syntax represent a range of token numbers to be passed to the FOR loop body.
    - The "k*" syntax designates that from token number "k" and on, use subsequent tokens implicitly in the FOR loop.
- usebackq → In this section, this option enables you to use the double quotes in the file names specified in the *file-set* parameter.

I know that most, if not all of the options above may not be very clear at the moment but bear with me because I will be dedicating individual sub-sections to illustrate each option and give you lots of examples.

The "tokens" option

In this section, I will be giving various examples to illustrate the use of the "tokens" option. All examples rely on the same input file (*text-tokens-1.txt*) with the following contents:

```
L1-Token1 L1-Token2 L1-Token3 L1-Token4 L1-Token5 L1-Token6
L2-Token1 L2-Token2 L2-Token3 L2-Token4 L2-Token5 L2-Token6
L3-Token1 L3-Token2 L3-Token3 L3-Token4 L3-Token5 L3-Token6
```

Example 1

Let's just output the second token from each line. Namely, we want the extract the values: "L1-Token2", "L2-Token2", and "L3-Token2".

That's how the "FOR /F" syntax would look like:

```
for /F "tokens=2" %%a IN (text-tokens-1.txt) DO (
	echo %%a
)
```

When executed, it yields the expected output:

```
L1-Token2
L2-Token2
L3-Token2
```

In simple terms, when we specified "tokens=2", we told the tokenizer to discard the first token and just pass the second token.

Example 2

Now assume we want to extract token #3 to token #5 from each line. That's how we do it:

```
for /F "tokens=3-5" %%a IN (text-tokens-1.txt) DO (
	echo %%a %%b %%c
)
```

The syntax from the example above warrants more explanation because you may be already wondering where did the "*%%b*" and "*%%c*" variables come from. They are automatically created by taking the first variable letter you specified and then creating more variables using the subsequent variable letters.

For instance, if you supplied the variable "%%d" in the **FOR** syntax, then "%%d" will be token #1, "%%e" will be token #2 and "%%f" will be token #3.

> *Note: According to the "FOR /?" command usage, only 52 total variables can be active at the same time.*

Let's see the output of that command:

```
L1-Token3 L1-Token4 L1-Token5
L2-Token3 L2-Token4 L2-Token5
L3-Token3 L3-Token4 L3-Token5
```

Note: please refer back to the sub-section entitled "Examples of valid FOR loop variable names" to see what variable names you can use in case you want to extract lots of tokens.

Example 3

Let's see how to extract token #2 and the remaining tokens thereafter:

```
for /F "tokens=2*" %%a IN (text-tokens-1.txt) DO (
      echo %%a %%b
)
```

We know that we have 6 tokens per line, and we wanted to extract token #2 and onwards. The first token to be retrieved will take the user provided variable name ("*%%a*" in this case). The remainder of the tokens will be assigned to the subsequent variable name ("*%%b*" in this case) and will contain the value of all the remaining tokens.

Note: You may intuitively think that when the asterisk is used then lots of variables will be created such as: "%%a %%b %%c %%d %%e", etc. If this was the case, then that will pose a problem because the tokenizer will not know how many tokens to expect when it is tokenizing the input and you (the script writer) will not know either.

Example 4

You may be wondering what happens if we want to extract tokens in random order. For example, assume we want to extract token #6, #5 and the tokens #1 to #3. You would intuitively think of using this syntax:

```
for /F "tokens=6,5,1-3" %%a IN (text-tokens-1.txt) DO (
      echo %%a %%b %%c %%d %%e
)
```

Before I explain more, let's see the output of the command above and then proceed with the explanation:

```
L1-Token1 L1-Token2 L1-Token3 L1-Token5 L1-Token6
L2-Token1 L2-Token2 L2-Token3 L2-Token5 L2-Token6
L3-Token1 L3-Token2 L3-Token3 L3-Token5 L3-Token6
```

We got an output that is not the one we intuitively expected! We specified the following options: "tokens=6,5,1-3" but instead, the output was as if we specified these options instead: "tokens=1-3, 5, 6".

See what happened? The interpreter re-arranged the tokens for us:

- %%a, %%b, %%c → token #1 through token #3
- %%d → token #5
- %%e→ token #6

Putting it all together

Putting all the snippets together in *for-file-lines-token.bat*:

```
@echo off

setlocal

echo Token #2 from each line:
echo -----------------------
for /F "tokens=2" %%a IN (text-tokens-1.txt) DO (
       echo %%a
)


echo Token #3 to Token #5 from each line:
echo ------------------------------------

for /F "tokens=3-5" %%a IN (text-tokens-1.txt) DO (
       echo %%a %%b %%c
)


echo Token #2 and onwards:
echo ---------------------

for /F "tokens=2*" %%a IN (text-tokens-1.txt) DO (
       echo %%a %%b
)
```

```
echo Token #6, #5 and #1 to #3:
echo -------------------------

for /F "tokens=6,5,1-3" %%a IN (text-tokens-1.txt) DO (
      echo %%a %%b %%c %%d %%e
)

endlocal
```

Note: If you attempt to use an erroneous or unspecified FOR loop variable then you won't get an error, instead the variable value will be resolved to the variable name instead.

The "delim" option

The delimiter option ("delim") is used to specify which delimiters are used when tokenizing the lines in the file. By default, if it was not specified then the delimiters are: the space and the tab characters.

It is also possible to specify various delimiters so that if one of the specified delimiters is first matched then a token is extracted. It is important to note that delimiter characters are case sensitive.

Example 1 – Single delimiter

Let's take the file *text-delims-1.txt* in our first example:

```
L1-token 1,L1-token 2,L1-token 3
L2-token 1,L2-token 2,L2-token 3
L3-token 1,L3-token 2,L3-token 3
```

The above file has 3 tokens per line, all comma separated. It is straightforward to tokenize each line with the following syntax:

```
for /f "delims=, tokens=1-3" %%a in (text-delims-1.txt) DO (
      ECHO #1=[%%a] #2=[%%b] #3=[%%c]
)
```

Notice how we specified two options this time. The first is "delims=," to tell the **FOR** keyword to replace its default delimiters and use the comma delimiter instead. The second option we used is "tokens=1-3" to extract 3 tokens, having "%%a" as the explicit variable name and "%%b" and "%%c" which will be implicitly created.

The output of the snippet above is:

```
#1=[L1-token 1] #2=[L1-token 2] #3=[L1-token 3]
#1=[L2-token 1] #2=[L2-token 2] #3=[L2-token 3]
#1=[L3-token 1] #2=[L3-token 2] #3=[L3-token 3]
```

Example 2 – Multiple delimiters

Let us now use another sample input file, *text-delims-2.txt*, that has values delimited by either the ";" or the "," separators:

```
L1-token 1,L1-token 2;L1-token 3
L2-token 1;L2-token 2,L2-token 3
L3-token 1,L3-token 2;L3-token 3
```

Tokenizing this file is a simple matter of adding one more delimiter to the "delims" option:

```
for /f "tokens=1-3 delims=,;" %%a in (text-delims-2.txt) DO (
      ECHO #1=[%%a] #2=[%%b] #3=[%%c]
)
```

> *Important: When you want to use many delimiter characters and one of them is the space character, then make sure you move the "delims" option to the end of the options list and put the space delimiter as the last character. For example: "tokens=1-3 delims=,; " (there's a trailing space at the end) means that the delimiters are the comma, semi-colon and the space character . If you swapped the order of the options like this: "delims=,; tokens=1-3" then you won't get the intended result.*

Example 3 – Reading the whole line

What if you don't want to specify any delimiters at all and instead read the whole line content?

Well, there are three methods to go about this. The first method is very simple and all we have to do is specify the "tokens=*" so that all tokens are allocated into the first variable. In that case you may simply omit the delimiters option (the "delims").

The second method involves specifying no delimiters at all with the syntax "delims=" at the end of the options list.

The third method involves using a delimiter character that we assume won't be present in the input file (this is a convoluted method but I mention it for the sake of completeness).

Assume the following input text file (*text-delims-3.txt*):

```
This is line 1, read in full
This is line 2, read in full
①This is line 3, with the delimiter on purpose¿this is the second token
This is line 4
```

Note: At marker ① in the input file, we put the "¿"character to illustrate method three.

Using the first method, we can read the whole line like this:

```
for /f "tokens=*" %%a in (text-delims-3.txt) DO (
      ECHO ^<%%a^>
)
```

Or using the second method, we can read the whole line like this:

```
for /f "delims=" %%a in (text-delims-3.txt) DO (
      ECHO ^<%%a^>
)
```

The output will include all the lines (surrounded by the angle brackets, as it was specified in the script):

```
<This is line 1, read in full>
<This is line 2, read in full>
<This is line 3, with the delimiter on purpose¿this is the second token>
<This is line 4>
```

Now to illustrate the third method, we assume that the inverted question mark character "¿" (ASCII code: 168) is the token delimiter. When this character is missing from the line, then there will be only one token: the whole line.

> *Note: You can type this symbol in your script using a full keyboard by holding the "Alt" key then punching-in 168 on the numeric pad. Alternatively, you can use the On-Screen keyboard to do the same.*

That's how the script would look like:

```
for /f "tokens=1 delims=¿" %%a in (text-delims-3.txt) DO (
	ECHO ^<%%a^>
)
```

And the output would be:

```
<This is line 1, read in full> <>
<This is line 2, read in full> <>
<This is line 3, with the delimiter on purpose> ①
<This is line 4> <>
```

Notice how all the lines except for line 3 (at marker ①) got printed in their entirety. The third line got broken into two tokens because of the presence of the inverted question mark delimiter. Since I only capture and display one token, the rest of the line is not printed. This method has its drawbacks, use it sparingly.

Example 4

Earlier, I mentioned that the delimiters are case sensitive. To illustrate that, let's assume the following file contents (*text-delims-4.txt*):

```
HelloLWorld,LHelloLFromLBellevue
```

The uppercase letter "L" will be used as a delimiter. The lower case L letters ('l') won't generate any tokens. That's how the **FOR** syntax would look like:

```
for /f "tokens=1-5 delims=L" %%a in (text-delims-4.txt) DO (
	ECHO ^<%%a %%b %%c %%d %%e^>
)
```

And it generates the following output:

```
<Hello World, Hello From Bellevue >
```

Putting it all together

Putting all the snippets together in *for-file-lines-delims.bat*:

```
@echo off

setlocal

ECHO Delimit with "," only:
ECHO ----------------------
ECHO.
for /f "delims=, tokens=1-3" %%a in (text-delims-1.txt) DO (
       ECHO #1=[%%a] #2=[%%b] #3=[%%c]
)

ECHO.
ECHO Delimit with "," or ";"
ECHO -------------------------
ECHO.
for /f "tokens=1-3 delims=,;" %%a in (text-delims-2.txt) DO (
       ECHO #1=[%%a] #2=[%%b] #3=[%%c]
)

ECHO.
ECHO Delimit using the inverted question mark
ECHO -----------------------------------------
ECHO.
for /f "tokens=1 delims=¿;" %%a in (text-delims-3.txt) DO (
       ECHO ^<%%a^>
)

ECHO.
ECHO Tokenizing everything into one variable
ECHO -----------------------------------------
ECHO.
for /f "tokens=*" %%a in (text-delims-3.txt) DO (
       ECHO ^<%%a^>
)


ECHO.
ECHO Tokenizing with uppercase L
ECHO ---------------------------
ECHO.
for /f "tokens=1-5 delims=L" %%a in (text-delims-4.txt) DO (
```

```
        ECHO ^<%%a %%b %%c %%d %%e^>
)
endlocal
```

The "eol" option

The end of line option ("eol") is used to specify a single character that causes the line to be skipped altogether if that character is present at its beginning. I know, I know the option's name ("eol") is counter-intuitive. The "eol" option is useful if you want to skip certain lines that start with a character of your choice. For instance, when the MS Windows INI files are parsed then all the lines that start with the semicolon character are treated as comment lines and skipped accordingly.

Example

Assume the following input file (*text-eol-1.txt*):

```
; This is a comment
Hello
; Another comment
From
; Once more
The other end of the world
; More comment
ohayou gozaimasu
```

To read all the lines except for the ones that start with a semicolon, we can use the following syntax (excerpt from *for-file-lines-eol.bat*):

```
setlocal enabledelayedexpansion
SET Line=1
for /f "eol=; tokens=*" %%a in (text-eol-1.txt) DO (
        ECHO Line^(!Line!^)=%%a ①
        SET /A Line=Line+1
)
endlocal
```

We expect to see 4 output lines like the following:

```
Line(1)=Hello
Line(2)=From
Line(3)=The other end of the world
Line(4)=ohayou gozaimasu
```

> *<u>Note:</u> We had to escape the parenthesis characters from the line at marker ①. In our case, we only have to escape the right parenthesis character (")").*

The "usebackq" option

By default, the "file-set" parameter is used to designate a set of files. The file names may also contain wildcards (as explained in the previous section entitled "File names and wildcards in the 'set' parameters").

When the "/F" option is used with the **FOR** loop to enable the extended syntax, then using the double quotes does not mean we are passing a file name containing space characters or wildcard characters, instead it means we are passing a literal string to be tokenized.

The "usebackq" option changes the semantics of how the **FOR** loop's "file-set" parameter is interpreted and in particular this will have effect on how the double-quotes character usage in the "file-set" parameter is interpreted. The "usebackq" option will prevent the double-quote presence (in the "file-set") from designating that a literal string is being tokenized. Instead, it will designate that long file names may have been passed.

Suppose we have a file named *"the long text file name.txt"* with the following contents:

```
line 1
line 2
line 3
line 4
```

Now, let's try to read its contents:

```
FOR /F "tokens=1-2" %%a IN ("the long text file name.txt") DO (
       echo Line: %%a %%b
)
```

The returned output is:

```
Line: the long
```

What happened? Why the file was not opened and its contents tokenized?

This is due to how the double-quotes character is interpreted with the "FOR /F" syntax. Instead of having all of the 4 lines returned from the file name that was passed, the "file-set" parameter was interpreted as a literal string because of the absence of the "usebackq" option.

To address this issue, we can use the "usebackq" option which will then allow the "FOR /F" syntax to interpret the "file-set" parameters that are enclosed inside double quotes as long file names.

In the example below, we will be able to read the contents of the referenced file or files and then tokenize their lines:

```
FOR /F "usebackq tokens=1-2" %%a IN ("the long text file name.txt") DO (
        echo Line: %%a %%b
)
```

Hence the following output:

```
Line: line 1
Line: line 2
Line: line 3
Line: line 4
```

In conclusion, the "usebackq" option makes it possible to list as many file names (long or short file names) in the "file-set" parameter:

```
FOR /F "usebackq tokens=1-2" %%a IN (
     "the long text file name.txt"
     text1.txt
     "the long text file name 2.txt"
) DO (
        echo Line: %%a %%b
)
```

The example above will read and tokenize the lines from all of the 3 file names in question.

All of the snippets used in this section are found in the Batch file script called: *for-file-lines-usebackq.bat*

Tokenizing output from a command execution

Now that we are equipped with the knowledge of how to tokenize lines from a file and were already exposed to the advanced syntax of the "FOR /F" syntax, let us now demonstrate how to tokenize output from a command execution.

When used from the command line, the syntax is:

```
FOR /F ["options"] %variable IN ('command') DO command [args]
```

And when used from inside a Batch file script, use a slightly modified syntax:

```
FOR /F ["options"] %%variable IN ('command') DO command [args]
```

Note the single quote character used in the "file-set" parameter.

When the "usebackq" option is used, then instead of using a single-quote to enclose the command to execute, use the backquote character instead ("`"):

```
FOR /F ["usebackq other-options"] %variable IN (`command`) DO command
```

<u>Note:</u> The backquote character was used in the "file-set" parameter instead of the single quote.

Let's illustrate command output tokenization using a simple example. Suppose we want to tokenize the output of the "time /t" command to get the hours, minutes and whether it is before or after midday.

The output of the "time /t" command looks like this:

```
C:\BatchProgramming>time /t
04:17 PM
```

To tokenize this output, we need to specify the space and the colon (": ") as delimiters and produce three tokens. Hence the syntax is:

```
for /f "tokens=1-3 delims=: " %%a in ('time /t') DO (
      echo hour=%%a mins=%%b ampm=%%c
)
```

The output produced is:

```
C:\BatchProgramming>for-command-output-time.bat
hour=04 mins=17 ampm=PM
```

When the "usebackq" is present in the options list then, the syntax becomes like this:

```
for /f "usebackq tokens=1-3 delims=: " %%a in (`time /t`) DO (
      echo tok1=%%a tok2=%%b tok3=%%c
)
```

> *The difference is that we enclosed the command inside the backquote character ("`").*

Tokenizing a string

Now we arrive at the final use case of the "FOR /F" command where we can use it to tokenize a string.

Tokenizing a string has two syntaxes:

```
FOR /F ["options"] %variable IN ("string-to-tokenize") DO command
[parameters]
```

And when the "usebackq" option is present, then the single quote should be used to enclose the string to be tokenized:

```
FOR /F ["usebackq options"] %variable IN ('string-to-tokenize') DO
command [parameters]
```

Let's illustrate the syntax using a simple example. Suppose we have this output and we want to extract the 4th token which is the name:

```
my name is Clark
^1 ^2   ^3 ^4
```

To extract the 4th token from such a string we can use this syntax (*for-string-token1.bat*):

```
for /f "tokens=4 delims= " %%a in ("my name is Clark") DO (
      echo The name is %%a
)
```

Or this syntax, if the "usebackq" option is used:

```
for /f "usebackq tokens=4 delims= " %%a in ('my name is Clark') DO (
       echo The name is %%a
)
```

Note: For literal string tokenization, all of the advanced syntax options apply except for the "eol" option.

The FORFILES command

We have seen in the previous sections that it is possible to enumerate files with the **FOR** keyword using both the regular and the extended syntax.

In addition to that, the operating system ships with a utility called **forfiles.exe**, located here:

```
C:\BatchProgramming>where forfiles
C:\Windows\System32\forfiles.exe
```

This utility's goal is to enumerate files based on two input criteria and then execute a command for each file that was matched. These criteria are:

- Path and file names mask
- File(s) modified date

This is a short list of the command line switches supported by this utility:

- /P → Specify the path to enumerate files from.
- /M → Specify the files names mask.
- /S → For matching recursively in sub-directories.
- /C → Specify the command to execute. Some special identifiers will become available to the command that will be executed. These special identifiers will be substituted with the proper information at each iteration for each file that is matched/returned.
- /D → Specify the number of days or the date after which or before the files to be matched have been modified.

The following are the special identifiers that can be used with the "/C" switch but are not present with the regular **FOR** keyword and its variables modifiers:

- @relpath → Returns the relative path of the file.
- @isdir → Returns "TRUE" if a file type is a directory, and "FALSE" for files.
- @fdate → Returns the last modified date of the file.
- @ftime → Returns the last modified time of the file. The returned time also includes the seconds.

> *Note: if you include a hexadecimal number (prefixed with "0x) inside the "/C" switch then that number is converted to its appropriate character representation.*

One more thing to note when using the "/C" switch is that you have to pass program names and not Batch file script keywords. However, if you plan to use Batch file script keywords then you have to prefix the commands to execute with "cmd /c", for example:

```
FORFILES /M *.*  /c "cmd /c echo @fname has a date of @fdate"
```

As a side effect of using "cmd /c", you won't be able to modify the environment variables of the parent command prompt. Therefore, in order to pass results from **FORFILES** to your scripts, you have to resort to other techniques, such as:

- Redirecting the output to a file and then parsing it.
- Using the **FOR** keyword to capture and tokenize the output of **FORFILES** in order to get the required information.

In the Chapter 4 of this book, there will be an example showing how to capture information from the **FORFILES** command output.

For more information about this command, please run it with the "/?" switch.

Nested FOR loops

It is possible to nest **FOR** loops the same way as it is possible to nest **IF** statements. For readability purposes, just make sure that the **FOR**'s body is a compound statement.

Let's assume we have this CSV file (*expenses.csv*) with the following contents:

```
Date,Total,Description,Category
11/27/2011,350,Google Nexus 5 phone,Electronics
11/27/2011,20,Dinner + tips,Food
11/27/2011,35,Grocery for the week,Grocery
11/28/2011,7,Sandwich,Food
11/29/2015,3,Mailed a book,Postage
11/29/2015,20,Lunch + tips,Food
11/29/2015,65,Tablet stylus,Electronics
11/29/2015,40,Refueled the car,Gas
01/29/2023,41781,Round trip to the moon with the kids,Transportation
```

Let's write a script that skips the header (the first line) and returns the sum total of all the 2nd tokens in the remaining lines (the "total" value).

For demonstration purposes, we are going to solve this problem using two nested **FOR** loops, but bear in mind that it can be solved in a single **FOR** loop. Both scripts are found in the *for-nest-sum-csv.bat* file.

Let's start with the nested **FOR** loop solution:

```
SET /A Total=0 ①
for /F "skip=1 tokens=*" %%a in (expenses.csv) do ( ②
      for /f "tokens=2 delims=," %%b in ("%%a") do ( ③
            set /a Total=Total+%%b ④
      )
)

echo Total = %Total% ⑤
```

Let's explain all the markers:

1. Use the "SET /A" to create a variable that will hold the total.
2. In the first outer FOR loop, we use the following options:
    a. "skip = 1" → Skip the first line, which is the header line.
    b. "tokens=*" → Don't tokenize, just return the whole line.
    c. Use the variable "*a*" to hold the line value.
3. In the inner **FOR** loop, we use the following options:
    a. "tokens=2" → Just extract the second token (it is the value of the "Total" column).
    b. "delims=," → Since we are dealing with a CSV file, use the comma as the delimiter character.

    c. Use the variable "*b*" to return the total.
4. For each iteration, update the total value.
5. After both loops are done, print the total value.

As I mentioned above, this can be done using a single loop like this:

```
SET /A Total=0
for /F "skip=1 tokens=2 delims=," %%a in (expenses.csv) do (
       set /a Total=Total+%%a
)

echo Total = %Total%
```

Throughout this book, there will be various real life examples illustrating how to use nested **FOR** loops.

Using the GOTO and IF

It is possible to simulate repetition control structures with a **GOTO** to repeat/loop and the **IF** conditional statement to decide when to break out of the loop.

This method, unlike using the **FOR** keyword, is not really structured and does not have to follow a certain syntax. It is up to you how you structure your code to achieve the repetition and how to break out of it.

In the following example, I demonstrate how to do forward counting and backward counting (*count-gotoif.bat*):

```
@echo off

SETLOCAL ENABLEEXTENSIONS

:: -----------------
:: Forward counting
:: -----------------

set /A I=1
set /A C=10
echo Counting from %I% to %C%:
echo.

:repeatcount1
       echo i = %I%
       SET /A I+=1
       if %I% GTR %C% goto donecount1
```

```
       goto repeatcount1
:donecount1

echo.
echo Done counting forward!

:: -----------------
:: Backward counting
:: -----------------
set /A I=10
set /A C=1
echo Counting from %I% down to %C%:
echo.

:repeatcount2
       echo i = %I%
       SET /A I-=1
       if %I% LSS %C% goto donecount2

       goto repeatcount2
:donecount2

echo.
echo Done counting backwards!

endlocal
```

When this script is executed, we get the following output:

```
C:\BatchProgramming>count-gotoif.bat
Counting from 1 to 10:

i = 1
i = 2
i = 3
i = 4
i = 5
i = 6
i = 7
i = 8
i = 9
i = 10

Done counting forward!
Counting from 10 down to 1:

i = 10
```

```
i = 9
i = 8
i = 7
i = 6
i = 5
i = 4
i = 3
i = 2
i = 1

Done counting backwards!

C:\BatchProgramming>
```

String operations

In the Batch files scripting language, it is possible to carry various string operations on environment variables with the help of special syntax modifiers.

String substitution

Apply string substitution operations on environment variables before they are evaluated using the following syntax:

```
%VarName:StringToBeMatched=StringToBeReplacedWith%
```

When DEVE is enabled, use this syntax when appropriate:

```
!VarName:StringToBeMatched=StringToBeReplacedWith!
```

So basically, instead of just wrapping the variable name with "%" (or "!") directly, you put the column character right after the environment variable name to specify that you want to start the substitution, then type the string value to be matched followed by the equal sign and the string to be replaced with.

Let me illustrate the syntax using a simple example (*str-substitute.bat*):

```
@echo off

SETLOCAL ENABLEDELAYEDEXPANSION

SET str1=Writing code using the Python scripting language. ①
ECHO Regular expansion: %str1:Python=Batch% ②
```

```
ECHO With DEVE: !str1:Python=Batch! ③

ENDLOCAL
```

Which produces the following output when executed:

```
Regular expansion: Writing code using the Batch scripting language.
With DEVE: Writing code using the Batch scripting language.
```

At marker ①, we create an environment variable called *str1* containing the string "Python" with the intent of replacing it with the word "Batch" (at markers ② and ③).

The string substitution syntax also allows you to start your search string with an asterisk ("*"). If that was the case, then everything from the beginning of the string up to your search string will be matched. Let me illustrate this with an example:

```
@echo off

setlocal enabledelayedexpansion

for %%a in (
	"01:31:2016 at 4:17AM - LOGENTRY: User 'Jane' has logged in"
	"01:31:2016 at 4:17AM - LOGENTRY: File 'payroll.db' has been
accessed"
	"01:31:2016 at 4:55AM - LOGENTRY: User 'Jane' logged out"
	) do (
	set V=%%~a ①
	set V=!V:*LOGENTRY: =! ②
	echo !V!
)
endlocal
```

> *Note: In the example above, we use a* **FOR** *loop just to provide us with three individual test strings to do string substitution on. In real life, those strings would come from an audit log file for example.*

Each test string has the following format: date/time stamp, followed by a hyphen, then the "LOGENTRY:" string and finally the actual log text. This structured line format makes it easy for us to extract just the log the text using the wildcard match-and-replace syntax as illustrated at marker ②.

Remember that string-substitution is only available for environment variables. Therefore, we have to transfer values to an environment variable first (code at marker ①) then do the string substitution. At marker ②, we match "*" (meaning anything) up to the "LOGENTRY: " text and then replace all that was matched with nothing; the DEVE syntax has been used because we are in a compound statement.

Let's run the *str-substitute-asterisk.bat* script and observe the output:

```
C:\BatchProgramming>str-substitute-asterisk.bat
User 'Jane' has logged in
File 'payroll.db' has been accessed
User 'Jane' logged out

C:\BatchProgramming>
```

The output is as expected and we managed to replace all the text prior to our match string ("LOGENTRY:") with an empty string (thus removing that text).

> *Note: At marker ①, we used the tilde "~" variable modifier to get rid of the enclosing double quotes.*

Sub-string

To extract parts (or substrings) of environment variables values, use the following syntax:

```
%VarName:~Position,Count%
```

The position is zero based; that is, you start counting characters from 0 instead of 1.

Let me illustrate with an example:

```
SET str1=ABCDEF
ECHO %str1:~0,1%
```

This prints just one character, the character "A", at position 0 from the environment variable *str1*.

In facsimile, the following:

```
ECHO %str1:~2,2%
```

would output two characters starting at position 2 (which is the 3rd character): "CD".

Another syntax of the substring is when "*Count*" is not specified:

```
%VarName:~Position%
```

In this case, the substring will return the remainder of the string starting from the passed position. Here's an example:

```
ECHO %str1:~3%
```

It would output all the characters starting at position 3 (i.e. from the 4th character): "DEF".

There's one more syntax to the string substring where "*Position*" or "*Count*" are passed as negative numbers.

When "*Position*" is a negative number, then the actual position used for the substring is the length of the string minus the positive value of "*Position*". That it is to say that we should extract the strings situated at "*Position*" characters from the end of the string.

Here's an example:

```
ECHO %str1:~-2%
```

Which extracts just 2 characters from the end of the string and returns the sub-string: "EF".

Therefore:

```
%str1:~-2%
```

...is equivalent to:

```
%str1:~4%
```

Similarly, when "*Count*" is negative then the actual count used for the substring is the length of the string minus the positive value of "*Count*" minus 1. Here's an example:

```
ECHO %str1:~1,-3%
```

...will return the substring "BC".

Let me explain: the "Position" value is 1, the count is -3, but the actual "Count" is the string length minus the positive value of "*Count*" (=3) minus 1. Thus the actual count used is "6 - 3 - 1= 2". Therefore, the previous substring is equivalent to:

```
ECHO %str1:~1,2%
```

More examples:

- From the end of the string, return one character ➔ %str1:~-1,1%
- Return all the string except the first two characters ➔ %str1:~2%
- Return all the characters except the last two ➔ %str1:~0,-2%

Here's the complete script (*str-substring.bat*):

```
@echo off

SETLOCAL

REM       012345
SET str1=ABCDEF

ECHO The string is: '%str1%'
ECHO [0, 1 ]  = %str1:~0,1%
ECHO [2, 2 ]  = %str1:~2,2%
ECHO [3,   ]  = %str1:~3%
ECHO [-2,  ]  = %str1:~-2%
ECHO [1, -3]  = %str1:~1,-3%

ECHO [1, -2]  = %str1:~1,-2%
ECHO [0, -1]  = %str1:~0,-1%
ECHO [0, -2]  = %str1:~0,-2%

ENDLOCAL
```

And when executed, the following output is produced:

```
The string is: 'ABCDEF'
[0, 1 ]  = A
[2, 2 ]  = CD
[3,   ]  = DEF
[-2,  ]  = EF
[1, -3]  = BC
[1, -2]  = BCD
[0, -1]  = ABCDE
[0, -2]  = ABCD
```

Check if a sub-string is in a string

One method we can test if a substring exists inside a larger string, without relying on external commands, is using a script like the following (*contains-str-1.bat*):

```
@echo off

:main
      setlocal

      set /p str=Enter text:
      set /p pattern=Enter pattern:
      call :str-contains "%str%" "%pattern%"
      echo found = %errorlevel%

      goto :eof

:str-contains <arg1=text> <arg2=pattern> -> errorlevel

      setlocal

      set copy=%~1
      set repl=%~2

      call set copy=%%copy:%repl%=%%

      (
        endlocal
        if "%~1"=="%copy%" (exit /b 0) else (exit /b 1)
      )
```

Let's run this script and see the result:

```
C:\BatchProgramming>contains-str-1.bat
Enter text: Batch file scripting
Enter pattern: Python
found = 0

C:\BatchProgramming>contains-str-1.bat
Enter text: Batch file scripting
Enter pattern: script
found = 1
```

The reasoning behind the "*str-contains*" function is that we attempt to find and replace the potential sub-string in the larger string. If the string match-and-replace operation succeeds, then it means the sub-string is part of the string.

String concatenation

To concatenate strings, we simply rely on the built-in mechanism of environment variable expansion. Let me illustrate using a simple example (*strcat-1.bat*):

```
@echo off

setlocal

set /P Fname=Enter your first name:
set /P Lname=Enter your last name:

set FULLNAME=%Fname% %Lname% ①

echo Full name is: %FULLNAME%
```

Notice how the *FULLNAME* environment variable was formed by assigning to it the value of the two environment variables *Fname* and *Lname* separated by the space character.

In the following example, I will illustrate how to concatenate strings inside a loop. For this hypothetical example, I will generate the numbers 0 to 9 (using the "FOR /L" syntax) and concatenate all the numbers into a single string.

For this to work, we will also rely on the DEVE syntax (*strcat-2.bat*):

```
@echo off

setlocal enabledelayedexpansion

set str=
for /L %%a in (0, 1, 9) do (
     set str=!str!%%a
)

echo str=%str%
endlocal
```

When executed:

```
C:\BatchProgramming>strcat-2
str=0123456789

C:\BatchProgramming>
```

String length

There is no built-in way to figure out a string's length, but using the substring method and repetition control structures we can compute the string length.

The basic idea is as follows:

1. Take a copy of the input string into an environment variable. This allows us to use the sub-string functionality. This copy variable will also be our work variable. We will modify it on each iteration.
2. Initialize a counter variable.
3. If the work variable becomes undefined (when it becomes empty), then break out of the loop because we are done and now we have the length in the counter variable.
4. Increment the length variable.
5. Shift the work variable to the left. That means, simply sub-string it from the 2nd character and on (thus skipping the first character and keeping all the rest).
6. Repeat from step 3.
7. When we break out of the loop, then we have the string's length.

The script *str-len.bat* is one way to express the algorithm described above:

```
:str-len (string, result-var) ①
      set len=0 ②
      set str=%~1 ③
      :str-len-repeat-1
            if not DEFINED str goto strlen-break-1 ④
            set str=%str:~1% ⑤
            set /a len+=1 ⑥
            goto str-len-repeat-1 ⑦

      :strlen-break-1
            set %~2=%len% ⑧
      goto :eof
```

Let me explain the algorithm above:

1. Define the function label.
2. Initialize the length variable to zero.
3. Use "*str*" environment variable as the string that we want to compute its length. It will also act as a work/temporary variable.

4. When we shift the string to the left in step 5, at one point it will become empty. When we set an empty value to an environment variable then that variable is deleted. Hence, we check if the variable is defined or not
5. Update the "*str*" environment variable and take all the characters except the first one. Effectively, we are shifting the contents to the left by one character.
6. Increment the length.
7. Repeat.
8. Return the length into the environment variable passed in the second argument.

Let's test the *str-len* function:

```
@echo off

:main

       setlocal

       call :str-len "Marco Polo" result ①

       echo result=%result% ②

       endlocal

       goto :eof
```

The test program above is explained as follows:

1. Call the *str-len* function and pass two arguments:
    a. The first argument is the string that we want to compute its length.
    b. The second argument is the environment variable name that will hold the result.
2. Display the string length that was returned in the "result" environment variable.

There's a small improvement we can makethat allows us to return a numeric result from functions using the "**EXIT /B** ReturnValue" syntax. After the function returns, the caller can then read the return value using the *%ERRORLEVEL%* pseudo-environment variable value (*str-len-2.bat*):

```
@echo off

:main

       setlocal enabledelayedexpansion

       set /p str=Enter a string:
```

```
    call :str-len %str%

    echo result=%errorlevel%

    endlocal

    goto :eof

:str-len string
   setlocal
    set len=0
    set str=%~1
    :str-len-repeat-1
           if not defined str goto strlen-break-1
           set str=%str:~1%
           set /a len+=1
           goto str-len-repeat-1

    :strlen-break-1
           exit /b %len%
           goto :eof
```

There's another efficient and faster method to compute the string length that I ran into while researching this book (*str-len-fast.bat*):

```
@echo off

:main
   setlocal
   set /P str=Enter string:
   call :strlen "%str%"
   echo length=%errorlevel%

   goto :eof

:strlen <1=string> => errorlevel
   setlocal enabledelayedexpansion
   set "s=%~1." ①
   set len=0 ②
   for %%P in (4096 2048 1024 512 256 128 64 32 16 8 4 2 1) do ( ③
       if "!s:~%%P,1!" NEQ "" ( ④
           set /a "len+=%%P" ⑤
           set "s=!s:~%%P!" ⑥
       )
   )
```

```
    ( ⑦
        endlocal
        exit /b %len% ⑧
    )
```

This script uses the divide-and-conquer algorithm. First, at marker ①, the algorithm appends a single character to the string; like this, the algorithm can still operate even if an empty string was passed (it will simply return the 0 in that case).

At marker ②, the *len* variable is initialized to 0. It will be updated in the loop as needed. At marker ③, we create a set of multiples of 2 starting by the largest string length supported by this function. The idea behind this set is to keep dividing the string in halves and deducing its length.

At marker ④, we probe (using the sub-string operation) to see if there is a character at the current probe length. If such a character exists, then the string's length is at least the probed length (marker ⑤). The script is then left-trimmed, thus getting rid of all the characters that were accounted for already by the current length probe iteration (marker ⑥).

Each time the loop (at marker ③) iterates, the length probe value decreases (by a multiple of two) until it reaches the value of 1 and the string can no longer be divided.

After the loop's end, at marker ⑦, a compound statement is used to persist the *len* variable's value past the **ENDLOCAL** call. More about the topic of persisting variables beyond the end of localization in Chapter 3.

Finally, at marker ⑧ we exit the function and return the string length back to the caller.

Using variable parameters with string operations

In the previous sections, I explained how we can use the special syntax of the environment variables expansion in order to achieve string substitution or string replacement.

So far we only used constant arguments with string operations. What if we need to pass a variable value to extract a substring for example?

Let me illustrate how to do that with a simple example (*str-substitute-var.bat*):

```
@echo off

set /P phrase=Enter string: ①
set /P match=Find what: ②
set /P replace=Replace with what: ③

echo The phrase is: %phrase%
call set phrase=%%phrase:%match%=%replace%%% ④
echo After substitution, the phrase is: %phrase% ⑤
```

In this script, I prompt the user for a phrase (at marker ①), then prompt for a string to match (at marker ②) and a string to replace with (at marker ③).

At marker ④, I use the string substitution syntax (as explained in the section above entitled "Sub-String"), however I used the **CALL** keyword to issue the substitution syntax.

The idea behind this syntax is that when the **CALL** keyword is used, then two-level environment variables expansion takes place. The first level is the immediate level where all the environment variables encapsulated inside the percent character are expanded first (prior to the **CALL** execution), then the second level of expansion takes place when **CALL** is executed. Also note that I escaped the percent character so it gets resolved during the second level expansion.

Let me walk you through how the two-level expansion take places when the script is executed with the following input:

```
C:\BatchProgramming>str-substitute-var.bat
Enter string: Hello from the C++ language
Find what: C++
Replace with what: Python
The phrase is: Hello from the C++ language
After substitution, the phrase is: Hello from the Python language
```

This is what happens behind the scenes:

1. Original statement → **call** set phrase=**%%**phrase:%match%=%replace%**%%**
2. First level expansion → **call** set phrase=**%**phrase:C++=Python**%**
    a. The double percent characters are now reduced to a single percent character.
    b. The *match* and *replace* environment variables are now expanded.
    c. The *phrase* variable is not expanded yet.

3. Second level expansion → The actual substitution takes place and the *phrase* environment variable is now expanded properly.

The following is another Batch file script example where we print each character in a given string. Obviously, we will need a loop with a counter to accomplish that.

Using the C programming language, the logic would look like this (*for-each-char-1.c*):

```
#include <stdio.h>
#include <stdlib.h>

int main()
{
        char buf[100];

        printf("Enter a string:");
        char *input = gets_s(buf, _countof(buf));
        if (input != NULL)
        {
                while (*input != '\0')
                        printf("%c\n", *input++);
        }
        return 0;
}
```

The same program can be expressed using the Batch files scripting language with something like the following (*for-each-char-1.bat*):

```
@echo off

:main
        setlocal

        set /p str=Enter a string:

        set i=0
        :repeat
                call set char_i=%%str:~%i%,1%% ①
                if not defined char_i goto break
                echo char[%i%]=%char_i%
                set /a i+=1
                goto repeat
        :break

        endlocal
```

In a similar fashion to the previous example above, we used the **CALL** keyword (at marker ①) to issue a substring operation. The variable "*i*" is expanded first (prior to the **CALL**) and then after the **CALL**, the second level expansion takes place and the "*char_i*" will contain a single character at the position designated by the value of the variable "*i*".

Let us print each individual character in the string but this time using the **FOR** keyword and the counting syntax (*for-each-char-2.bat*):

```
@echo off

:main
      setlocal enabledelayedexpansion

      rem set /p str=Enter a string:
      set str=A string is 123

      for /l %%a in (0,1,4096) do (
            set char_i=!str:~%%a,1! ①
            if not defined char_i goto break
            echo char[%%a] is '!char_i!'
      )
      :break
      echo Done!

      goto :eof
      endlocal
```

Note: Using the DEVE syntax when applicable can help you avoid using the two-level expansion syntax and still accomplish the same results. Check marker ① in the code above.

String sorting

String sorting is provided to the Batch files scripting language using the external utility called "**SORT**". It is located in the Windows system directory:

```
C:\BatchProgramming>where sort
C:\Windows\System32\sort.exe
```

Here's a partial help output from the "**SORT /?**" command execution:

```
SORT [/R] [/+n] [/M kilobytes] [/L locale]
     [/REC recordbytes]
     [[drive:][path]filename] [/T [drive:][path]]
     [/O [drive:][path]filename3]

  [drive:][path]filename Specifies the file to be sorted.  If not
                         specified, the standard input is sorted.

  /+n                    Specifies the character number, n, to
                         begin each comparison.
  /R[EVERSE]             Reverses the sort order; that is,
                         sorts Z to A, then 9 to 0.
  /O[UTPUT]
    [drive:][path]filename
                         Specifies the file where the sorted input is
                         to be stored.  If not specified, the data is
                         written to the standard output.   Specifying
                         the output file is faster than redirecting
                         standard output to the same file.
```

In short, the **SORT** command will let you:

1. Sort strings from the standard input (if received through piped output) or an input file (specified in the parameter).
2. Store the result into an output file (with the "/O" switch) or write it to the standard output (if no output file is specified).
3. Skip characters in a line before doing the comparison (with the "/+n" switch). That's useful to sort lines while disregarding fixed length prefixes.
4. Control whether to sort in ascending or descending order (if the /R switch is present).

Example 1 - Sorting commands output

Let's illustrate this by outputting a bunch of unordered numbers which will then be piped to the **SORT** command:

```
C:\BatchProgramming>(echo 6 & echo 3 & echo 2 & echo 1) | sort
1
2
3
6
```

Similarly, we could have sorted them in descending order using the "/R" switch:

```
C:\BatchProgramming>(echo 6 & echo 3 & echo 2 & echo 1) | sort /R
6
3
2
1
```

Here's another example where we sort the output of the "**DIR /B**" command:

```
C:\BatchProgramming>dir /b *.txt | sort
findstr-test.txt
ftp-resp.txt
more-lines.txt
text-delims-1.txt
text-delims-2.txt
text-delims-3.txt
text-delims-4.txt
text-eol-1.txt
text-tokens-1.txt
text1.txt
the long text file name 2.txt
the long text file name.txt
```

Example 2 - Sorting file contents

Let's take the *wa-plates.txt* text file that contains a bunch of Washington State plate numbers. To sort this file, we can issue the following command:

```
C:\BatchProgramming>sort wa-plates.txt
ALJ-0493
AVP-1645
BCJ-6808
EOV-6287
GTR-7960
GXA-0259
JDS-1869
JUM-6327
KOL-7693
KOR-2027
MBW-5007
AGW-4585
NDR-6273
PIO-1704
QKU-0946
QZW-8690
RGL-2899
```

```
WTW-3852
XGU-0334
ZNQ-3360
ZXB-6459
```

To sort just the numeric part, we can use the "/+4" switch:

```
C:\BatchProgramming>sort /+4 wa-plates.txt
GXA-0259
XGU-0334
ALJ-0493
QKU-0946
AVP-1645
PIO-1704
JDS-1869
KOR-2027
RGL-2899
ZNQ-3360
WTW-3852
MBW-5007
NDR-6273
EOV-6287
JUM-6327
ZXB-6459
BCJ-6808
KOL-7693
GTR-7960
QZW-8690
```

Using the FINDSTR command

Unlike most of the keywords that have been explained in the previous sections, the **FINDSTR** is an external command:

```
C:\BatchProgramming>where findstr
C:\Windows\System32\findstr.exe
```

This command is very helpful because it provides complementary string operations, especially string matching facilities. If you are familiar with UNIX based operating systems, this command is akin to the **grep** command.

Here's a partial help output of the **FINDSTR** command:

```
C:\BatchProgramming>findstr /?
Searches for strings in files.
FINDSTR [/B] [/E] [/L] [/R] [/S] [/I]
        [/X] [/V] [/N] [/M] [/O] [/P] [/F:file]
        [/C:string] [/G:file]
        [/D:dir list] [/A:color attributes] [/OFF[LINE]]
        strings [[drive:][path]filename[ ...]]
  /B         Matches pattern if at the beginning of a line.
  /E         Matches pattern if at the end of a line.
  /L         Uses search strings literally.
  /R         Uses search strings as regular expressions.
  /S         Searches for matching files in the current directory and all
             subdirectories.
  /I         Specifies that the search is not to be case-sensitive.
  /X         Prints lines that match exactly.
  /V         Prints only lines that do not contain a match.
  /N         Prints the line number before each line that matches.
  /M         Prints only the filename if a file contains a match.
  /O         Prints character offset before each matching line.
  /P         Skip files with non-printable characters.
  /OFF[LINE] Do not skip files with offline attribute set.
  /A:attr    Specifies color attribute with two hex digits.
             See "color /?"
  /F:file    Reads file list from the specified
             file(/ stands for console).
  /C:string  Uses specified string as a literal search string.
  /G:file    Gets search strings from the specified
             file(/ stands for console).
  /D:dir     Search a semicolon delimited list of directories
  strings    Text to be searched for.
  [drive:][path]filename
             Specifies a file or files to search.
```

With this command, it will be possible to search for strings in a file (or piped output) with criteria controlled by the following switches:

- /B or /E → Look for strings at the beginning or end of a line. The same can be achieved with the "^" and "$" regular expression characters.
- /I → Case insensitive string matching.
- /X → Only print the lines that have an exact match.
- /V → Print all the lines except those that have a match.
- /L → Search for strings literally.
- /R → Search for strings using regular expressions.

- /N → Display the matching line number.
- /O → Display the matching file offset.

In Chapter 4, there will be various recipes that illustrate the use of the **FINDSTR** command. For now, let me illustrate how to use this command with a few examples.

Let's assume the following input file (*findstr-test.txt*):

```
This is a simple example file
With a few lines
123
Of Various formats
//<Begin
Line 1
Line 2
Line 3
//>End
This line contains a fox
This line contains a chicken
And this one contains a bird
456
module!offset: 00 00 00 00 00 00 00 00 00 01
kernel32!77441122: 00 00 00 00 00 00 00 00 00 02
user32!6A112233: 00 00 00 00 00 00 00 00 00 03
@echo Directive 1
@echo Directive 2
@echo Directive 3
789
Some other lines
```

This file has various lines which we will extract using a combination of built-in commands and **FINDSTR** command calls.

Example 1 – Extracting text between two markers

In this example, we want to extract the lines between the "//<Begin" and the "//>End" begin and end markers respectively.

I will use the **FINDSTR** command to figure out the line numbers of the beginning and end markers, subtract the two lines to get the count of lines in between. Afterwards, I will use the "**FOR /F**" syntax with the "skip" option to read the lines in between the two markers.

Let me illustrate how to grab the begin marker's line number:

```
C:\BatchProgramming>findstr /B /N /C:"//<Begin" findstr-test.txt
4://<Begin
```

Note: The "/B" switch was used to match the string at the beginning of the file, the "/N" switch was used to display the line numbers and the "/C" switch was used to specify the text to be matched.

In facsimile, we can retrieve the end marker's line number like this:

```
C:\BatchProgramming>findstr /B /N /C:"//>End" findstr-test.txt
8://>End
```

Now we need to tokenize the output in order to extract the line numbers. We can use the **FOR /F** syntax like this:

```
C:\BatchProgramming>for /f "usebackq delims=: tokens=1" %a in (
      `findstr /b /n /c:"//>End" findstr-test.txt`) do @echo %a

8

C:\BatchProgramming>
```

Note: I used the "usebackq" option in order to tokenize the output of a command (the FINDSTR 's output), the "delims=:" option, and the "tokens=1" option to express that I am interested in a single token (the first token that indicates the line number).

Putting it all together (*findstr-extract-between-markers.bat*):

```
@echo off

setlocal enabledelayedexpansion

set FN=findstr-test.txt
call :get-line-no "//<Begin" "%FN%" ①
set MBEGIN=%errorlevel% ②

call :get-line-no "//>End" "%FN%"
set MEND=%errorlevel%

if "%MBEGIN%"=="-1" goto error ③
if "%MEND%"=="-1"   goto error

set /A C=MEND-MBEGIN-1 ④
```

```
for /f "useback skip=%MBEGIN% tokens=* delims=" %%a in ("%FN%") DO ( ⑤
       echo %%a ⑥
       SET /A C-=1 ⑦
       if !C!==0 goto :eof ⑧
)
goto :eof

:get-line-no <1=string> <2=file> ⑨
⑩
for /f "useback tokens=1 delims=:" %%a in (
    `findstr /N /C:"%~1" "%~2"`) DO (
    EXIT /B %%a  ⑪
)
EXIT /B -1 ⑫

:error
       echo Could not find markers!
       exit /b
```

And a short explanation of the markers:

1. Call the *get-line-no* function to retrieve the begin marker's line number. The return value is stored in the *ERRORLEVEL* pseudo-environment variable (with the **EXIT /B** invocation).
2. Store the result in the *MBEGIN* environment variable. In the subsequent two lines, we do the same for the end marker.
3. Check if we matched both markers. If a marker was not found, then -1 is returned by the *get-line-no* function. The script would then go to the *error* label and terminate the script.
4. Compute the embedded lines count using the **SET /A** syntax to carry a subtraction operation.
5. Open the input file, skip past the begin marker's line number. Do not specify any delimiters so we take the line as is (no spaces will be trimmed).
6. Echo each line read.
7. Decrement the variable "*C*" that denotes the remaining-lines -to-read counter.
8. When the lines counter reaches zero then terminate the script → Mission accomplished.
9. Define the *get-line-no* function.
10. This step has been explained in the snippets above. It simply tokenizes the output of **FINDSTR** to extract the line number from the output.
11. Use **EXIT /B** to return the token (which is the line number) as an exit code.
12. If no match was found, return the -1 exit code.

When we run this script, we observe the desired output:

```
C:\BatchProgramming>findstr-extract-between-markers.bat
Line 1
Line 2
Line 3

C:\BatchProgramming>
```

Example 2 – Print all the lines beginning with a certain character

Let's assume we want to print all the lines from the sample text file above that begin with the "@" symbol but we want to display the lines without that symbol.

This is a simple one to pull:

```
C:\BatchProgramming>findstr /B /C:"@" findstr-test.txt
@echo Directive 1
@echo Directive 2
@echo Directive 3
```

Now to omit the "@", we can use the sub-string operation along with the "**FOR /F**" syntax.

That's the full script (*findstr-substr.bat*):

```
@echo off

setlocal enabledelayedexpansion

for /f "useback tokens=*" %%a in (
  `findstr /b /c:"@" "findstr-test.txt"`) do (
        set line=%%a ①
        set line=!line:~1! ②
        echo !line!
)
endlocal
```

Some explanation:

1. Take all the tokens into a single variable "*a*".
2. Use the sub-string operation with the DEVE syntax to strip out the first character in that line.

When we run it, we get the expected output:

```
C:\BatchProgramming>findstr-substr.bat
echo Directive 1
echo Directive 2
echo Directive 3
```

Example 3 – Print all the lines that contain numbers only

Let us illustrate how to use **FINDSTR** with a simple regular expression to find all the lines that contain numbers only.

The correct regular expression is "^[0-9]+$" but **FINDSTR** does not support the "+" character which designates one or more matches. We shall use the "^[0-9][0-9]*$" regular expression which is equivalent to the original regular expression:

```
C:\BatchProgramming>findstr /r /c:"^[0-9][0-9]*$" findstr-test.txt
123
456
789
```

If we did not enclose the expression in double quotes with the "/C" switch, then we would need to escape the caret character like this:

```
C:\BatchProgramming>findstr /r ^^[0-9][0-9]*$ findstr-test.txt
```

Example 4 – Printing lines that have a specific format

Often times, as a system administrator, you have to deal with parsing log files and generating reports. The following example can give you some more ideas on what **FINDSTR** is capable of.

In the *findstr-test.txt* text file from above, we also have the following lines:

```
module!offset: 0f 00 00 00 00 00 00 00 00 01
kernel32!77441122: 00 00 00 00 00 00 00 00 00 02
user32!6A112233: 00 00 00 00 00 00 00 00 00 03
```

Let's write a regular expression to match an address line that begins with a module name, followed by an exclamation mark and offset followed by a colon. The regular expression supported by **FINDSTR** is like the following:

```
C:\>findstr /r /c:"^[a-z][a-z0-9]*![0-9a-z][0-9a-z]*:" findstr-test.txt
module!offset: 00 00 00 00 00 00 00 00 00 01
kernel32!77441122: 00 00 00 00 00 00 00 00 00 02
user32!6A112233: 00 00 00 00 00 00 00 00 00 03
```

Example 5 - Finding strings from piped output

The **FINDSTR** command can also be used to find strings in piped output.

Let's group a bunch of **ECHO** commands and then pipe the output to **FINDSTR** like this:

```
(echo line 1 && echo skip && echo line 2 && echo skip) | findstr /r
/c:"line [0-9][0-9]*"
```

Let's run it and observe the output:

```
line 1
line 2
```

A few things to note here:

1. I used the parenthesis to group all the **ECHO** commands and have the output emitted once.
2. The pipe ("|") is used to connect the output of the grouped **ECHO** commands to the **FINDSTR** input.
3. A simple regular expression is used to only print output of the form: "line N" (where *N* is a number).

In the following example, to parse out the volume serial number of drive C using the "`dir /w`" command output, we can use the **FINDSTR** command with pipes like this:

```
C:\BatchProgramming>dir /w c:\ | findstr /c:"Volume Serial Number"
 Volume Serial Number is 2419-9694
```

Here's another example where we use the following syntax to print all the lines except those that start with "@":

```
C:\BatchProgramming>type findstr-test.txt | findstr /V /B /C:"@"
This is a simple example file
With a few lines
123
Of Various formats
//<Begin
Line 1
Line 2
Line 3
//>End
This line contains a fox
This line contains a chicken
And this one contains a bird
456
module!offset: 0f 00 00 00 00 00 00 00 00 01
kernel32!77441122: 00 00 00 00 00 00 00 00 00 02
user32!6A112233: 00 00 00 00 00 00 00 00 00 03
789
Some other lines
```

Example 6 - Multiple filters

It is possible to pipe the output of various commands into **FINDSTR** or even the output of **FINDSTR** back to itself.

For instance, in this command, we omit all the lines beginning with "@" or with "Line N", and finally we sort the following output:

```
findstr /v /b /c:"@" findstr-test.txt | findstr /v /r /c:"[a-z]*!" | sort
```

When executed, we observe the following output:

```
//<Begin
//>End
123
456
789
And this one contains a bird
Line 1
Line 2
Line 3
Of Various formats
Some other lines
```

```
This is a simple example file
This line contains a chicken
This line contains a fox
With a few lines
```

Example 7 – Processing a C++ source file and generate C# constants

Imagine you have a C++ file that defines some string constants that you want to share in your C# program.

Let's suppose that this C++ file (*transform-me-1.cpp*) contains the following constants:

```
#include <stdio.h>

//
// XML constants begin
//
static LPCWSTR XML_PROVIDERS = L"Providers";
static LPCWSTR XML_PROVIDER = L"Provider";
static LPCWSTR XML_NAME = L"Name";
static LPCWSTR XML_GUID = L"Guid";
static LPCWSTR XML_METADATA = L"Metadata";
static LPCWSTR XML_OPCODES = L"Opcodes";
static LPCWSTR XML_OPCODE = L"Opcode";
static LPCWSTR XML_VALUE = L"Value";
static LPCWSTR XML_VERSION = L"Version";
static LPCWSTR XML_KEYWORDS = L"Keywords";
static LPCWSTR XML_KEYWORD = L"Keyword";
static LPCWSTR XML_TEMPLATE = L"Template";
static LPCWSTR XML_TASK = L"Task";
//
// XML constants end
//
```

These strings declaration syntax cannot be used as-is in C#. Instead, we have to transform each declaration line from:

```
static LPCWSTR XML_STR = L"Value"
```

To:

```
public const string XML_STR = "Value"
```

To achieve that, we can follow the following steps:

1. Invoke **FINDSTR** to match the XML constant definitions lines.
2. Use "**FOR /F**" to capture the output of the **FINDSTR** invocation (from the previous step) and tokenize the variable name and its value.
3. Use the string substitution syntax on each match and replace/fix the syntax as required.

To express this logic using the Batch files scripting language, we can use something like this (*transform-me-1.bat*):

```
for /F "usebackq tokens=3*" %%a in (
    `findstr /B /C:"static LPCWSTR XML_"  transform-me-1.cpp`) DO (
  set Z=%%b
  set Z=!Z: L"= "!
  echo public const string %%a !Z!
)
```

Let's run the script and test it:

```
C:\BatchProgramming>transform-me-1.bat
public const string XML_PROVIDERS = "Providers";
public const string XML_PROVIDER = "Provider";
public const string XML_NAME = "Name";
public const string XML_GUID = "Guid";
public const string XML_METADATA = "Metadata";
public const string XML_OPCODES = "Opcodes";
public const string XML_OPCODE = "Opcode";
public const string XML_VALUE = "Value";
public const string XML_VERSION = "Version";
public const string XML_KEYWORDS = "Keywords";
public const string XML_KEYWORD = "Keyword";
public const string XML_TEMPLATE = "Template";
public const string XML_TASK = "Task";
```

We can see that the C++ declaration syntax was changed to C# and the "L" prefix (that designates Unicode C strings) disappeared.

Basic data structures

The Batch files scripting language does not have formal data structures support, however it has enough primitives that allow us to build data structures such as the following:

- Stacks
- Arrays
- Associative arrays
- Sets

In the following sub-sections, we will be using string operations (tokenization, sub-strings, etc.), environment variables, repetition control structures to build all the aforementioned data structures and their basic operations.

Arrays

An array is a data structure that holds a list of values (usually all of the same type), referenced by the same variable name and whose values are accessed using a numerical index. It can be compared to a table with a single column and multiple rows. Each row contains a value, but all values belong to the same table.

Suppose we have three separate variables to store three values:

```
V1=5, V2=10 and V3=15
```

We can use an array named "*V*" to store all the values, which can later be referenced by an index (or a position):

```
Index/Value
-----------
0   / 5
1   / 10
2   / 15
```

In high-level languages, the array value at a given index is expressed using the variable name followed by a pair of square brackets that enclose the desired index value. For instance, the value of "*V1*" is equivalent to the value of "*V[0]*" (read as V of zero).

In the Batch files scripting language, we will use environment variables to store the array values:

```
set V[0]=5
set V[1]=10
set V[2]=15
```

While these are 3 separate environment variables, we can effectively enumerate them using a counting **FOR** loop and an indexing mechanism similar to the following:

```
for /L %%a in (0, 1, 2) do (
       echo V[%%a]=!V[%%a]! ①
)
```

Notice how at marker ① I used the DEVE syntax to expand *V*'s value at the index *%%a*. Had I used the regular expansion method (with the percent "%" character), then I would not get the appropriate result because of the embedded *%%a*. The *%%a*, if used, would confuse the environment variable expansion mechanism because of the preceding percent character that was used to expand "*V*".

In fact, the expansion mechanism will think that we are expanding the variable "*%V[%*" instead:

```
set V[=Wrong ①
for /L %%a in (0, 1, 2) do (
       echo V[%%a]=%V[%%a]% ②
)
```

The code above displays the value of variable "*V[*" three times:

```
V[0]=Wrong
V[1]=Wrong
V[2]=Wrong
```

If you want to use the regular expansion syntax (with "%"), then you have to rely on the two-level expansion syntax like this:

```
for /L %%a in (0, 1, 2) do (
       call echo V[%%a]=%%V[%%a]%% ①
)
```

Before concluding this section, it is worthwhile noting that you are not obliged to use the "Variable[Index]" syntax. You can use the "*Variable.Index*", "*Variable(Index)*" or anything else that allows you to easily enumerate and compute the environment variable name using an index.

> *Note: If you use the "Variable(Index)" syntax, make sure you escape the parenthesis properly, otherwise the command interpreter will think you started or closed a compound statement.*

If you wish to delete or clear the array, you can simply use the:

```
SET Variable=
```

syntax on each element like this:

```
for /L %%a in (0, 1, 2) do (
	set V[%%a]=
)
```

The source code of the snippets used above can be found in the script *array-1d.bat*.

Before moving to the next section, it is worthwhile noting that in high-level languages or other scripting languages, an array's size is usually maintained in an attribute/property (a member variable of the array) or retrieved using a special operator or function.

For instance, in JavaScript, the "length" attribute denotes the elements count in the array:

```
<script language="Javascript">
	var Arr = new Array();

	for (var i=1; i<= 3;i++)
		Arr.push(i);

	alert(Arr.length);
</script>
```

Accessing the "*Arr.length*" attribute would return the value 3.

In Batch file scripts, instead of re-computing the array's length (which is costly), we can compute the length and then cache its value in an additional attribute variable. This require us to carry all the array management through helper functions which will guarantee that the length attribute stays up-to-date after each operation.

Building management functions for one-dimensional arrays

In this section, I will illustrate how to use the Batch files scripting language to build array support functions that will allow us to mimic JavaScript's array functionality.

These are the functions that we will be building together:

1. Create a new array.
2. Append a value to the end of the array.
3. Insert a value into the array at a position between zero and the length-1.
4. Delete a value from the array at a position within the array's bounds.
5. Find a value in the array and return its position.
6. Return the array's length.

Let's get started with the *array-create* function.

The create-array function

The reason we introduce this function is to enforce a set of naming conventions to the array variables and to initialize and maintain the *length* attribute.

```
::
:: Create an empty array (or with the given size if specified)
::
:array-create <1=ArrayName> <2=size>
      if defined %~1.length call :array-destroy %1 ①

      :: No size specified?
      if "%~2" equ "" ( ②
            set %~1.length=0 ②
      ) else (
            :: Create an array with the size
            set /a array_create_len=%~2-1 ③
            for /l %%a in (0, 1, !array_create_len!) do ( ④
                  set %~1[%%a]=0 ⑤
            )
            set %~1.length=%~2 ⑥
            set array_create_len= ⑦
      )

      goto :eof
```

This function takes the array name as the first argument and an optional second argument which is used to specify the array's initial size. However, if no size argument was passed then we simply create the array by setting its *length* attribute to zero (at marker ②) and return to the caller.

At marker ①, we check to see if the array is defined by looking for the *length* attribute and if we found it then we call the *array-destroy* function. It is a good idea to destroy any previous arrays with the same name before attempting to create new ones.

If a size was passed to the *array-create* function, then we create a loop (marker ④) to iterate from 0 to *size*-1 (as computed at marker ③) and start creating each array variable (at marker ⑤).

At the end of the loop, at marker ⑥, we update the *length* attribute with the user given size. At marker ⑦, we clean the work variable we employed earlier at marker ③.

> *Note: it is difficult to localize the environment block in the array functions that we are building. This is because we will be heavily modifying the environment while working with the user passed arrays. Therefore, we employ unique work variable names as it shall be explained in the section entitled "Variables naming conventions" in Chapter 3.*

Destroy the array

In a long program, it is a good practice to destroy arrays once you are done using them. This ensures that the environment variable block does not run out of space.

The following *array-destroy* function will delete all the variables inside an array:

```
::
:: Destroy the array (and all its elements)
::
:array-destroy <1=ArrayName>
    :: Compute the length
    call set /a len=%%%~1.length%%%-1 ①
    :: Clear array values
    for /L %%a in (0, 1, %len%) do (
        set %~1[%%a]=
    )
    :: Clear the length attribute
    set %~1.length=

    goto :eof
```

Apart from deleting all the array's variables, the one thing worth noting is how we get the length of the array using the syntax at marker ①:

```
call set /a len=%%%~1.length%%%-1
```

It uses the two-level expansion syntax: the first level resolves the first argument ("%1") to the array name and the second level returns the actual value. With the "**SET /A**" syntax, we decrement the returned length, so it can be used with a 0-based **FOR** loop.

Appending values to the array

Now that we are done with the creation and destruction functions, we are ready to explore how to add new values at the end of the array while properly maintaining the *length* attribute along the way:

```
::
:: Append an element into the end of the array
::
:array-append <1=ArrayName> <2=Value> [<3=another value>]
       :array-append-repeat ①
              call set %~1[%%%~1.length%%]=%~2 ②
              set /A %~1.length+=1 ③
              shift /2 ④
              if "%~2" NEQ "" goto array-append-repeat ⑤
       goto :eof
```

The gist of the code is to create a new variable containing the value of the second argument ("%2") and adding it to the end of the array as indicated by marker ②. After adding the value to the array, we make sure that the length is incremented (marker ③).

We attempt to **SHIFT** the arguments by 2 (at marker ④) in order to see if more values are passed in the arguments. Marker ⑤ checks if more values were passed and if so, then we loop again to marker ①. The reason we shift by 2 is because we don't want to touch the first argument ("%1") which is the array's name, because we still need it in the loop (at markers ② and ③).

Inserting values at a given position

To insert a value into the array at a given position, we have to shift to the right by one position all the variables in the array past the user supplied position value. Afterwards, we increment the *length* attribute.

Here's how the *array-insert* function looks like:

```
::
:: Insert an element at a given position into the array
::
:array-insert <1=ArrayName> <2=Position> <3=Value>
	call set array_insert_len=%%%~1.length%%
	if %~2 GEQ %array_insert_len% ( ①
		echo Error: out of bounds!
		exit /b -1
		goto :eof
	)

	:: Shift items to the right
	set /a array_insert_pa=%~2+1 ②
	for /L %%a in (%array_insert_len%, -1, %array_insert_pa%) do ( ③
		set /a array_insert_pa=%%a-1 ④
		call set %~1[%%a]=%%%~1[!array_insert_pa!]%% ⑤
	)

	:: Insert the new value
	set %~1[%~2]=%~3 ⑥

	:: Increase the length
	set /a %~1.length+=1 ⑦

	set array_insert_len=
	set array_insert_pa=

	goto :eof
```

> *Note: The code above uses a bunch of temporary work variables. It also makes sure that all of them are discarded when the function terminates.*

At marker ①, we start by doing sanity checks to see if we are trying to insert at a position greater than the actual array's length. If it is the case, then we display an error message and exit the function.

At marker ②, we initialize a variable to denote the position beyond the user supplied position. This will be the starting position where all the variables will be shifted to. At marker ③, we start a reverse loop that counts from the array's length (and not "*length* -1", thus treating it as the new length) down-to the new shift position. By using the reverse loop, we save ourselves the hassles of having to swap variables from left to right as we move them up one position in the array. Inside the loop at marker ④, we compute the position that will be the source value that we will be copying from. At marker ⑤, we copy the value over to its new location. At marker ⑥ we insert the value at the desired position (after having shifted to the right all the previous slots). Finally, at marker ⑦, we increment the *length* attribute. The function ends by deleting all the work variables.

Deleting a value at a given position

This functionality is similar to the insertion functionality, except that it shifts the elements to the left while overwriting the value at the user supplied position:

```
::
:: Delete an element from the array at a given position
::
:array-delete <1=ArrayName> <2=Position>
       call set /a array_delete_len=%%%~1.length%%
       if %~2 GEQ %array_delete_len% (
              echo Error: out of bounds!
              exit /b -1
              goto :eof
       )

       set /a array_delete_len-=1

       :: Shift items to the left
       for /L %%a in (%~2, 1, %array_delete_len%) do (
              set /a array_delete_pa=%%a+1
              call set %~1[%%a]=%%%~1[!array_delete_pa!]%%
       )

       :: Purge the last element (since we shifted to the left)
       set %~1[%array_delete_len%]=

       :: Decrease the length
       set /a %~1.length-=1

       set array_delete_len=
       set array_delete_pa=

       goto :eof
```

Finding the position of a value in an array

The function that finds a value's position in an array is passed two mandatory arguments and a third optional one. The first two being the array name and the value to be matched, while the third one being the start position of where we want to start looking at.

If the start position was not provided, then we start searching from the beginning of the array at position 0 (marker ①). If the value was found then its position is returned (marker ②), otherwise we return -1 (marker ③).

Here's the *array-find* routine:

```
::
:: Find an element in the array and return the position
::
:array-find <1=ArrayName> <2=Value> <3=Start Pos> =>
<errorlevel=foundpos>
     :: Set a default position if not set
     set array_find_p=%~3 ①
     if not defined array_find_p set array_find_p=0 ①

     :: Get the length
     call set /a array_find_len=%%%~1.length%%

     :: Check the bounds of the start position
     if %array_find_p% GEQ %array_find_len% (
          echo Error: out of bounds!
          exit /b -1
          goto :eof
     )


     :: Search all items
     set /a array_find_len-=1
     for /L %%a in (%array_find_p%, 1, %array_find_len%) do (
          call set array_find_len=%%%~1[%%a]%%
          if "!array_find_len!" equ "%~2" ( ②
               set array_find_len=
               set array_find_p=
               exit /b %%a ②
          )
     )

     set array_find_len=
     set array_find_p=
     exit /b -1 ③
```

Testing the array functions

In this section, we will demonstrate how to use and test these functions (*array-1d-funcs.bat*). Let's start by creating an array, adding some values, displaying them and then destroying the array:

```
call :array-create A1
call :array-append A1 "elias" "peter" "mike"

echo The values are:
set A1[

call :array-destroy A1
echo The values after destruction are:
set A1[
```

Let's execute the test code and observe the output:

```
C:\BatchProgramming>array-1d-funcs.bat
The values are:
A1[0]=elias
A1[1]=peter
A1[2]=mike
The values after destruction are:
Environment variable A1[ not defined

C:\BatchProgramming>
```

It works as expected!

Now let us update the code above and try to insert the name "Mary" at position 1, in between "Elias" and "Peter":

```
call :array-insert A1 1 "mary"
echo The new values are:
set A1[
```

And its output is:

```
The values are:
A1[0]=elias
A1[1]=mary
A1[2]=peter
A1[3]=mike
```

Now let us exercise the delete functionality and remove "Peter" (from position 2):

```
call :array-delete A1 2
echo The values after deletion:
set A1[
```

And the output is:

```
A1[0]=elias
A1[1]=mary
A1[2]=mike
```

Works like a charm, but unfortunately, we have now ended up with a ménage à trois. No worries, we can solve that by using the *array-find* function, to find "Mike" and remove him from the equation:

```
call :array-find A1 "mike"
if "%errorlevel%" equ "-1" (
        echo Mike is hiding somewhere! Oh man!
) else (
        call :array-delete A1 %errorlevel%
        echo Mike's busted.
        echo New values are now:
        set A1[
)
```

And the output is:

```
Mike's busted.
New values are now:
A1[0]=elias
A1[1]=mary
```

Now we have a better love story between Elias and Mary.

Multi-dimensional arrays

Multi-dimensional (or N-dimensional) arrays have the same concept as single dimensional arrays except that they can be compared to a table with *N* columns and any number of rows. Each row contains *N* values. If there are *M* rows in an N-dimensional array, then there is total of *M* x *N* elements.

In high-level languages, a value inside a multi-dimensional array is referenced using the syntax "Array[Dim1Index][Dim2Index][Dim3Index][...]". In the Batch files scripting language, we can also use the same terminology and store the values in the corresponding environment variables, or we can equally use another terminology such as "Array.Dim1Index.Dim2Index.Dim3Index" etc. for example.

I won't be expanding much on this topic because the ideas are the same as single dimensional arrays which have been previously explained in details.

Let us assume you have a table containing two columns: one for the first name and another for the last name. This table can be expressed using a two dimensional array like this:

```
set TABLE[0][0]=Elias
set TABLE[0][1]=Ashmole
set TABLE[1][0]=John
set TABLE[1][1]=Smith
set TABLE[2][0]=Mary
set TABLE[2][1]=Jane
```

The row is denoted by "*TABLE[n]*", therefore both "*TABLE[0][0]*" and "*TABLE[0][1]*" designate the first row, etc. The first column indicates the first name and the second row holds the last name.

To list the elements, we can use the following syntax:

```
echo The names we have in the table are:
echo -----------------------------------
for /L %%a IN (0, 1, 2) do (
call echo [%%a] FirstName: '%%TABLE[%%a][0]%%' LastName:
'%%TABLE[%%a][1]%%'
)
```

It has been explained previously that instead of using the two-level expansion syntax to expand the values from the "*TABLE*" variable, we can use the DEVE syntax like this:

```
echo [%%a] FirstName: '!TABLE[%%a][0]!' LastName: '!TABLE[%%a][1]!'
```

Let's run the *array-2d.bat* script and observe its output:

```
C:\BatchProgramming>array-2d
The names we have in the table are:
-----------------------------------
[0] FirstName: 'Elias' LastName: 'Ashmole'
[1] FirstName: 'John' LastName: 'Smith'
[2] FirstName: 'Mary' LastName: 'Jane'

C:\BatchProgramming>
```

Associative arrays

An associative array is also known as a dictionary, map or a symbol table. Unlike the array whose values are accessed using a numerical index, the values of an associative array are referenced by a key. In the Batch files scripting language, the key can be either a string or a number.

A numeric key index that is used to access values in an associative array, unlike regular arrays, does not have to be between 0 and the array's length minus 1. That means that *"ARR[123]"* and *"ARR[9999]"* are valid entries in the associative array, whereas *"ARR[123]"* is not valid in a regular array unless that array has 124 elements or more.

Use an associative array to easily map one value (the key) to another (the actual value). For example, let's assume the following associative array that maps usernames to full user names like this:

```
set USERS[moeh]=Moe Howard
set USERS[shemph]=Shemp Howard
set USERS[larryf]=Larry Fine
```

Usually, when enumerating the values in an associative array, you require the key/value pairs. Therefore, a regular counting **FOR** loop ("**FOR /L**") won't be useful. Instead, we have to use something like the following to enumerate the key/value pairs:

```
for /f "usebackq delims=" %%a in (`set USERS[`) do ( ①
        for /f "usebackq tokens=1,2 delims==" %%m in ('%%a') do ( ②
                set __k=%%m& set __k=!__k:*[=!& set __k=!__k:]=! ③
                set __v=%%n ④
                echo key = '!__k!' value = '!__v!'
        )
)
```

Since we are using one environment variable per key/value pair, at marker ① we had to invoke the **SET** keyword while passing part of the name of our associative array ("USER[") to enumerate all of the pairs. In the outer **FOR** loop, we will get 3 individual lines passed to the **FOR**'s body, each line containing something like this:

```
USERS[KeyName]=TheSavedValue
```

At marker ②, we compose another **FOR** loop, but this time we use it to tokenize each line. We use the equal sign ("=") to split the line into two tokens.

At marker ③, just for brevity, we issue multiple unconditional joined commands on one line that do the following:

1. Transfer the first token, the key, from the **FOR** loop variable to an environment variable. This will let us do string substitution.
2. Cut out all the strings prior to and including the square bracket ("[") character. This will eventually take out the "USER[" string from the line and leave us with "KeyName]" string.
3. Finally, take out the remaining closing square bracket ("]"). This will leave us with the name of the key.

At marker ④, we conveniently transfer the second token (the value) to an environment variable. This step is optional, but I did it just to have the *__k* and *__v* variables denote the key/value pairs.

If you know the key and you want to look up the associated value, then you can directly access the environment variable like this: *ARRAYNAME[key]*.

To illustrate how to retrieve a value from an associative array, let's prompt the user for a key and then look up the value associated with it:

```
set /p user=Enter user name:
if not defined USERS[%user%] (
      echo User '%user%' was not found in the system!
) else (
      echo %user%'s full name is: !USERS[%user%]!
)
```

Let's run the snippet above two times, once with a valid key value and another with an invalid key value:

```
C:\BatchProgramming>array-assoc-1.bat
Enter user name:larryf
larryf's full name is: Larry Fine


C:\BatchProgramming>array-assoc-1.bat
Enter user name:Mary
User 'Mary' was not found in the system
```

In this section, I showed how to work with associative arrays that are easily updatable. In the following section, I will illustrate how to create a read-only associative array for the purpose of lookups only.

Working with encoded associative arrays

In the previous section, we used individual environment variables for each key/value pair. However, there is a better way that just requires using one environment variable to store all the key/value pairs.

We will use a special encoding to achieve that. Instead of using the previous method like this:

```
set FRUITS[b]=banana
set FRUITS[a]=apple
set FRUITS[o]=orange
set FRUITS[k]=kiwi
```

We can use the following encoding (or a similar one instead):

```
set FRUITS=k@kiwi$a@apple$b@banana$o@orange
```

In the latter example above, we used a single environment variable (*FRUITS*) that contains a set of strings that are separated by the dollar sign ("$"). Each string consists of a key/value pair separated by the at-sign ("@").

Intuitively, we deduce that to retrieve a value given the key, we have to use two **FOR** loops (one being nested in the other). The outer loop will tokenize by the dollar sign ("$") and the inner loop will tokenize by the at-sign ("@").

To enumerate the key/value pairs, we can use something like this:

```
FOR %%a in (%FRUITS:$= %) do ( ①
      FOR /F "usebackq tokens=1,2 delims=@" %%b in ('%%a') do ( ②
            echo key=%%b value=%%c ③
      )
)
```

At marker ①, we replace the dollar sign with the space character. When we do that, the regular (non-extended syntax) **FOR** keyword will iterate as much as there are space-separated items in its set.

So for example, this code alone:

```
echo FRUITS split by the space character: %FRUITS:$= %

for %%a in (%FRUITS:$= %) do (
      echo %%a
)
```

Produces this output:

```
FRUITS split by the space character: k@kiwi a@apple b@banana o@orange
k@kiwi
a@apple
b@banana
o@orange
```

Now that we can have as many iterations (in the outer loop) as the count of associative array elements, we proceed with the inner loop at marker ②.

Within the inner loop, we take two tokens that are separated by the at-sign ("@"). Upon each outer iteration we get a new key/value pair that will be parsed in the inner loop.

Let's run the code and see the output, as produced by marker ③:

```
key=k value=kiwi
key=a value=apple
key=b value=banana
key=o value=orange
```

To use an even simpler method, we can directly encod the key/value pairs in the outer loop itself like this:

```
for %%a in ("k=kiwi" "a=apple" "b=banana" "o=orange") do ( ①
      for /f "usebackq tokens=1,2 delims==" %%b in ('%%~a') do ( ②
            echo key=%%b value=%%c
      )
)
```

Note: Make sure you enclose the items in the "set" with double quotes when using the equal character ("=") as the key/value separator.

Notice that since we are doing the encoding ourselves in the outer loop, at marker ①, we had the freedom to choose how to formulate the **FOR** loop's "set" parameter.

The code at marker ② is trivial, except that we trim the enclosing quotes in the set parameter with the tilde modifier like this: "%%~a".

The output of the snippet above should be the same as the output from the first method.

The last thing left to explain in this section is how to extract a value given its key. The following code explains how to do that:

```
set FRUITS=k@kiwi$a@apple$b@banana$o@orange
call :get-by-key FRUITS a R ①
echo get by key result=%R% ②
goto :eof

:get-by-key <1=assoc-array-name> <2=key> => <3=result> ③
        setlocal
        call set __t=$%%%~1%%$ ④
        set __t=!__t:*$%~2@=! ⑤
        for /f "useback tokens=1* delims=$" %%a in ('%__t%') do ( ⑥
                endlocal
                set %~3=%%a ⑦
        )
        goto :eof
```

At marker ①, we call the *get-by-key* function (at marker ③) and pass to it the array name, the key value and the output environment variable name. At marker ②, we display the result of the function call which is the value of the desired key.

The trick behind this function is to surround the encoded associative array variable (at marker ④) with the chosen key/value pairs separator (the dollar-sign in our case). By doing that, we ensure that the algorithm works with corner cases: the first and the last key/value pairs which normally do not have a preceding or trailing separator.

At marker ⑤, we get rid of all the strings up to the matched key and the key/value separator (the at sign). So for example, if the key we are looking for is "a", then "*__t*", after marker ⑤ becomes:

```
__t=k@kiwi$a@apple$b@banana$o@orange
```

At marker ⑥, we tokenize the string previously obtained using the key/value pairs separator (the dollar sign). By only taking the first token, we obtain the desired value (marker ⑦):

```
get by key result=apple
```

Additionally, we can improve upon the code above by getting rid of the **FOR** loop (at marker ⑥) and use yet another string replacement operation to get rid of the remaining key/value pairs ("b@banana$o@orange") like this:

```
:get-by-key2 <1=assoc-array-name> <2=key> => <3=result>
        setlocal
        call set __t=$%%%~1%%$
        set __t=!__t:*$%~2@=! [⑤ same code as the previous snippet]
        set __t=!__t:$=^&::! [⑥ improved]
        endlocal & set %~3=%__t%
        goto :eof
```

At the new marker ⑥, we replace the dollar sign with joined comment statements. Essentially, the string:

```
apple$b@banana$o@orange
```

Becomes:

```
apple&::b@banana&::o@orange&::
```

Notice how each dollar sign is now replaced with "&::" which comments out the remaining string after it. What we are left with is the value "apple".

The full source code of the associative array examples can be found in the following two scripts: *array-assoc-1.bat* and *array-assoc-2.bat*.

Stacks

A stack is a last-in-first-out structure (LIFO). It allows us to store values for later use, by pushing and popping values from the stack.

Last-in-first-out means that if we push the values 1, 2, 3 to the stack and then pop the stack 3 times, we would get the values in the reverse order of the push: 3, 2, 1.

Let's us construct the *PUSH* function that takes the name of the stack variable and a series of values to be pushed to the stack.

The function can be written as such:

```
:push <1=variable> <2=value> [3=value, 4=value, ...] ①
      :push-more ②
            call set %~1=%~2~%%%1%% ③
            shift /2 ④
            if "%2" NEQ "" goto push-more ⑤
      goto :eof
```

And the explanation for the code markers is as follows:

1. Define the function label and describe its input and output arguments (if any).
2. Define a repetition label in the function. We will loop and jump again to that label in order to push more values.
3. Create the stack variable or prepend to it the value to be pushed. The **CALL** keyword is used for the two-level expansion (as explained in the previous section entitled "Two-level environment variables expansion").
4. Keep the first argument fixed and shift %3 to %2, %4 to %3, and so on. We do this so we refer to the remaining arguments using the same "%2" alias.
5. If no more arguments were passed to the *PUSH* function, then don't loop.

Basically, we use a string to store all the pushed values; the values are separated them with the "~" character.

Each pushed character is prepended to the beginning of the stack variable. This will facilitate the creation of the *POP* function that tokenizes the value of the stack variable and returns the first token:

```
:pop <1=variable> => <2=out-variable>
      :: Clear previous output variable
      set %~2=

      setlocal
      :: Expand the value of the input variable
      call set VAL=%%%~1%%
      :: Tokenize, take two tokens: first token and the remaining ones
      for /F "usebackq tokens=1* delims=~" %%a in ('%VAL%') DO (
            endlocal
            :: Pop off the value
            set %~1=%%b
            :: Return the popped value
            set %~2=%%a
      )

      goto :eof
```

The *POP* operation tokenizes the stack variable values into two tokens: the first token contains the last pushed value and the second token contains the remainder of stack value. Each *POP* operation will throw away the first token. When all the values are popped, the stack will become empty because the underlying environment variable becomes empty.

Let's test the stack functions using a **FOR** loop to count from 1 to 10 and push those values to the stack and then pop them back again:

```
for /L %%a in (1, 1, 10) DO (
        echo Push %%a
        call :push STK %%a
)

echo.
echo.
:test-pop-more
        call :pop STK V
        if not defined V goto test-pop-no-more
        echo Pop -^> %V%
        goto test-pop-more
:test-pop-no-more
```

Let's run the *ds-stacks.bat* script and observe the output:

```
C:\BatchProgramming>ds-stacks.bat
Push 1
Push 2
Push 3
Push 4
Push 5
Push 6
Push 7
Push 8
Push 9
Push 10


Pop -> 10
Pop -> 9
Pop -> 8
Pop -> 7
Pop -> 6
Pop -> 5
Pop -> 4
Pop -> 3
Pop -> 2
```

```
Pop -> 1

C:\BatchProgramming>
```

Indeed, the pop order came out as expected: LIFO!

Sets

A set is a collection of unique values; therefore, we can choose to store the values anyway we wish as long as we ascertain that the set always contains unique values even if we attempt to add duplicates.

For that, we can use individual environment variables each containing a single value, and just for the fact that the environment variable exists, it means that value exists in the set.

Alternatively, we can use a single environment variable and encode all the values in it. The former is much easier to code and the latter requires writing more code to maintain the no-duplicate-values property of the set.

Let's imagine we have the following numeric set: (5, 1, 10, 91, 17) and the following strings set: ("Mars", "Jupiter", "Pluto", "Earth", "Saturn").

To express these sets using the first method (using an individual variable for each set member), we can use something like this:

```
set NUMSET.5=1
set NUMSET.1=1
set NUMSET.10=1
set NUMSET.95=1
set NUMSET.17=1

set PLANETSET.Mars=1
set PLANETSET.Jupiter=1
set PLANETSET.Pluto=1
set PLANETSET.Earth=1
set PLANETSET.Saturn=1
```

As you can see, we used the "SetVariableName.Value" terminology. We could have equally used any other terminology as long as it would be easy to check if a value belongs to a set.

To test if a number is in a given set, we can use the following code:

```
:set-contains <1=Set name> <2=Value>
       if defined %~1.%~2 (exit /b 1) else (exit /b 0)
```

To test the code, we can write something like this:

```
:repeat-n-set
set /P N=Enter a number to see if it is in the set:
call :set-contains NUMSET %N%
if %errorlevel% EQU 1 (
      echo '%N%' is in the set!
) else (
      echo '%N%' is NOT in the set!
      goto repeat-n-set
)

:repeat-p-set
set /P P=Enter planet name to see if it exist in the set:
call :set-contains PLANETSET %P%
if %errorlevel% EQU 1 (
      echo '%P%' is in the set!
) else (
      echo '%P%' is NOT in the set!
      goto repeat-p-set
)
```

Let's run it and observe the output:

```
C:\BatchProgramming>ds-sets-1.bat
Enter a number to see if it is in the set: 55
'55' is NOT in the set
Enter a number to see if it is in the set: 123
'123' is NOT in the set
Enter a number to see if it is in the set: 10
'10' is in the set
Enter planet name to see if it exist in the set:venus ①
'venus' is NOT in the set
Enter planet name to see if it exist in the set:Venus ①
'Venus' is NOT in the set
Enter planet name to see if it exist in the set:mARS ②
'mARS' is in the set
```

All the output with marker ① show how environment variable names are case insensitive: the value "venus" or "Venus" do not exist in the set. On the other hand, the code at marker ②, shows that the value "mARS" exists in the set, even though it was inserted as "Mars".

Without going too much into details, implementing the functions: *set-remove*, *set-add*, and *set-destroy* should be trivial:

```
:set-remove <1=Set name> <2=Value>
       set %1.%2=
       goto :eof

:set-add <1=Set name> <2=Value>
       set %1.%2=1
       goto :eof

:set-destroy <1=Set name>
       for /f "usebackq" %%a in (`set %1.`) do (
              for /f "usebackq tokens=1 delims==" %%b in ('%%a') do (
                     set %%b=
              )
       )
```

The second method to encode values in a set looks like this:

```
       set NUMSET=5 1 10 95 17
       set PLANETSET=Mars Jupiter Pluto Earth Saturn
```

To check if a value exists in the set, we can use the following code:

```
:set-contains <1=Set name> <2=Value>
       call set __V=%%%~1%%
       for %%a in (%__V%) do (
              if %%a EQU %~2 ( ①
                     exit /b 1
              )
       )
       set __V=
       exit /b 0
       goto :eof
```

Note: that at marker ①, if we were dealing with strings then the **`IF`** *check is case sensitive. We should replace with "***`IF /I`***" to make it case insensitive check.*

I will only implement the *set-destroy* function while leaving the *set-add* and *set-remove* functions as an exercise for the reader:

```
:set-remove <1=Set name> <2=Value>
       :: Exercise for the user
       echo NOT IMPLEMENTED
       goto :eof

:set-add <1=Set name> <2=Value>
       :: Exercise for the user
       echo NOT IMPLEMENTED
       goto :eof

:set-destroy <1=Set name>
       set %~1=
```

The full source code used in this section can be found in the following two scripts: *ds-sets-1.bat* and *ds-sets-2.bat.*

Summary

This chapter contained lots of new material. I did my best to make everything I explained accessible to you. It is a good idea to spend time playing with the sample code in this chapter and modifying them until you feel comfortable.

Here is a summary of what was covered in this chapter:

- Conditional statements: the basic and the extended syntax of the **`IF`** keyword.
- Repetition control structures: all the various **`FOR`** keyword usages has been covered: counting, enumerating files and directories, tokenization, etc.
- String operations were covered: string substitution, sub-strings, string concatenation, string search and replace.
- Finding strings in files or piped output.
- Sorting files or piped output.
- Data structures were covered in details: you learned how to build single, multi-dimensional and associative arrays along with how to create stacks and sets.

The next chapter will cover programming concepts, conventions, debugging tips and testing methodologies.

Test your skills

Here are some problems for you to solve in the hope that they will cement all the newly learned concepts:

- Implement the "array-find" function.
- Implement an associative array library with the following functions:
    - map-create(name)
    - map-add(name, key, value)
    - map-get(name, key) → value
    - map-destroy(name)
- Implement the set functionality by encoding and managing the set values in a single environment variable.

CHAPTER 3

Coding Conventions, Testing And Troubleshooting Tips

There are so many tips and tricks to learn in the Batch files scripting language. The two previous chapters covered the basics along with the more advanced topics. This chapter will cover various tips and tricks that are not very obvious. For instance, I will be using various keywords together to achieve a new functionality. In addition, in this chapter, I will show you how to pick a coding convention, how to write various kind of functions, how to systematically parse command line arguments, and how to build a re-useable Batch file scripting library.

Finally, I will give you some debugging and troubleshooting tips that will help you fix programming and logic issues while dealing with large and complex Batch file scripts.

Coding conventions

Batch files scripting is not really different than programming in high-level languages. Therefore, writing complex Batch file scripts can become counterproductive and hard to maintain if you don't follow a consistent coding convention or style as you do with other programming languages.

It is well established that there is not just a single correct coding convention, therefore adopting one convention or style as opposed to another is a matter of personal choice; different programmers follow different styles. However, all conventions have a single goal behind their logic: to keep the script consistent and easy to maintain.

From my own programming background and from looking at other Batch file scripts, I decided to adopt a certain coding style which I will describe in this section. Let me give you some ideas:

1. Unless you are debugging your script, start your script by turning the command echo off → use "@echo off".
2. Define an "*end*" label where you do cleanup and de-initialization. Otherwise, just use the special "*:eof*" label to terminate your script (if no cleanup is needed).

3. After defining each label, increase the indentation. Use similar indentation principles as you would when programming in other languages (take Python for instance).
4. After creating a new code block (due to an **IF**, **FOR** or a nested label), also increment the indentation level. Decrement it when leaving the previous code block.
5. Choose which capitalization style you want to adopt with the keywords or the commands: all lower case, all UPPER CASE, CamelCase, etc.). It is best to be consistent and not mix styles.

The following is an example script showing my favorite coding style. It encompasses most of the points I covered above (*coding-style.bat*):

```
@echo off

:start
      rem Usually, parameters are parsed here

      if "%1"=="help"              goto usage
      if "%1"=="compress"          goto compress

      goto usage

:usage
      echo.
      echo Example usage:
      echo ----------------
      echo %0 help          - Shows the help screen
      echo %0 compress      - Start the compression
      goto end

:compress
      if "%PROCESSOR_ARCHITECTURE%"=="AMD64" (
            echo Sorry, this tool requires an x86 operating system
            goto end
      )

      rem Do the compression
      goto end


:end
```

Variables naming conventions

In your Batch file script, you might need to use various environment variables: some of them you want to export back to the caller's environment block and some you want to discard when your script finishes execution. Plan ahead how you want to export persistent variables and how to name/work with local variables and then discard them properly.

Additionally, if you plan to interact with other scripts and internal functions, then make sure you do not overwrite environment variables of other functions. This is especially true when working with recursive functions.

It is advisable that you use the **SETLOCAL** keyword to localize all the changes that will affect the environment block. This will ensure all changes or addition that are encapsulated between the **SETLOCAL** and **ENDLOCAL** are local to the executing script (or function) only.

In a later section in this chapter, I will show you how to persist changes beyond the call to the **ENDLOCAL** keyword.

Avoid environment variable collision

When using work/temporary environment variables inside functions, it is advisable that you prefix all the variables with the function name.

Take for example the following script (*env-group-naming.bat*):

```
@echo off

       setlocal
       call :add-two 5 10
       echo Result=%errorlevel%
       goto :end

:add-two <1=num1> <2=num2> => result => %errorlevel%
       set addtwo.n1=%1 ①
       set addtwo.n2=%2 ②
       set /A addtwo.result="%addtwo.n1% + %addtwo.n2%"

       exit /b %addtwo.result%

:end
       endlocal
```

In the example above, all the variables pertaining to the *add-two* function are prefixed with "*addtwo*" to ensure that each function have its own unique variable names.

Of course, this will not work for recursive functions though. The fool proof method is to enable environment block localization inside functions as well.

Labels naming conventions

Labels serve a dual purpose in Batch file scripts: as a jump location/bookmark (invoked with the **GOTO** syntax) to another part in your script, with no intention of resuming the execution on the subsequent lines; or as functions declarations (invoked with the "**CALL** :" syntax) with the ability to return back to the caller (with the "**GOTO :EOF**" or "**EXIT /B**" syntax).

Because label names are global in a Batch file script (there are no local labels per function), a redundant label name will cause problems. You have to make sure your label names do not repeat and occur once only in the script. If you follow a consistent naming convention, not only you will make your Batch file script readable and easy to maintain but you will also have no difficulty coming up with descriptive and unique label names.

Here are some guidelines:

- Define the "*:main*" label where you do initialization, argument parsing and dispatching to other parts of your script.
- Define the "*:usage*" label where you display a help screen in case your Batch file script requires arguments that need to be explained to the user.
- Define the "*:end*" label where you jump to for cleaning up and proper script termination.

If you use simple and non-descriptive label names such as "*L1*", "*L2*", "*L3*", or even just numbers such as "1", "55", "22", etc., then you will have a hard time maintaining your script in the future. Instead, use descriptive names such as: "*copy-files-to-temp-folders*", "*delete-old-files*", etc.

Since labels can also be called as functions with the "**CALL** :" syntax, then any label site may also be considered a function definition. Whether a label is a function or a regular label depends on how you use that label in your script.

If the label was intended to be used as a function, then it makes sense to append extra information after the label definition (on the same line) to annotate the input arguments and the return values. It is also pleasant to use the "::" style comments on the line preceding the function label to describe the function using free-style and human friendly descriptions.

Below is a function that sorts a file's contents into another file. Here's how I suggest you have its label and description defined:

```
:: Sort an input file into an output file in ascending order
:: If you pass the optional third argument then descending
:: order will take place.
:sort-file <1=input file> <2=output file> <3=optional: DESC>
```

Often times, a function may have its own nested labels that you also want to make sure they are descriptive and unique. The simple rule to achieve this, is to prefix the nested label names with the function name itself.

Here's an example to illustrate how to name local labels in a function (*func-label-conventions.bat*):

```
:: Computes the total sum of numbers between the start and end numbers
:sigma <1=start number> <2=end number> => %result%
       if "%1"=="" goto sigma-usage
       if "%2"=="" goto sigma-usage

       setlocal

       :: start of counter
       set /a i=%1
       set /a sum=0

       :sigma-repeat
              :: done with the loop
              if %i% GTR %2 goto sigma-break

              set /a sum+=i
              set /a i+=1
              goto sigma-repeat

       :sigma-break
              for %%a in (%sum%) do (
                     endlocal
                     set result=%%a
              )
       goto :eof

       :sigma-usage
              endlocal
              set result=Error!
              goto :eof
```

Note: This time, for the sake of illustration, I used the "FOR" syntax to return the result past the end of the localization.

Persisting changes beyond the ENDLOCAL call

We have already established that any changes to the environment block will not persist if those changes took place inside a localized environment block (i.e. code executing between **SETLOCAL** and **ENDLOCAL**).

So the question becomes: how would your script use temporary environment variables inside a localized environment block but finally export one or more variables to the caller?

Well, the classical and simplest way to achieve this is to join the **ENDLOCAL** and the **SET** keyword calls in a single command line, using the ampersand ("&"). This is illustrated at marker ① in the *env-export-and.bat* script:

```
@echo off

setlocal

set variable1=1
set variable2=2
set /A result=variable1 + variable2
endlocal & set result=%result% ①

echo The result is: %result%
```

While this method works in many cases, it fails when you are using the DEVE syntax to export a variable's value (*env-export-and-fail.bat*):

```
@echo off

set result=
setlocal enabledelayedexpansion ①

for /l %%a in (1, 1, 5) do (
      set result=%%a
      if "%%a"=="2" (
            endlocal & set result=!result! ②
            goto :eof
      )
)
```

In the example script above, we use the DEVE syntax (as noted in marker ①), and therefore we can no longer use "*!varName!*" syntax past the **ENDLOCAL** call (at marker ②). Therefore, when this script is executed, the exported "*result*" value is not expanded properly:

```
C:\BatchProgramming>set result
Environment variable result not defined

C:\BatchProgramming>env-export-and-fail.bat

C:\BatchProgramming>set result
result=!result!

C:\BatchProgramming>
```

In the following sub-sections, I will illustrate three additional methods that show how to solve this problem:

1. Using **ENDLOCAL** inside (or with) a compound statement to persist one or more variables.
2. Transfer the variables you want to export to the **FOR** loop's variables. The **FOR** loop's variables are not affected by the end of environment block localization.
3. If you plan to export a single numeric value, then return it as an exit code in the *ERRORLEVEL* pseudo-environment variable.
4. Use a temporary file to store the environment variables prior to the **ENDLOCAL** call, and then read that file and update the environment post the **ENDLOCAL** call.

Using compound statements

This method uses the same logic as the classical method explained above, except that instead of joining the commands with ampersand ("&"), we use the parenthesis to compound the commands.

In a nutshell, the syntax looks like this (*env-export-compound-simple.bat*):

```
@echo off

:: Clear previous values
set result1= ①
set result2= ①

:: Start localization
setlocal ②
```

```
set r1=Hello ③
set r2=World ③

:: Compound statement
( ④
      :: End localization
      endlocal ⑤
      set result1=%r1% ⑥
      set result2=%r2% ⑥
)
```

The explanation is as follows:

1. Clear previous result variables. We don't want biased results.
2. Start localization.
3. Compute the two values that we want to return. Store them in internal work/temp variables.
4. That's the most important thing: to start a compound statement.
5. End the localization. Even if we end the localization in the compound statement, the environment variables that were already created will still be available until the block ends, and will be reverted or deleted afterwards.
6. Other variables that we create or update, post the environment block localization end, will persist.

Let's test it:

```
C:\BatchProgramming>set result
Environment variable result not defined

C:\BatchProgramming>env-export-compound-simple.bat

C:\BatchProgramming>set result
result1=Hello
result2=World
```

Now, let's illustrate using a more elaborate example in which we want to export delayed variables and **FOR** loop variables (*env-export-compound.bat*) script:

```
@echo off

      setlocal
      :: Make sure no result is set previously
      set result1= ①
```

```
    set result2= ①
    set result3= ①

    :: Call the function
    call :get-results ②

    :: Check results
    set result ③

    goto :eof

:get-results
    setlocal enabledelayedexpansion ④
    set s= ⑤
    for /l %%a in (1, 1, 5) do (
        set s=!s!%%a ⑥
        if "%%a"=="4" ( ⑦
            set /a retval1=!s! ⑧
            set /a retval2=%%a * 2 ⑨
            set /a retval3=%%a * 4 ⑨
            goto get-result-return ⑩
        )
    )
    goto :eof

    :get-result-return
    (
        endlocal ⑪
        set result1=%retval1%
        set result2=%retval2%
        set result3=%retval3%
    )
```

And the explanation is as follows:

1. For the sake of demonstration, make sure no environment variables with the same name existed before.
2. Call the function that will return three environment variables back: *result1* through *result3*.
3. After the function call, verify that we receive three output variables as expected.
4. Localize the environment block and enable the DEVE syntax inside the "*get-results*" function.
5. Create a temporary variable that we will use with the DEVE syntax. This variable is just to illustrate that we can still export values while DEVE is enabled.

6. Update the variable "*s*" using the DEVE syntax.
7. In the counting **FOR** loop, use the 4th iteration as the break condition. At this stage, we prepare to return back to the caller.
8. Capture the value of "*s*" using the DEVE syntax into a temporary variable (*retval1*). It is not necessary to do this step, because "*s*" won't be changing and it makes no sense to take a copy of it. Do this step if you plan to keep using "*s*" as a work/temporary variable that you will be changing before returning to the caller.
9. For the sake of demonstration, capture two more variables to return as results. The results we capture are from the counting **FOR** loop. This scenario is pretty common in real world scripts.
10. That's the tricky part. We break out of the loop by jumping to an external label. In this case, we jump to the label containing the compound statement.
11. End localization and start exporting the variables *result1*, *result2* and *result3*.

The compound statement method is by far the most intuitive and easy method, therefore use it whenever possible.

Using the exit code

This method has already been mentioned in previous examples in this book, but I will mention it again for the sake of completing this topic of discussion.

Often times, if you just have a single numeric variable that you want to pass back to the calling environment, then you can use the following syntax:

```
EXIT /B Value
```

The caller would pick that value using the "*%ERRORLEVEL%*" pseudo-environment variable.

Let's take a look at *env-export-exitcode.bat* script:

```
@echo off

setlocal ①

set variable1=1 ②
set variable2=2

set /A result=variable1 + variable2 ③
exit /B %result% ④
```

The explanation is as follows:

1. Start the environment block localization.
2. Create some temporary variables.
3. Compute result.
4. This Batch file script will return the value of the desired variable back to the caller using "/B" switch. When the script finishes, all other variables will be discarded.

> *Note: We did not issue an* **ENDLOCAL** *call, this is because the environment block localization will end when the script ends.*

Let's test this script and see if the *ERRORLEVEL* pseudo-environment variable is reflecting the desired value and none of the work variables were exported (*"result"*, *"variable1"* or *"variable2"*) despite the fact that we did not explicitly end the environment block localization:

```
C:\BatchProgramming>set variable ①
Environment variable variable not defined

C:\BatchProgramming>set result ①
Environment variable result not defined

C:\BatchProgramming>env-export-exitcode.bat ②

C:\BatchProgramming>echo %errorlevel% ③
3

C:\BatchProgramming>set variable ④
Environment variable variable not defined

C:\BatchProgramming>set result ④
Environment variable result not defined
```

Here's the explanation of the output above:

1. Test that no previous remnants of the work variables exist.
2. Call the script.
3. Directly display the exit code variable, otherwise it will be overwritten if you call other commands that overwrite the exit code.
4. Test again for environment variables remnants after the script has executed. Good! The environment is clean as intended.

Using the FOR loop variables

In this method, we will use the "**FOR /F**" syntax to store the variable we want to export into one of the **FOR**'s tokens, then we will end the localization. Finally, while still inside the **FOR**'s body, we will create the environment variable which will then persist.

> *Note: This method makes sense to use if you already plan to return the FOR loop's variables values. It is a bit cumbersome to create a **FOR** loop just to endure the end of localization. Instead, use the compound statements technique.*

This method is illustrated inside the *env-export-for.bat* script:

```
@echo off

setlocal ①

set variable1=hello
set variable2=world

set result=%variable1% %variable2% ②

for /f "usebackq tokens=* delims=" %%a in ('%result%') do ( ③
     endlocal ④
     set result=%%a ⑤
     goto :eof ⑥
)
```

Let me explain the code markers:

1. Start the environment block localization.
2. Compute a value and store it in a variable that we want to export.
3. Use the "**FOR /F**" such as:
    a. Take the whole string as a single token with the "tokens=*" option.
    b. Use the "usebackq" syntax and enclose the "file-set" parameter of the **FOR** loop in a single quote. This means we are tokenizing a literal string.
    c. The variable "*%%a*" will contain the value of "*%result%*"
4. Terminate the environment block localization.
5. Re-create the "*result*" environment variable, post the environment block localization, which will persist this time.
6. Terminate the script and go back to caller.

Let's run the script:

```
C:\BatchProgramming>set result
Environment variable result not defined

C:\BatchProgramming>env-export-for

C:\BatchProgramming>set result
result=hello world
```

From the output above, we can see that the script executes as intended.

> *Note: To export multiple values using this method, you may resort to using nested* **FOR** *loops in order to capture each variable inside a* **FOR** *loop variable.*

Using temporary files

In this method, we will localize the environment block, do some calculations and then export a single environment variable back to the caller (thus having it survive past the localization). This method is similar to the recipe entitled "Stateful Batch files" (from Chapter 4), and it will be handy to easily export a bunch of variables at once.

The script *env-export-temp-files.bat* is as follows:

```
@echo off

setlocal ①

set variable1=1 ②
set variable2=2 ②

set /A result=variable1 + variable2 ③

echo set result=%result% >%~dpn0-state.bat ④

endlocal ⑤

call %~dpn0-state.bat ⑥
del %~dpn0-state.bat ⑦
```

Let's explain the code markers:

1. Start the environment block localization. All environment changes will be undone at marker ⑤.
2. Create some temporary variables.
3. Compute the result value that we plan to export.
4. Generate a temporary Batch file that will re-create the "*result*" environment variable when it is called.
5. Terminate the environment block localization.
6. Call the temporary Batch file to restore the environment variables that we wanted to export (re-create) to the calling environment. In our case, the variable will be available to the calling command prompt.
7. Delete the temporary Batch file.

When executed, we can see that we do have a "*result*" variable exported to the command prompt:

```
C:\BatchProgramming>set result ①
Environment variable result not defined

C:\BatchProgramming>env-export-temp-files.bat

C:\BatchProgramming>set result ②
result=3

C:\BatchProgramming>
```

Note how at marker ①, prior to the script execution, we had no environment variable "*result*". Post execution, at marker ②, we can see that the "*result*" variable did indeed persist.

Writing recursive functions

In this section, I will illustrate how to write the *Fibonacci* function recursively. It will serve as a model for writing other recursive functions.

This will illustrate three things:

1. Using nested environment block localization.
2. Issuing recursive calls (to the same function) with different arguments and how to break out of the recursion.
3. Exporting results that survive the end of the environment block localization.

In the C language, the recursive Fibonacci function is expressed like this (*fib.c*):

```
int fib(int n)
{
	if (n == 0 || n == 1)
		return n;
	else
		return fib(n-2) + fib(n-1);
}
```

The *fib.bat* script implements the recursive Fibonacci function:

```
@echo off

	setlocal enabledelayedexpansion

	for /l %%a in (1, 1, 8) do ( ①
		call :fib %%a
		echo fib^(%%a^)=!errorlevel! ②
	)

	goto :eof

:fib <1=n> => %errorlevel% ③
	:: Break recursion when n==0 or n==1
	if %1 LSS 0 ( ④
		echo Error: Cannot be called with a negative number!
		exit /b 0
	)
	if "%1"=="0" exit /b 0 ⑤
	if "%1"=="1" exit /b 1 ⑤

	setlocal ⑥

	:: r1 = fib(n-1) ⑦
	set /a arg=%1-1 ⑦
	call :fib %arg% ⑧
	set r1=%errorlevel% ⑨

	:: r2 = fib(n-2) ⑦
	set /a arg=%1-2 ⑦
	call :fib %arg% ⑧
	set r2=%errorlevel% ⑨

	:: return result
	set /a r=r1+r2 ⑩
	exit /b %r% ⑪
```

Let me explain the important aspects of the script at the following code markers:

1. That's the driver part of the script. Set up a **FOR** loop counter that counts from 1 to 8.
2. Upon each loop iteration, call the "*fib*" function. We intend to compute the *fib(1)* to *fib(8)*.
3. Define the "*fib*" function. Denote the function input arguments and return value method as part of the label's comments.
4. Sanity checks. Do not allow computations of negative numbers. Display an error message and exit.
5. The special input values 0 and 1 are the terminating cases. They are important conditions to break out of recursion.
6. Enable environment block localization in this function before attempting to change or create new environment variables.
7. Prepare to call self with argument value "*n - 1*" and "*n - 2*" respectively. Therefore, create a temporary variable called "*arg*" with "**SET /A**". Because environment variable localization is enabled, then modifying the variable "*arg*" (if it was previously defined) in the "*fib*" function will not mess it up for the caller.
8. Call self with "*n - 1*" and "*n - 2*".
9. The "*ERRORLEVEL*" is volatile, it is important to save its value immediately after the function call. Store its value into "*r1*" and "*r2*" respectively.
10. Use the "**SET /A**" to compute the summation of "*r1*" and "*r2*" variables.
11. Return to the caller the final result.

That's the script! Let's call it and observe its output:

```
C:\BatchProgramming>fib
fib(1)=1
fib(2)=1
fib(3)=2
fib(4)=3
fib(5)=5
fib(6)=8
fib(7)=13
fib(8)=21
```

Parsing command line arguments

The majority of Batch file scripts you end up writing may require user parameters so they function properly. In this section, I will show you how to design the usage screen and how to validate and parse the required command line arguments and switches.

One way to design the command line arguments/switches is to think what kind of input arguments the script requires, and what would the help or usage screen look like if the script is executed without arguments. This proves to be an effective process because it lets you first write the help screen in plain English and then worry about how to write the underlying parser later.

Having said that, let's look at this script's hypothetical usage screen:

```
Usage:
------

parse-args action [/option value] [/option]

To display help, run it as:

parse-args /? | parse-args /help


Actions:
--------

* adduser /user username /password password

Adds a user to the system with the designated password.

* removeuser /user username [/force]

Removes a user from the system. If the /force flag is set then
the current user is logged off and the account is removed.

* initscript /user username /script <script name>

Sets the user's initialization script. The script file should exist,
or the command may fail.
```

With the usage screen above, we outlined what are the mandatory arguments and what are the options that each action takes. In this case, we notice that the first argument is always an action which is followed by the different arguments that each action takes.

For example, the "*removeuser*" action takes a username and optionally the "*/force*" switch, while the "*initscript*" action also takes a username and a path to a script file name.

The usage screen is really nothing but a bunch of "**ECHO**" statements. Conventionally, your script is supposed to show the usage screen under three circumstances:

- When arguments are required in order to run the script but no arguments were passed.
- When either of the "*/?*" or "*/help*" are passed.
- When an unrecognized argument or when incomplete arguments are passed.

To display the usage screen, use code like this:

```
:Main
   setlocal enabledelayedexpansion

   if "%1"==""          goto Usage
   if "%1"=="/?"        goto Usage
   if "%1"=="/help"     goto Usage

   set ForceFlag=0 ①
   goto ParseActions
```

After checking if no arguments were passed or if the help switch is passed, we proceed to parse the actions part of the arguments (which is "*%1*"):

```
:ParseActions
   if /I "%1"=="adduser" set action=adduser ①
   if /I "%1"=="removeuser" set action=removeuser ①
   if /I "%1"=="initscript" set action=initscript ①

   if "%action%"=="" goto Usage ②

   shift ③
   goto ParseOptions ④
```

At markers ①, we check if we recognize any action value. If so, the "*action*" variable is set accordingly.

At marker ②, check if the "*action*" variable is set or not. If it was not set, then that means no recognizable action was passed and therefore we should display the usage screen.

At marker ③, we shift the arguments so that "*%1*" is positioned at the switches and ready for further parsing.

At marker ④, we proceed to parse the option switches as dictated by the usage screen:

```
:ParseOptions
    set S=
    if "%1"=="" goto Handle-%action% ①

    if "%1"=="/user" ( ②
        if "%2"=="" ( ③
        :ErrNoUserPassed
            echo No username passed!
            goto Usage
        )
        set Username=%~2 ④
        set S=2
    )

    if "%1"=="/password" (
        if "%2"=="" (
        :ErrNoPasswordPassed
            echo No password was specified
            goto Usage
        )
        set Password=%~2
        set S=2
    )

    if "%1"=="/force" (
        set S=1
        set ForceFlag=1
    )

    if "%1"=="/script" (
        if "%2"=="" (
        :ErrNoScriptPassed
            echo No script file specified
            goto Usage
        )
        if not exist "%~2" (
            echo The script file is not found!
            goto Usage
        )
        set Script=%~2
        set S=2
    )

    if not defined S (
        echo Invalid switch!
        goto Usage
    )
```

```
    FOR /L %%a in (1, 1, %S%) DO SHIFT ⑤

    goto ParseOptions
```

In the code snippet above, all the option switches are parsed (marker ②), validated (marker ③) and their values stored in appropriate variables (marker ④). When no more option switches are found, then the appropriate action handler is dispatched (marker ①).

Finally, what you do at each action handler is script specific. In the following example, we simply check (markers ①) if all the needed options are passed, and then carry on and execute the action (marker ②):

```
:Handle-adduser
    if "%Username"=="" goto ErrNoUserPassed ①
    if "%Password%"=="" goto ErrNoPasswordPassed ①

    ②
    echo Adding user '%username%' with password '%Password%'
    goto :eof
```

The complete script code can be found in the *parse-args.bat* file.

Batch files calling other Batch files

So far we have seen how to call a function inside the Batch file itself. If you plan to invoke other Batch files and continue execution, then make sure you invoke the other Batch file using the "**CALL** BatchFileName args…" syntax.

The **CALL** keyword ensures that your script won't terminate when the called script terminates.

> *Note: If you just execute the other Batch file script without using the* **CALL** *keyword, then when the called Batch file terminates, then the caller will terminate also.*

We will use two scripts (the caller and the callee) to illustrate how to call other Batch files. *call-script0.bat* is the first script:

```
@echo off

:: Call the script and invoke a soft quit
call call-script1.bat softquit ①
echo after script

:: Call the script and have it terminate at its last line
call call-script1.bat hello world ②
echo after script, default exit

:: Call the script with no arguments, we know it will fail!
call call-script1.bat ③
echo This line will not execute! ④
```

call-script1.bat is the second script:

```
@echo off

if "%1"=="" (
      echo FATAL ERROR! No arguments passed!
      :: Terminate the caller as well
      EXIT
)

echo script1 called with: %*

if "%1"=="softquit" (
      :: Terminate this script only
      exit /b
)

:: Even if no EXIT is passed, script will terminate
:: w/o terminating the caller!
```

At the first marker, we call the second script which will terminate itself using an **`EXIT /B`**. This won't terminate the executing script and therefore the line after will execute.

At marker ②, we call the second script again, however it will reach its end (no **`EXIT /B`** is used) and the execution flow returns back to the caller. We will get the same behavior as if an **`EXIT /B`** was present at the end of the script.

At marker ③, the called script (*call-script1.bat*) will use the **`EXIT`** keyword thus terminating the calling script (*call-script0.bat*) and exiting its interpreter session, therefore the command at marker ④ won't even have a chance to execute.

Let's run the *call-script0.bat* script and observe the output:

```
C:\BatchProgramming>cmd && echo after CMD!
Microsoft Windows [Version 10.0.10240]
(c) 2015 Microsoft Corporation. All rights reserved.

C:\BatchProgramming>call-script0.bat ← called without arguments
script1 called with softquit
after script
script1 called with hello world
after script, default exit
FATAL ERROR! No arguments passed!
after CMD!

C:\BatchProgramming>
```

> *Note: Because the called script will issue an "**EXIT**", it will terminate the command interpreter. This is why we invoke an additional interpreter prompt as the first command. It is really not advisable to issue an "**EXIT**" from a Batch file script because it will inconveniently terminate the user's interpreter.*

If you don't use the **CALL** keyword, then you can still invoke another Batch file by typing its name. However, this will be akin to "including" the second Batch file into the context of the executing Batch file. When the "included" Batch file terminates, then your script terminates as well.

Let's assume we have two scripts: a caller script (*use-script0.bat*) and a called script (*use-script1.bat*).

The caller script:

```
@echo off

echo line 1 from main script
echo will execute second script without a CALL

use-script1.bat

①
echo After using the second script. This line should not execute!
```

The called script:

```
@echo off

echo this is the second script!

:: exit /b will not only terminate this script, but the calling script.
exit /b ②
```

Let's execute the caller script and observe the output:

```
C:\BatchProgramming>use-script0
line 1 from main script
will execute second script without a CALL
this is the second script!

C:\BatchProgramming>
```

Did you notice how the code at marker ① in the caller script did not execute? Here's the reason why: the second script was included into the first one and therefore the **EXIT /B** will have the same effect as if it was present in the caller script.

> *Note: If the called script did not even have the "EXIT /B" keyword, when it terminates, it will also terminate the caller with it. Therefore, the code at marker ② in the called script can be removed (or commented out) and still we won't see the output of the code at marker ① in the calling script.*

Building, testing and using a utility Batch file script library

A very important facet of programming and code maintainability is the ability to re-use code. In the Batch files scripting language, you can also write Batch file scripts that act as libraries that contain functionality that can be used by other Batch file scripts. Throughout this book, we have seen scripts that are self-contained: they were using local functions residing in the same file.

In this section, I will be taking some of the useful routines (string functions, parsing functions, etc.) and put them into a re-useable Batch file script library, showing you along the way how to design a Batch file script library and how to use it.

While the Batch files scripting language does not have a mechanism to "#include" (like in the C language) or "import" (like in Python) other files, you can instead **CALL** other scripts while specifying which function in the script to call and what are arguments to pass.

There are many ways you can use to create a Batch file script library, but most importantly, it is vital that you establish a single convention with which you call external functions (residing in the library), pass the input arguments and receive output values.

With the above points in mind, let's devise the methodology for building a Batch file script library:

1. The called library guarantees that all environment changes are local to the library itself. No environment variables will be exported except for the return values. Do not use obscure internal temporary/work variable names thinking that they are unique enough to your function. This leads to errors if the function is recursive. To be on the safe side, always localize the environment block.
2. We assume that the first argument that will be passed to the library is always going to be the name of the function to be invoked. All the subsequent arguments passed thereafter are the arguments of that particular function.
3. Functions that return a single numeric value use the exit code mechanism to pass the return value. Functions that return one (non-numeric) or more values use the caller's designated output variable names to return the results.
4. No library function calls are supposed to fatally terminate the caller's script (perhaps except for the library initialization function). The caller is responsible for terminating execution if there are conditions that warrant such a case.

With those concepts in mind, let us design a Batch file script library containing the following functions:

1. Get the serial number of a logical disk
2. Check if a number is odd
3. Compute a string's length
4. Get a temporary file name

The library that we will be building resides in the *lib-batch.bat* file. The first thing to do in this script is to parse the first argument which denotes the name of the function to be called:

```
@echo off

setlocal
set function= ①

if /I "%1"=="volserial"    set function=volserial ②
if /I "%1"=="is-odd"       set function=is-odd ②
if /I "%1"=="strlen"       set function=strlen ②
if /I "%1"=="get-tempfile" set function=get-tempfile ②
```

```
if "%1"=="__test__"          set function=__test__ ③

if not defined function ( ④
       endlocal
       echo FATAL ERROR: Invalid function call '%1'
       exit /b -1
)

shift ⑤
(
       endlocal
       goto %function%-function ⑥
)
```

In the beginning of the library, we temporarily localize the environment block while we decide which function to call. We make sure we end the localization before jumping to the required library function. The variable called "*function*" is used to hold the parsed function name to be called (at marker ① and ②).

Optionally, we may add a hidden/internal function that allows us to test the library script itself (marker ③). Nonetheless, for performance reasons, it is better not to include this functionality in the script file itself and instead delegate it to a separate file (see "Testing the library" topic in this chapter).

When marker ④ is reached and no function has been recognized, then we exit back to the caller. Theoretically, this should never happen in production environment because you are supposed to test your scripts.

At marker ⑤, we discard the first argument (the function name) with the **SHIFT** syntax, thus all the remaining arguments will be starting from "*%1*". This is useful from the point of view of the called functions because they expect to receive arguments starting from "*%1*" and onwards.

Finally, at marker ⑥, we go to the function in question. We assume that all the present functions are defined by a label having the "*FunctionName*-function" format.

The easiest function to implement is the "*is-odd*" function:

```
:is-odd-function => errorlevel
       set /A RESULT="(%1 & 1)"
       exit /B %result%
```

The second easiest function to implement is the volume serial number retrieval function. We rely on the internal command that is called **VOL**:

```
C:\BatchProgramming>vol /?
Displays the disk volume label and serial number, if they exist.

VOL [drive:]

C:\BatchProgramming>
```

When we run it, it produces two output lines and the second line contains the volume serial number:

```
C:\BatchProgramming>vol C:
 Volume in drive C is store
 Volume Serial Number is 3231-1102
```

Therefore, we can easily parse the output using "**FOR /F**" like this:

```
	for /f "usebackq skip=1 tokens=5" %%a in (`vol %1:`) do (
		echo serial=%%a
	)
```

The whole function would look like this:

```
:volserial-function <1=drive letter> <2=result-variable>
	for /f "usebackq skip=1 tokens=5" %%a in (`vol %1:`) do (
		endlocal
		set %2=%%a
	)
	goto :eof
```

And finally, we implement the "*get-tempfile*" function which takes two input arguments and returns the full path of a temp file name:

```
:get-tempfile-function <1=prefix> <2=extension> <3=out-temp-filename>
	setlocal
	:get-tempfile-repeat
		set FN=%TEMP%\%~1-%RANDOM%.%~2
		if exist "%FN%" goto get-tempfile-repeat

	(
		endlocal
		set %3=%FN%
```

```
    )
    goto :eof
```

Note: If the generated file name coincides with an existing file name, then the script will keep looping until a non-existent temporary file name is generated.

Now, let me illustrate how to use this library (*use-lib.bat*):

```
@echo off
setlocal enabledelayedexpansion

set /P "S=Enter string: "
call lib-batch strlen "%S%"
echo The string "%S%" length is %errorlevel%

echo.
set /P "N=Enter number: "
call lib-batch is-odd %N%
if %errorlevel%==1 (
  echo The number %N% is Odd!
) ELSE (
   echo The number %N% is even!)

echo.
call lib-batch get-tempfile tmpfil tmp S
echo Generated temp file name at: %S%

echo.
set /P "S=Enter drive letter: "
call lib-batch volserial %S% N
echo The volume serial number of drive %S% is: %N%
endlocal
```

Which outputs the following when executed:

```
C:\BatchProgramming>use-lib.bat
Enter string: hello
The string "hello" length is 5

Enter number: 2
The number 2 is even

Generated temp file name at: C:\Temp\tmpfil-21554.tmp

Enter drive letter: c
The volume serial number of drive c is: 1324-6579
```

```
C:\BatchProgramming>
```

Testing the library

When developing and maintaining a library, Batch file script or not, it is important that you do no introduce bugs or incompatible changes. This is where the testing discipline comes into play: to ensure that the functionality/changes work as intended and that the previous code relying on the library also keeps on working as expected.

If the test fails, you have a chance to investigate the problems: either the driver code needs to be adapted to the new changes, or you introduced bugs in the library code.

Like any other programming language, testing usually consists of calling the functions to be tested, capturing the results and comparing them against a set of known and accepted results. Any mismatch in the results will cause the test to fail. Additionally, the test code is supposed to exercise/test corner cases, boundary cases and invalid inputs, etc.

In the script *test-lib.bat*, we test both the *strlen* and the *is-odd* functions.

The *strlen* function is executed in a loop and tested against a set of string/length pairs (marker ①). An inner loop will tokenize each string/length pair and extract the string itself and the expected length (marker ②). If the returned result does not match the expected result (marker ③), then the script will report an error and terminate:

```
for %%a in ("abcdefg~7" "hello world~11" "hello~5" "a~1" "ab~2") do ( ①
        for /f "tokens=1,2 delims=~" %%b in (%%a) do ( ②
                echo Checking length for "%%b"
                call lib-batch strlen "%%b"
                set R=!errorlevel!
                echo Length is: !R! , expected length: %%c
                if !R! NEQ %%c ( ③
                :ErrStrlenfailed
                        echo String length function failed.
                        EXIT /B -1
                )
        )
)
```

Additionally, the *strlen* function is tested against an empty string (a corner case):

```
echo Testing empty string length
call lib-batch strlen
if %errorlevel% neq 0 goto ErrStrlenfailed
echo Empty string length is zero
```

In facsimile, we can also test the *is-odd* function in a loop. However, instead of storing the expected oddness result, after each iteration, we use an alternating variable (called "*Odd*", at marker ①) whose value will flip (marker ③) between 0 to denote that the number is even and 1 to denote the odd case:

```
set Odd=0 ①
FOR /L %%a IN (10, 1, 20) DO (
      call lib-batch is-odd %%a
      set R=!errorlevel!
      echo Is odd '%%a'? =^> !R!
      if !R! NEQ !Odd! ( ②
            echo Odd test failed.
            EXIT /B -1
      )
      if !Odd!==0 (set Odd=1) else (set Odd=0) ③
)
```

Let's run the test script, *test-lib.bat*, and see the output:

```
C:\BatchProgramming>test-lib
Checking length for "abcdefg"
Length is: 7 , expected length: 7
Checking length for "hello world"
Length is: 11 , expected length: 11
Checking length for "hello"
Length is: 5 , expected length: 5
Checking length for "a"
Length is: 1 , expected length: 1
Checking length for "ab"
Length is: 2 , expected length: 2
Testing empty string length
Empty string length is zero
Is odd '10'? => 0
Is odd '11'? => 1
Is odd '12'? => 0
Is odd '13'? => 1
Is odd '14'? => 0
Is odd '15'? => 1
Is odd '16'? => 0
```

```
Is odd '17'? => 1
Is odd '18'? => 0
Is odd '19'? => 1
Is odd '20'? => 0
-------------------
All tests passed
-------------------
```

Note: While this test script is not comprehensive, I leave it up to you to write more code coverage for complex script functions that will be used in production environment.

Debugging and troubleshooting tips

When you are writing Batch file scripts, you are bound to encounter errors of all sorts:

1. Unexpected script behaviors.
2. Logic errors.
3. Batch file syntax errors.
4. Errors from other scripts.
5. Real obscure errors.

Therefore, it is essential to learn how to be able to debug your script and figure out what's wrong.

ECHO is your friend

The best way to debug your script is to temporarily re-enable the command echo if you had it turned off at the top of the script (with "@echo off"). I use this technique all the time.

If you turn on the command echo at the beginning of the script, you may see lots of output and therefore making it hard to sift through all the output in order to see what the issue is. For that reason, you may want to enable the command echo near the suspected problematic code sites and then turn it back off afterwards. By tweaking the command echo (from off to on) you can spot the error and eliminate it.

When the command echo is turned on, then each command in the Batch file script is displayed first (having all the environment variables values expanded if they were present) then the output of the command is displayed thereafter.

Compound statements will be echoed in their entirety (even if a conditional compound statement's condition is not met) and they won't necessarily look as nicely formatted as you had them in the original script.

Let's take the *debug-1.bat* script as an example to illustrate how the echoed commands are displayed with the absence of "**`@echo off`**":

```
setlocal

:: statement #1
if "%1"=="" ( ①
      echo ^>^>no argument
      echo ^>^>was passed
) else (
      echo ^>^>argument passed!
) ①

echo ^>^>this is 2nd statement ②

if "%2"=="" echo ^>^>no second argument passed && goto :eof ③

echo this is 3rd statement ④

rem check the third argument
if "%3"=="" ( ⑤
      echo ^>^>3rd arg not passed
) else (
      echo ^>^>1
      if "%3"=="abc" (
            echo ^>^>abc
      )
) ⑤
```

The script above contains various types of statements: single line, conditional compound and joined statements. It expects one to three arguments to be passed and it outputs a different message accordingly.

Let's run the script with no arguments first:

```
C:\BatchProgramming>debug-1.bat

C:\BatchProgramming>setlocal ①

C:\BatchProgramming>if "" == "" ( ②
echo >>no argument
 echo >>was passed
```

```
)  else (echo >>argument passed! ) ②
>>no argument ③
>>was passed ③

C:\BatchProgramming>echo >>this is 2nd statement ④
>>this is 2nd statement

C:\BatchProgramming>if "" == "" echo >>no second argument passed   &&
goto :eof ⑤
>>no second argument passed

C:\BatchProgramming>
```

The first thing to observe is that all the label-style comments and empty lines are omitted and not displayed (with the exception of the **REM** style comments). Also notice how after each command is reached in the Batch file script, the prompt is shown (in this case it is "C:\BatchProgramming>") followed by the command to be executed (marker ① for instance). This behavior is the essence of Batch file scripts: to automate/script the commands instead of having you manually type them each time.

At marker ②, the whole multi-line compound statement is echoed first before we can see the result of its execution. Notice how the first argument "*%1*" (which is absent) got expanded to an empty string and how it led the **IF** check to resolve to true, hence the **IF**'s body was executed as observed by the output at marker ③.

At marker ④, we had a single statement so we first see the prompt followed by the command, then on the subsequent line we see the output of the command.

At marker ⑤, the script was checking for the presence of a 2nd argument ("%2") and if it was not present then it terminated the script (using "**goto :eof**"). This explains why we never saw the remainder of the script.

Now let us re-run the same script with all of the three arguments:

```
C:\BatchProgramming>debug-1 abc 123 abc

C:\BatchProgramming>setlocal

C:\BatchProgramming>if "abc" == "" (
echo >>no argument
 echo >>was passed
)  else (echo >>argument passed! )
>>argument passed!
```

```
C:\BatchProgramming>echo >>this is 2nd statement
>>this is 2nd statement

C:\BatchProgramming>if "123" == "" echo >>no second argument passed   &&
goto :eof

C:\BatchProgramming>echo this is 3rd statement
this is 3rd statement

C:\BatchProgramming>rem check the third argument

C:\BatchProgramming>if "abc" == "" (echo >>3rd arg not passed )  else (
echo >>1
 if "abc" == "abc" (echo >>abc )
)
>>1
>>abc
```

Let's take another script (*debug-2.bat*) as an example to illustrate what happens with repetition keywords:

```
setlocal enabledelayedexpansion

set N=3

FOR /l %%a in (1, 1, !N!) do (
	set s=
	for /l %%b in (1,1, %%a) do (
		set s=!s!*
	)
	echo !s!
)

echo The script is terminating now!
endlocal
```

This script has two nested loops. The output will differ based on how the variables expand in each statement before it gets executed:

```
C:\BatchProgramming>debug-2

C:\BatchProgramming>setlocal enabledelayedexpansion

C:\BatchProgramming>set N=3

C:\BatchProgramming>for /L %a in (1 1 !N!) do ( ①
set s=
```

```
 for /L %b in (1 1 %a) do (set s=!s!* ) ②
 echo !s!
)

C:\BatchProgramming>(
set s=
 for /L %b in (1 1 1) do (set s=!s!* )
 echo !s!
)

C:\BatchProgramming>(set s=!s!* ) ③
*

C:\BatchProgramming>(
set s=
 for /L %b in (1 1 2) do (set s=!s!* )
 echo !s!
)

C:\BatchProgramming>(set s=!s!* ) ④

C:\BatchProgramming>(set s=!s!* )
**

C:\BatchProgramming>(
set s=
 for /L %b in (1 1 3) do (set s=!s!* )
 echo !s!
)

C:\BatchProgramming>(set s=!s!* ) ⑤

C:\BatchProgramming>(set s=!s!* )

C:\BatchProgramming>(set s=!s!* )
***
⑥
C:\BatchProgramming>echo The script is terminating now!
The script is terminating now

C:\BatchProgramming>endlocal
```

A few things to observe at each numbered output marker:

1. The DEVE variable *"!N!"* (or any other DEVE variable in general) is not expanded and displayed when the echo is on. Instead you have to explicitly echo the variable if you want to see its value when debugging the script.

2. Notice how the commas disappeared from the outputted **FOR** loop syntax. This is just a small example of how the input script syntax differs when it is being echoed before it is being interpreted.
3. This marker denotes the first outer loop iteration and the inner loop's body is executed once.
4. This marker denotes the second outer loop iteration and the inner loop's body is executed twice. You only observe the body of the inner loop being echoed. At the end of the inner loop, the last statement in the inner loop gets executed and that's why we can see "**".
5. The same logic applies here, etc.
6. The outer loop has finished and we are back to the main script's execution scope.

Takeaways:

1. Loops make it hard to debug because there will be so much output generated. This is especially true in case long compound statements were present in the body of the **FOR** loop.
2. DEVE style variables won't expand to their real values. That's not so helpful for debugging: use explicit echoes.

Making your script debug-ready

We learned from the previous section that relying on a simple "**ECHO ON**" or "**ECHO OFF**" is not as powerful when debugging a long script that generates lots of output.

What if I told you we can conditionally and quickly enable our script to turn debugging features on or off by tweaking some environment variables before executing the script? I will be illustrating a couple of tricks showing you how to do that!

The first trick relies on globally enabling the command echo for the whole script by starting the script with the following line (*debug-3.bat*):

```
→ @if NOT DEFINED _ECHOON (echo off) ①

echo Hello from this script
for /l %%a in (1, 1, 3) do (
      echo i=%%a
)
```

At the beginning of the script, instead of using the usual "`@echo off`", we check if the caller's environment block had a special variable called *_ECHOON* already defined. If it was defined, then we don't issue the "`@echo off`" and therefore the echo will be on by default:

Let's test the script without that special variable being defined:

```
C:\BatchProgramming>set _ECHOON
Environment variable _ECHOON not defined

C:\BatchProgramming>debug-3
Hello from this script
i=1
i=2
i=3

C:\BatchProgramming>
```

The output of the script shows the expected results: no command echo. Now let us set that special variable and try again:

```
C:\BatchProgramming>set _ECHOON=1

C:\BatchProgramming>debug-3

C:\BatchProgramming>echo Hello from this script
Hello from this script

C:\BatchProgramming>for /L %a in (1 1 3) do (echo i=%a )

C:\BatchProgramming>(echo i=1 )
i=1

C:\BatchProgramming>(echo i=2 )
i=2

C:\BatchProgramming>(echo i=3 )
i=3

C:\BatchProgramming>
```

The echo was not turned off and we could see what's being executed inside the script.

The second trick is to conditionally redirect the debug output to one of the following:

1. The **NUL** device when you want to turn off debug messages.
2. To the **CON** device when you want to redirect all the debug output to the screen (the console/standard output).
3. To a file (usually referred to as "a log file") for later examination. This case is useful when you are troubleshooting a script that is deployed on a remote machine. Later, when a problem is detected in the script, you can ask your client to send you the debug log file.

In order to conditionally redirect the debug output/messages, we will rely on a special environment variable that we opt to call "*_CNDECHO*", which means conditional **ECHO**. To achieve any of the three desired output redirection options mentioned above, we can use one of the following syntaxes:

1. set _CNDECHO=^>*NUL*
2. set _CNDECHO=^>*CON*
3. set _CNDECHO=^>^>*A_file_name.log* ← any file or device name of your choosing.

> *Note: For the 3rd case, where we redirect the output to a file, it makes no sense to use a single redirection character (">") because it will overwrite the log file each time we output something. Instead, we use the ">>" to create a new log file and append to an existing one if it was found.*

For the sake of simplicity, in our debug-ready scripts, we will define a default *_CNDECHO* value at the top of the script and leave it up to the caller to specify another value from the calling environment (*debug-4.bat*):

```
@echo off

setlocal

if NOT DEFINED _CNDECHO (set _CNDECHO=^>NUL) ①
echo Hello world
for /l %%a in (1,1,3) do (
      echo this is a debug line #%%a %_CNDECHO% ②
      echo i=%%a
)
echo Script terminating
```

Note: You want to keep using the regular environment variable expansion syntax and not the DEVE one because we defined the _CNDECHO *at the top of the script and we are not going to change it (that's why the DEVE syntax becomes futile in this case).*

At marker ①, we set the default echo condition value to display nothing (by redirecting the output to the *NUL* device).

```
C:\BatchProgramming>debug-4
Hello world
i=1
i=2
i=3
Script terminating
C:\BatchProgramming>
```

As we observe from the output above, all the commands (in our case, just at marker ②) that were terminated by a trailing *%_CNDECHO%* had their output redirected appropriately. In this case all the output went to the **NUL** device.

Now let us tweak the *_CNDECHO* variable and see what happens:

```
C:\BatchProgramming>set _CNDECHO=^>CON ①
C:\BatchProgramming>debug-4
Hello world
this is a debug line #1
i=1
this is a debug line #2
i=2
this is a debug line #3
i=3
Script terminating
C:\BatchProgramming>
```

At marker ①, before running the script again, we changed the conditional echo value so it writes to the standard output. Afterwards, when the script was executed, we could see all the debug lines!

Finally, let's use the same script but this time redirect the output to a log file:

```
C:\BatchProgramming>del test.log ①
Could Not Find test.log

C:\BatchProgramming>set _CNDECHO=^>^>test.log ②
```

```
C:\BatchProgramming>debug-4
Hello world
i=1
i=2
i=3
Script terminating

C:\BatchProgramming>type test.log ③
this is a debug line #1
this is a debug line #2
this is a debug line #3

C:\BatchProgramming>
```

We optionally delete the previous log file (at marker ①), then we change the conditional echo value so it emits to the *test.log* file (at marker ②). We tested this behavior by running the script and checking its log file (at marker ③).

> *Note: you can always edit your script and change the value of the* _CNDECHO *variable so it always redirects the output to the standard output (the* CON *device) by default.*

Dumping the values of the work and state variables

It is very useful to be able to dump the values of the state variables, loop variables or other variables (DEVE style variables) when debugging and troubleshooting a faulty or complicated script that you want to understand how it works.

For the sake of demonstration, I want to take the *str-len-fast.bat* script, rename it to *debug-5.bat* and inject various conditional echo statements inside of it. We are doing this to illustrate how handy it is to output/dump internal state variables so we understand the inner workings of a script or to spot a bug:

```
@echo off

setlocal enabledelayedexpansion

@if NOT DEFINED _CNDECHO (set _CNDECHO=^>NUL)

:main
    setlocal
    set /P str=Enter string:
    echo DBG: the string value is %str% %_CNDECHO%
```

```
    call :strlen "%str%"
    echo length=%errorlevel%

    goto :eof

:strlen <1=string> => errorlevel
    set "s=%~1."
    echo DBG: inside str-len, initial value is ^<%s%^> %_CNDECHO%
    set len=0
    for %%P in (4096 2048 1024 512 256 128 64 32 16 8 4 2 1) do (
       echo DBG: P=%%P str part is ^<!s:~%%P,1!^> %_CNDECHO%

        if "!s:~%%P,1!" NEQ "" (
            set /a "len+=%%P"
            echo DBG: string length so far: !len! %_CNDECHO%
            set "s=!s:~%%P!"
            echo DBG: truncated string so far is: !s! %_CNDECHO%
        )
    )

    (
        endlocal
        exit /b %len%
    )
```

Notice how we inserted lots of debugging output at strategic locations to help us understand how the state variables of the script are changing.

Let's adjust the *_CNDECHO* variable value so it outputs messages to the console and then run the script and observe its output:

```
C:\BatchProgramming>set _CNDECHO=^>CON
C:\BatchProgramming>debug-5.bat
Enter string: 1234567
DBG: the string value is 1234567
DBG: inside str-len, initial value is <1234567.>
DBG: P=4096 str part is <>
DBG: P=2048 str part is <>
DBG: P=1024 str part is <>
DBG: P=512 str part is <>
DBG: P=256 str part is <>
DBG: P=128 str part is <>
DBG: P=64 str part is <>
DBG: P=32 str part is <>
DBG: P=16 str part is <>
DBG: P=8 str part is <>
DBG: P=4 str part is <5>
DBG: string length so far: 4
```

```
DBG: truncated string so far is: 567.
DBG: P=2 str part is <7>
DBG: string length so far: 6
DBG: truncated string so far is: 7.
DBG: P=1 str part is <.>
DBG: string length so far: 7
DBG: truncated string so far is: .
length=7
```

See how useful it is to dump the internal state variables? It lets you see how the *str-len* function works by showing you its internal state variables during each iteration.

When you are done debugging or troubleshooting a script, you have three choices:

1. Clean out all the conditional debug outputs completely. Even if they are conditional statements, they take space in the script and look unprofessional especially if you want to ship your script to your customers (more especially if you have no intentions to troubleshoot the scripts remotely).
2. Prepend to the conditional commands a "REM" or "::" to transform those commands (that had their output redirected) to simple comment statements.
3. Or just keep all the conditional output statements but make sure they redirect to the *NUL* device by default.

Note: My advice is to clean out all the conditional debug output when you are done writing the script and then make sure you have test scripts that ensure that the script keeps working as intended during its development cycle.

If you feel adventurous, you may also write a Batch file script that strips all the lines that have the conditional echo syntax automatically!

Other tips

When the script generates lots of output, you may want to insert the **PAUSE** command strategically into your script file to pause the display (until you hit ENTER) and have a chance to read the output.

Additionally, you can run your script and pipe the output to the **MORE** command:

```
C:>MyScript.bat | MORE
```

If you have a full keyboard, instead of using the **PAUSE** command, you can hit the **PauseBreak** key on your keyboard.

If for any reason you want to stop your script at any point, you can interrupt it by pressing the **Ctrl+PauseBreak** or the **CTRL+C** keys on your keyboard.

Summary

This chapter focused more on high-level and design concepts as opposed to the two other chapters before it. It covered the following topics:

- Coding conventions: general program layout and variable/label naming conventions.
- How to avoid pollution the environment block and how to have variables survive after the end of the environment block localization.
- How to write more advanced functions such as recursive functions and how to properly return values to the caller.
- Building a Batch file scripting library for use with other scripts in the future.
- Various testing and debugging tips.

We are approaching the end of this book. The last chapter contains a bunch of recipes aiming at solving real life problems with the Batch files scripting language and further demonstrating the power and versatility of what is seemingly a very basic and simple scripting language.

CHAPTER 4

Batch Files Recipes

In this last chapter of this book, I present you with a bunch of useful scripts which will exercise various Batch files scripting language features. I call those scripts "recipes", some of them are hypothetical and others solve real world problems faced by developers or system administrators alike. In the same fashion as all the previous code samples from the other chapters, all the recipes therein will also be annotated and explained in details.

Simple console text editor

This is a simple example (*console-editor.bat*) showing how to redirect the **CON** (console input) to a file using the file **COPY** command. This will let us create a very simple console based text editor:

```
@echo off

if "%1"=="" (
	echo Please specify the file name to create.
	goto :eof
)

echo Please start typing. Press Ctrl+Z to finish.

copy CON %1 >nul

echo.
echo Excellent. You typed the following:
if exist %1 type %1
```

In this example, we used the **COPY** command by specifying that the console device (*CON*) is the input and the file passed in the arguments is the output. Finally, we use the **TYPE** command to display the newly created file.

Check if the script has administrative privilege

Often times, you may need to write a Batch file script that requires elevated or administrative privileges. Instead of having your script fail some time later because of the lack of privileges, you can check if it has enough privilege in the script's beginning before doing any actual work.

In the subsequent examples below, I will illustrate various ways you can use to check if the script is running with elevated privileges or not.

Looking for a specific privilege

To check if the current user has a specific privilege, we can use the external command **WHOAMI** with the "/PRIV" switch.

Here is the output of this command from a non-privileged user command prompt:

```
C:\BatchProgramming>whoami /priv

PRIVILEGES INFORMATION
----------------------

Privilege Name                Description
============================= ====================================
SeShutdownPrivilege           Shut down the system
SeChangeNotifyPrivilege       Bypass traverse checking
SeUndockPrivilege             Remove computer from docking station
SeIncreaseWorkingSetPrivilege Increase a process working set
SeTimeZonePrivilege           Change the time zone
```

Notice how that a regular user has few privileges, whereas the same command when executed by a privileged user, we get more privileges:

```
C:\BatchProgramming>whoami /priv

PRIVILEGES INFORMATION
----------------------

Privilege Name                  Description
=============================== =========================================
SeIncreaseQuotaPrivilege        Adjust memory quotas for a process
SeSecurityPrivilege             Manage auditing and security log
SeTakeOwnershipPrivilege        Take ownership of files or other objects
SeLoadDriverPrivilege           Load and unload device drivers
SeSystemProfilePrivilege        Profile system performance
SeSystemtimePrivilege           Change the system time
```

```
SeProfileSingleProcessPrivilege Profile single process
SeIncreaseBasePriorityPrivilege Increase scheduling priority
SeCreatePagefilePrivilege       Create a pagefile
SeBackupPrivilege               Back up files and directories
SeRestorePrivilege              Restore files and directories
SeShutdownPrivilege             Shut down the system
SeDebugPrivilege                Debug programs
SeSystemEnvironmentPrivilege    Modify firmware environment values
SeChangeNotifyPrivilege         Bypass traverse checking
SeRemoteShutdownPrivilege       Force shutdown from a remote system
SeUndockPrivilege               Remove computer from docking station
SeManageVolumePrivilege         Perform volume maintenance tasks
SeImpersonatePrivilege          Impersonate a client after authentication
SeCreateGlobalPrivilege         Create global objects
SeIncreaseWorkingSetPrivilege   Increase a process working set
SeTimeZonePrivilege             Change the time zone
SeCreateSymbolicLinkPrivilege   Create symbolic links
```

There are some privileges that can help the script decide if the user has enough administrative privileges. In particular, we can rely on the presence of the *SeLoadDriverPrivilege* or the *SeTakeOwnershipPrivileg* privileges.

We can write a script like the following to check if any of the aforementioned privileges are present (*is-admin-1.bat*):

```
Whoami.exe /priv ① | find "SeTakeOwnershipPrivilege" > nul ②

if errorlevel 1 ( ③
      echo Requires admin!
      goto :eof
)

echo Script running as admin...
```

At marker ①, we invoke the "**whoami**" command and then pipe its output to the "**find**" utility at marker ②. The find command returns 0 if there's a match and 1 if there is no match.

If you remember from the previous section entitled "Conditionally executing multiple commands on the same line", the error code 0 is considered success, therefore at marker ③, we check if the *ERRORLEVEL* is 1 (not success) and then bail out and print a message saying that this script requires administrative privileges. With this in mind, let's simplify this script so it uses a long statement combining conditional commands and output piping like this:

```
whoami.exe /priv | find "SeTakeOwnershipPrivilege" >nul && goto start
echo Require admin privileges!
goto :eof
:start
echo The script has administrative privileges.
```

The trick here is that we jump to the *start* label using the conditional statement if the "**FIND**" succeeded (returned 0).

Checking if system directories are writable

I have observed this method being used quite often by other scripts. A script would attempt to create a file in the system folders (say in "%windir%\system32"), and then check if the file is created successfully. If the file was created, then the script assumes that it has enough privileges (*is-admin-2.bat*):

```
@echo off
setlocal

set TEMPFN=%WINDIR%\test-admin-%~nx0-%RANDOM%.tmp ①
copy "%~f0" "%TEMPFN%" /y >nul 2>&1 ②
if %ERRORLEVEL% equ 0 ( ③
       del "%TEMPFN%" ④
) else (
       echo Requires admin privilege! ⑤
       goto :eof
)
echo The rest of the script goes here...
```

Explanation:

1. Generate a unique temporary file name in the Windows folder. Normally that folder is protected against writes.
2. Copy the current script's contents to the temp file path. Redirect both the standard output and the standard error to the *NUL* device. We don't want to display any output at all on failure (when not enough privileges are present).
3. Check the *ERRORLEVEL* variable (the error code returned from the **COPY** operation). An error code of 0 means success and therefore the script is running with administrative privileges.
4. Delete the temporary file. We don't want to pollute the system.
5. Not enough privilege (*ERRORLEVEL* not equal to 0). Bail out.

Using known commands that fail to run without elevated privileges

One last trick to see if administrative privileges are available, is to invoke commands that directly fail if the privileges are not present. One such command is the "**NET SESSION**" command.

Let's run it from a non-admin user command prompt and observe its output:

```
C:\BatchProgramming>net session
System error 5 has occurred.

Access is denied.


C:\BatchProgramming>echo %errorlevel%
2

C:\BatchProgramming>
```

And now let us run it from an elevated command prompt:

```
C:\BatchProgramming>net session
There are no entries in the list.

C:\BatchProgramming>echo %errorlevel%
0
```

Do you see the difference? The exit code is 0 when administrative privileges are present. Let us write another script and test this approach (*is-admin-3.bat*):

```
@echo off

net session >nul 2>&1 ①

if %errorlevel% neq 0 ( ②
      echo Requires administrative privilege.
      goto :eof
)

echo Script starts here...
```

At marker ①, we run the "**NET SESSION**" command and redirect both the standard output and standard error streams to the *NUL* device. At marker ②, we check for the success exit code and bail out otherwise.

Stateful Batch file scripts

Imagine you have a Batch file script that runs the whole day in a loop while backing up files and tracking jobs on the system. If the system crashes, it takes down the Batch file script with it. Now the next time you need to run the Batch file script, its internal state variables are lost and the script would start the beginning all over again.

In this recipe, I will show you how to save the environment variables that were computed and used during the life-time of the Batch file script and then how to load them again when the script is executed again.

If you follow a consistent variables naming convention (as advised in Chapter 3, in the section entitled "Coding and variable naming conventions") then it will be really easy for your script to enumerate all the environment variables with a single command.

Let us assume that we group all the environment variables that are used to store internal states under the "*script*" prefix like this:

```
set script.v1=1
set script.v2=2
set script.v3=3
set script.v4=4
set script.inited=1
```

We can list all the variables like this:

```
C:\BatchProgramming>set script.
script.inited=1
script.v1=1
script.v2=2
script.v3=3
script.v4=4
```

This kind of variables grouping is all we need to build a stateful script: the save variables operation will run the "**`SET script.`**" command and redirect the output to the state text file, and the load variables operation will enumerate each line, prefix it with the "**`SET`**" keyword and execute that line.

Here's the annotated script (*load-save-states.bat*):

```
@echo off

setlocal

set statefile=%~dpn0-state.txt ①

:main
      call :loadvariables "%statefile%" ②

      :: Initialize variables
      if "%script.inited%" NEQ "1" (
            set script.inited=1 ③
            set script.v2=2
            set script.v3=3
            set script.v4=4
            set script.v1=1
      )

      :: Dump variables after load
      call :dumpvars The loaded script state variables are: ④

      ::decrement and flip
      set /a script.v2=-script.v2 ⑤
      set /a script.v4-=1 ⑥

      :: Dump variables after load
      echo.
      call :dumpvars The script state variables at script end: ⑦

      :: Save the variables
      call :savevariables "%statefile%" script ⑧

      goto :eof


:dumpvars <message*>
      echo.
      echo ---------------------------------------------------
      echo %*
      echo ---------------------------------------------------
      set script.
      goto :eof


:loadvariables <1=statefile>

      if not exist "%~1" goto :eof
```

```
        for /f "usebackq" %%a in ("%~1") do (
                set %%a ⑨
        )

        goto :eof

:savevariables <1=statefile> <2=state-prefix>
        :: Dump all the state environment variables
        set %2.>"%~1" 2>nul ⑩
        goto :eof
```

Let me explain all the numbered markers in the script before running and testing it:

1. Compute the state file name. It is the script's file path and name without the extension but instead having the string "*-state.txt*" appended to it.
2. Attempt to load the state variables by calling the load function with one argument: the state file name. If the state file does not exist, then nothing will be loaded.
3. Check if the initialization variable "*inited*" is properly set. If not, we use the "*script.*" variables prefix to initialize and group all the hypothetical state variables.
4. For demonstration purposes, let us dump all the state variables directly after we loading them.
5. Negate the variable "*v2*". This is just to demonstrate how the state persist on each run. On each run, the variable "*v2*"'s sign will alternate from positive to negative, then negative to positive.
6. The variable "*v4*" will be decremented on each run. After 4 runs, it will become negative.
7. Dump the state variables again to show the modifications.
8. Save the state variables after the modifications are made. We call the save function and pass two arguments: the state file name and the state variables prefix.
9. Loading the state variables is as simple as reading each line in the state file (with a "**`FOR /F`**") and recreating the variables with the "**`set`**" command.
10. Conversely, saving the environment variables is a simple call to the "**`set`**" command while passing the variable prefix value. Make sure you redirect the output to the state file and the *stderr* to the *NUL* device to mask out error messages.

Let's assume that this is the first run of the script and no state file existed before. The output will be like the following (take note of markers ① to ④):

```
-------------------------------------------------
The loaded script state variables are:
-------------------------------------------------
script.inited=1
script.v1=1
script.v2=2 ①
script.v3=3
script.v4=4 ②


-------------------------------------------------
The script state variables at script end:
-------------------------------------------------
script.inited=1
script.v1=1
script.v2=-2 ③
script.v3=3
script.v4=3 ④
```

Notice how the variable "*v2*" got negated between marker ① and marker ③. Similarly, the variable "*v4*" got decremented.

The second run of the same script yields different results (also take note of markers ① to ④):

```
-------------------------------------------------
The loaded script state variables are:
-------------------------------------------------
script.inited=1
script.v1=1
script.v2=-2 ①
script.v3=3
script.v4=3 ②


-------------------------------------------------
The script state variables at script end:
-------------------------------------------------
script.inited=1
script.v1=1
script.v2=2 ③
script.v3=3
script.v4=2 ④
```

Note how the variable "*v2*" at marker ① was loaded exactly like it was stored in the previous run (with value -2), and how the variable "*v4*" got decremented once more (it has the value 2 now).

These were the basics of writing a stateful Batch file scripts. In the next recipe, I will show you how to write a resumable Batch file script that, not only it will be able to save its state variables, but it will also be able to continue execution from where it was interrupted or left off.

Resumable Batch files

Imagine you want to do a long and time consuming operation, however if the Batch file script is interrupted, you want the operation to resume from where it was last interrupted.

To achieve this, the Batch file script has to be designed in such a way that it has a well-defined set of tasks or execution stages. Each stage, when it finishes execution, saves the state variables and the execution stage name in a file. If and when the script gets interrupted, then the script picks up where it left off by re-loading the state variables (using similar concepts as the ones used in the previous recipe), reading the current execution stage from a file and finally jumping to the appropriate execution stage and resuming execution thereon.

Let's assume that a hypothetical Batch file script called *resumable-script.bat* has the following five stages of execution:

1. *step-create-files* → Creates files and prepares them for the next step.
2. *step-process-files* → Processes the files created in the previous step.
3. *step-create-report* → Creates reports from all the files that were processed.
4. *step-compress* → Compresses the previously generated reports.
5. *step-email* → Emails the reports.

Now that we have all the steps properly defined, we need to write a small prologue in our script that has the following duty:

1. Find all the steps in the Batch file script and generate a "stages" file (if it was not already present on the disk). In order for the script to figure out what are the available stages, it has to define execution stages using label names with a known prefix. We use the "*step-*" prefix. We also use one special label called "*step-done*" to denote the end of the steps.
2. Load the state variables once.
3. Load the stages file and look for the step that last executed. Skip the steps that previously executed and continue executing the remainder of the steps.

4. After each execution stage finishes, store the stage's name in a file that denotes the current progress/stage name and also save the state variables in a different file.

That's the source code of the *resumable-script.bat* script:

```
@echo off

:prologue
      setlocal enabledelayedexpansion

      ::
      :: Initialize global variables here
      ::
      set stagesfile=%~dpn0-stages.txt ①
      set progressfile=%~dpn0-progress.txt ②
      set exec= ③

      ::
      :: The stages file does not exist, create it!
      ::
      if not exist "%stagesfile%" ( ④
            findstr /b ":step-" "%~f0">%stagesfile% ⑤

            rem Reset progress
            if exist "%progressfile%" del "%progressfile%"
      )

      ::
      :: Execute each step in progression
      ::

      :: Read the current stagesfile
      if exist "%progressfile%" (
      for /f "usebackq" %%a in ("%progressfile%") do set curstep=%%a ⑥
      ) else (
            set exec=1 ⑦
      )

      ::
      :: Dispatcher loop
      ::
      :: Go over all the stages
      for /f "usebackq" %%a in ("%stagesfile%") do ( ⑧
            :: Should we execute from here and on?
            if "!exec!"=="1" ( ⑨
                  :: Execute the step
```

```
                call %%a ⑩

                :: Remember the step as executed
                echo %%a>%progressfile% ⑪

                :: Last step? Delete the progress file
                if "%%a"==":step-done" del "%progressfile%" ⑫
            ) else (
                :: Now that we did not execute this step,
                :: signal execution for next step
                if "%%a"=="%curstep%" set exec=1 ⑬
            )
        )
        :: All done!
        goto :eof ⑭

:step-create-files ⑮
        echo (1) creating files
        timeout /t 2 >nul
        goto :eof ⑯

:step-process-files
        echo (2) processing files
        timeout /t 2 >nul
        goto :eof


:step-create-report
        echo (3) creating report
        timeout /t 2 >nul
        goto :eof

:step-compress
        echo (4) compressing report
        timeout /t 2 >nul
        goto :eof

:step-email
        echo (5) emailing the report
        timeout /t 2 >nul
        goto :eof


:step-done
        echo (6) All steps done! Script terminated!
        goto :eof
```

Note: For brevity, I have omitted the code that saves/load the script's state variables.

While this script seems long, the gist of it is in its prologue. Let me explain all the worthwhile code markers:

1. Compute the file that will hold all the stages (or steps) of execution. This file's name is the scripts file name but with "*-stages.txt*" termination instead.
2. Compute the file that will hold the last executed step name.
3. The *exec* variable is a control variable. If it is set, then steps execution will take place. As long as it is not set, then each step read from the steps file will be simply skipped.
4. If the stages file does not exist, then it will be created.
5. Use the "**`FINDSTR /B`**" command to match the "*:step-*" string at the beginning of the line in the script itself. All the matches that are returned are redirected to the stages file. This is how we figure out all the stage names.
6. Read the single line containing the last executed step and store into the "*curstep*" variable.
7. If no progress file was found, then let us set the *exec* flag early on. This will let the script start executing the first stage and onwards.
8. Open the steps file and start reading it line by line.
9. Is the execution flag set? If so, execute each step.
10. **`CALL`** each step found in the stages file. Each step is defined by its own label. Steps act like functions and they are supposed to return to the caller accordingly. Note that the "*%%a*" token variable already contains the ":" symbol (as read from the stages file).
11. Remember the step name that was executed. When the script is re-run, then this step and all the steps preceding it will be skipped.
12. Is this the last step? If so, delete the progress file. This will cause the script to start from the beginning again when it is executed.
13. As each step name is read, compare its name against the last step that is stored in the progress file. Once found, set the execution flag (*exec*) so that the subsequent steps start executing instead of being skipped.
14. This marks the end of the dispatcher loop. You can do generic de-initialization in here (perhaps deleting the stages file). The "*step-done*" step is meant to clean-up/de-initialize after all the steps have executed. The script does not have to end when this label is reached, instead the script can continue its non-resumable logic from here on.
15. This is the first step because it is the first label in the Batch file script with the "*:step-*" prefix. In fact, that's how steps execution order is defined.

16. End of the step. Each step, upon completion, is expected to issue a "**GOTO :EOF**" or an "**EXIT /B**" to return back to the dispatcher (at marker ⑧).

Now that we are done with the explanation, let us run the script then interrupt it with *Ctrl+C* and see how it behaves:

```
C:\BatchProgramming>resumable-script.bat
(1) creating files
(2) processing files
^CTerminate batch job (Y/N)? y
```

Note that we interrupted it before it completed step #2, therefore, when we run it again, we expect it to resume at step #2 until its completion:

```
C:\BatchProgramming>resumable-script.bat
(2) processing files
(3) creating report
(4) compressing report
^CTerminate batch job (Y/N)? y
```

Note how when the script is executed again, it automatically picked up at execution at step #2. This time, we interrupted it a step #4.

Let us list both the stages file and the progress file:

```
C:\BatchProgramming>dir resuma*.txt /b
resumable-script-progress.txt
resumable-script-stages.txt
```

Now let us then see their contents:

```
C:\BatchProgramming>type resumable-script-stages.txt
:step-create-files
:step-process-files
:step-create-report
:step-compress
:step-email
:step-done
```

And:

```
C:\BatchProgramming>type resumable-script-progress.txt
:step-create-report
```

We can see how the progress file contains the name of the 3rd step, which means if we resume the script, it should continue from the 4th step (*step-compress*):

```
C:\BatchProgramming>resumable-script.bat
(4) compressing report
(5) emailing the report
(6) All steps done
```

The script completed execution all the way to the end. If we run it again, it will start all over from the beginning.

Converting ordinals to characters

Often times, it is useful to convert ordinals to their corresponding character values. If you have used Python before, we are talking about the **ORD()** function. For example, the ordinal 65 is the character "A", and the ordinal 48 is the character "0".

To convert ordinals to characters in a Batch file script, we will need a mechanism that allows us to map a number to a character. Fortunately, such mechanism exists and is called a dictionary (a map, or an associative array) and has been explained in the "Basic data structures" section in Chapter 2.

The script *ord2chr.bat* illustrates how to get the character given its ordinal:

```
:ord2chr <1=ordinal value> => %result%
       for %%a in ("65=A" "66=B" "67=C" "68=D" ①
                     "69=E" "70=F" "71=G" "72=H"
                     "73=I" "74=J" "75=K" "76=L"
                     "77=M" "78=N" "79=O" "80=P"
                     "81=Q" "82=R" "83=S" "84=T"
                     "85=U" "86=V" "87=W" "88=X"
                     "89=Y" "90=Z" "97=a" "98=b"
                     "99=c" "100=d" "101=e" "102=f"
                     "103=g" "104=h" "105=i" "106=j"
                     "107=k" "108=l" "109=m" "110=n"
                     "111=o" "112=p" "113=q" "114=r"
                     "115=s" "116=t" "117=u" "118=v"
                     "119=w" "120=x" "121=y" "122=z"
                     "48=0" "49=1" "50=2" "51=3"
                     "52=4" "53=5" "54=6" "55=7"
                     "56=8" "57=9") do (
       for /f "usebackq tokens=1-2 delims==" %%b in ('%%~a') do ( ②
                     if "%1"=="%%b" ( ③
                            set result=%%c ④
                            goto :eof
```

```
                )
            )
    )
```

In the first marker, we use the regular **FOR** loop syntax, with a set of key/value pairs. The key is the ordinal number and the value is the character value.

At the second marker, we further tokenize each key/value pair using the equal sign ("=") as the delimiter.

At marker ③, we check if the current key (the ordinal) matches the parameter's ("%1") value that was passed. If so, then at marker ④, we return the value of the character (which is the second token) to the caller.

Let's now use the "*ord2chr*" function in a useful manner, for instance to generate a random string:

```
:gen-rand-str <1=length> <2=mod> <3=base> => %result%
        set str=
        for /l %%a in (1, 1, %1) do (
                set /A N="(!RANDOM! %% %2) + %3"
                call :ord2chr !N!
                set str=!str!!result!
        )
        set result=%str%

        goto :eof
```

The first argument is the length of the string we want to generate. The second argument ("*mod*") denotes the exclusive upper boundaries of the random number. The third parameter ("*base*") is added to the generated random number and therefore letting us chose what is the lowest random number value generated.

Using mathematical terminology, the random number that will be generated, given "*mod*" and "*base*", will be within the following range: *[base → base+mod[*.

Finally, the random string is returned into the "*result*" environment variable. Let's now use the "*gen-rand-str*" function to generate a bunch of Washington State car plate numbers:

```
:get-plate-number
        call :gen-rand-str 3 26 65
        set P=%result%

        call :gen-rand-str 4 10 48
        set N=%result%
```

```
    set result=%P%-%N%

    goto :eof
```

Let's run the full script, *ord2chr.bat*, and observe the output:

```
C:\BatchProgramming>ord2chr.bat
QDR-8857
NZX-0249
WKQ-2986
QQS-8448
OVW-3967
KWT-7558
FVJ-4775
MBR-4128
KBW-9071
```

Convert a string from upper case to lower case and vice versa

This recipe is really simple because it relies on the same logic used in the previous recipe. We encode the case mappings in a **FOR** loop and do string substitution. We need two mappings: one for upper case to lower case conversion and another from lower case to upper case.

To assist us in building the mapping, I created the "*gen-tables.py*" Python script to do just that. Let me run the script and extract the mappings from its output:

```
C:\BatchProgramming>python gen-tables.py
:: gen_upper2lower
("A=a" "B=b" "C=c" "D=d" "E=e" "F=f" "G=g" "H=h" "I=i" "J=j" "K=k" "L=l"
"M=m" "N=n" "O=o" "P=p" "Q=q" "R=r" "S=s" "T=t" "U=u" "V=v" "W=w" "X=x"
"Y=y" "Z=z")

:: gen_lower2upper
("a=A" "b=B" "c=C" "d=D" "e=E" "f=F" "g=G" "h=H" "i=I" "j=J" "k=K" "l=L"
"m=M" "n=N" "o=O" "p=P" "q=Q" "r=R" "s=S" "t=T" "u=U" "v=V" "w=W" "x=X"
"y=Y" "z=Z")
```

With those two tables, we can now easily write the *change-str-case.bat* script:

```
:upper2lower <1=str> <2=result-var>
	setlocal

	set V=%~1

	for %%a in ("A=a" "B=b" "C=c" "D=d" "E=e" "F=f"
	            "G=g" "H=h" "I=i" "J=j" "K=k" "L=l"
	            "M=m" "N=n" "O=o" "P=p" "Q=q" "R=r" "S=s"
	            "T=t" "U=u" "V=v" "W=w" "X=x" "Y=y" "Z=z") DO (
		for /f "usebackq tokens=1,2 delims==" %%b in ('%%~a') DO (
			set V=!V:%%b=%%c! ①
		)
	)
	(
		endlocal
		set %~2=%V%
	)

	goto :eof

:lower2upper <1=str> <2=result-var>
	setlocal

	set V=%~1

	for %%a in ("a=A" "b=B" "c=C" "d=D" "e=E" "f=F" "g=G"
	            "h=H" "i=I" "j=J" "k=K" "l=L" "m=M" "n=N"
	            "o=O" "p=P" "q=Q" "r=R" "s=S" "t=T"
	            "u=U" "v=V" "w=W" "x=X" "y=Y" "z=Z") DO (
		for /f "usebackq tokens=1,2 delims==" %%b in ('%%~a') DO (
			set V=!V:%%b=%%c! ①
		)
	)
	(
		endlocal
		set %~2=%V%
	)

	goto :eof
```

The code at both markers ① used the string replacement syntax to replace the first token value with the second token value. This is akin to exchanging the uppercase character value with its lowercase counterpart (and vice versa).

Let us try both functions with the following test code:

```
@echo off

setlocal enabledelayedexpansion

set /P str=Please enter a string:

call :upper2lower "%str%" lower
echo Converted to all lowercase ^>^> %lower%

call :lower2upper "%str%" upper
echo Converted to all uppercase ^>^> %upper%
```

Let's run the script and see the output:

```
C:\BatchProgramming>change-str-case.bat
Please enter a string:Hello WORLd
Converted to all lowercase >> hello world
Converted to all uppercase >> HELLO WORLD
```

Note: Other languages (such as French) have characters with accents and you may want to include them in your mapping tables.

Extracting embedded text files

Let's suppose that your Batch file script embeds a bunch of configuration scripts used for setting up the environment. For instance, it contains: one configuration XML file, another file containing project compilation instructions, a skeleton source code file and a *Makefile*.

As part of setting up the environment, you instruct your users to run the Batch file script and it will get everything ready (create the project directory, create the *Makefile* and other files). Such a script is really handy for setting up a build system for programmers or for deploying/applying configurations and policies on behalf of system administrators.

In the following recipe, *extract-embedded-files.bat*, we are going to illustrate how to achieve that. Feel free to take a copy of the script, modify it and embed other text files inside of it.

The concept that explains how to extract text contained between two markers from a text file has been explained in one of the examples in the section entitled "Using the FINDSTR command" in Chapter 2. For this reason, I won't spend time explaining that again but instead, I will show you how to put the whole script together and then I will highlight new aspects of the script that have not been explained before:

```
@echo off

      setlocal enabledelayedexpansion
      echo Extracting all embedded files...
      call :extract-all-files ①

      goto :eof


:extract-one-by-one ②

      call :extract-embedded-file "Configuration-XML" f1.xml
      echo Return value: %errorlevel%

      call :extract-embedded-file "Readme" f2.xml
      echo Return value: %errorlevel%

      goto :eof


:extract-all-files
      setlocal
      for %%a in ( ③
            "Configuration-XML=Config.xml"
            "Readme=README.txt"
        ) do (
            for /f "usebackq tokens=1-2 delims==" %%b in ('%%~a') do (
                  set MSG=Extracting '%%b' to '%%c'...
                  call :extract-embedded-file %%b %%c ④
                  if %errorlevel% EQU 0 (
                        set MSG=!MSG!done.
                  ) else (
                        set MSG=!MSG!failed.
                  )
                  echo !MSG!
                  )
            )

    endlocal
      goto :eof


:extract-embedded-file <1=SectionName> <2=OutFile>
      setlocal

      call :get-line-no "//<Begin-%~1" "%~f0" ⑤
```

```
      set MBEGIN=%errorlevel%

      call :get-line-no "//>End-%~1" "%~f0" ⑤
      set MEND=%errorlevel%

      :: By default, we assume failure
      set err=1 ⑥

      if "%MBEGIN%"=="-1" goto :extract-embedded-file-end
      if "%MEND%"=="-1"   goto :extract-embedded-file-end

      :: Delete previous output file
      if exist "%~2" del "%~2"

      set /A C=MEND-MBEGIN-1

  for /f "useback skip=%MBEGIN% tokens=* delims=" %%a in ("%~f0") DO (
            echo %%a >>"%~2"
            SET /A C-=1
            if !C!==0 (
                  :: Success
                  set err=0 ⑦
                  goto :extract-embedded-file-end
            )
      )

      :extract-embedded-file-end
      (
            endlocal ⑧
            exit /b %err%
      )


:get-line-no <1=string> <2=file>
      for /f "useback tokens=1 delims=: " %%a in (
           `findstr /N /C:"%~1" "%~2"`) DO (EXIT /B %%a)

      EXIT /B -1
      goto :eof


//<Begin-Configuration-XML ⑨
<Provider>
   <Name>Microsoft-Windows-DesktopWindowManager-Diag</Name>
   <Metadata>
      <Guid>{31F60101-3703-48EA-8143-451F8DE779D2}</Guid>

<ResourceFilePath>C:\windows\system32\dwmcore.dll</ResourceFilePath>
```

```
<MessageFilePath>C:\windows\system32\dwmcore.dll</MessageFilePath>
        <PublisherMessage>Microsoft-Windows-DesktopWindowManager-
Diag</PublisherMessage>
    </Metadata>
    <EventMetadata>
        <Event>
            <Id>1</Id>
            <Channel>Microsoft-Windows-DesktopWindowManager-
Diag/Diagnostic</Channel>
            <Level>Information</Level>
            <Task>DesktopWindowManager_DiagStats</Task>
            <Keyword>DesktopWindowManager-WDI</Keyword>
        </Event>
    </EventMetadata>
</Provider>
//>End-Configuration-XML ⑩

//<Begin-Readme ⑨
This README file contains various information about this utility.
Please refer to the online manual for more details.
//>End-Readme ⑩

echo You can write more Batch file commands in here.
```

This is a bit of a long script because it embeds two files that will be extracted and written to disk, however its logic is simple as you shall see in the following explanation.

At marker ①, we call the "*extract-all-files*" function which will extract all the embedded files with their names encoded in the **FOR** loop at marker ③. That **FOR** loop uses the same trick we used to encode associative arrays (as described in the section "Basic data structures" in Chapter 2).

At marker ④, we call the "*extract-embedded-file*" function and pass the two necessary arguments to extract each file individually: the embedded file identifier and the output file name. At markers ⑤, form the full names of the beginning and end markers by appending the "//<Begin" and "//>End-" strings before calling the *get-line-no* function.

If you want to add more embedded files inside the script, you have to assign a unique identifier (or a string) for each file and then paste the file's contents between the following markers like this:

```
//<Begin-IDENTIFIER
File contents go here
...
//>End-IDENTIFIER
```

All the code with marker ⑨ designate the beginning of an embedded file and the code with marker ⑩ designate the end. Please note that you cannot nest embedded files: each begin and end marker must contain a single file.

At marker ⑥, the script sets the environment variable *"err"* to 1 to designate that the extract function will fail by default and succeed if it goes inside the block (at marker ⑦) when all the lines are extracted properly.

At marker ⑧, we return to the caller the result of the extraction operation in the form of an error code to be checked via the *ERRORLEVEL* pseudo-environment variable after the call.

Embedding and extracting binary files and executables

This recipe borrows a lot from the previous recipe which extracts embedded text files. Batch files are essentially text files and they do not fare well with binary content. Therefore, in order to embed binary content, we need to encode the content as text first.

To extract the binary content back again, we extract the textual representation that we previously encoded and decode it back to binary form.

If you are using Windows Vista or Windows Server 2003 and above, then your system has a utility called **`certutil.exe`** which allows you to work with certificate files ("*.cer" files). In this recipe, we will abuse this utility and have it encode an arbitrary file to base64 text and then decode it back from base64 to its binary form.

To encode a binary file, use the following syntax:

```
C:\BatchProgramming>CertUtil [Options] -encode InFile OutFile
```

And to decode a base64 encoded file, use the following:

```
C:\BatchProgramming>CertUtil [Options] -decode InFile OutFile
```

Therefore, let us encode a file, decode it and see if it decoded properly:

```
C:\BatchProgramming>certutil -encode test.exe test.txt
Input Length = 94720
Output Length = 130300
CertUtil: -encode command completed successfully.

C:\BatchProgramming>certutil -decode test.txt test.exe.1
Input Length = 130300
Output Length = 94720
CertUtil: -decode command completed successfully.

C:\BatchProgramming>FC /b test.exe test.exe.1
Comparing files test.exe and TEST.EXE.1
FC: no differences encountered
```

The encoded text file has contents similar to the following:


```
-----BEGIN CERTIFICATE-----
TVqQAAMAAAAEAAAA//8AALgAAAAAAAAAQAAAAAAAAAAAAAAAAAAAAAAAAAAAAAAA
AAAAAAAAAAAAAAAA8AAAAA4fug4AtAnNIbgBTM0hVGhpcyBwcm9ncmFtIGNhbm5v
…
…snipped…
…
8DP0M/gz/DMANAQ0CDQMNBA0FDQYNCA0UDRgNHA0gDSQNKg0tDS4NLw02DTcNAg3
CDoMOhA6FDoYOhw6IDokOig6LDo4Ojw6QDpEOkg6TDpQOlQ6xDrMOtQ63DrkOuw6
AAAAAAAAAAAAAAAAAAAAAA==
-----END CERTIFICATE-----
```


It is then evident that the start and end embedding markers are the "*-----BEGIN CERTIFICATE-----* " and "*-----END CERTIFICATE-----*" respectively.

Let us now borrow the guts of the *extract-embedded-files.bat* script and modify it so it extracts the embedded certificate text and decode it into binary form on disk. The new script*, extract-embedded-bin.ba*t, assumes that there's only one embedded encoded binary in the script and its base64 encoded text is located right past the end of the Batch file script code and occupies the remaining of the script:

```
@echo off

      setlocal enabledelayedexpansion

      set FN=test.bin
      echo Extracting embedded binary file '%FN%'
      call :extract-embedded-bin "%FN%"
```

```
	goto :eof

:extract-embedded-bin <1=OutFileName>
	setlocal

	set MBEGIN=-1
	for /f "useback tokens=1 delims=: " %%a in (
 `findstr /B /N /C:"-----BEGIN CERTIFICATE-----" "%~f0"`) DO ( ①
		set /a MBEGIN=%%a-1 ②
	)

	if "%MBEGIN%"=="-1" (
		endlocal
		exit /b -1
	)

	:: Delete previous output files
	if exist "%~1.tmp" del "%~1.tmp" ③
	if exist "%~1" del "%~1" ④

 for /f "useback skip=%MBEGIN% tokens=* delims=" %%a in ("%~f0") DO ( ⑤
		echo %%a >>"%~1.tmp"
	)

	certutil -decode "%~1.tmp" "%~1" >nul 2>&1 ⑥
	del "%~1.tmp" ⑦

	endlocal
	exit /b 0
```


```
-----BEGIN CERTIFICATE-----
TVqQAAMAAAAEAAAA//8AALgAAAAAAAAAQAAAAAAAAAAAAAAAAAAAAAAAAAAAAAAA
AAAAAAAAAAAAAAAA8AAAAA4fug4AtAnNIbgBTM0hVGhpcyBwcm9ncmFtIGNhbm5v
dCBiZSBydW4gaW4gRE9TIG1vZGUuDQ0KJAAAAAAAAACd3fm32byX5Nm8l+TZvJfk
Nstl5M68l+Q2y2bk0LyX5DbLZOSuvJfkBENc5Nq8l+TZvJbkjbyX5DTrlOXJvJfk
xDDMMNQw3DDkMOww9DD8MAQxDDEUMRwxJDEsMTQxPDFEMUwxVDFcMWQxbDF0MXwx
…snipped…
RDJMMlQyXDJkMmwydDJ8MoQyjDKUMpwypDKsMrQyvDLEMswy1DLcMuQy7DL0Mvwy
BDMMMxQzHDMkMywzNDM8M0QzTDNUM1wzZDNsM3QzfDOEM4wzlDOcM6QzrDO0M7wz
AAAAAAAAAAAAAAAAAAAAA==
-----END CERTIFICATE-----
```

And the explanation of the annotated code is as follows:

1. **FINDSTR** is used to find the encoded text start. Notice how I used the "/B" switch to ensure that we only match the lines that begin with the marker and not those who contain the marker (such as the code at marker ① itself).
2. The line where the marker is found is saved. We want to remember the encoding marker start so we decrement the returned line number (because the "SKIP" option of the "**FOR /F**"' keyword is 1-based).
3. The extracted text goes to the output file name with a ".tmp" extension appended.
4. The output file name itself is used to store the binary (and not the decoded text).
5. Keep extracting all the encoded lines all the way down to the end of the script.
6. Execute the **certutil** utility to decode the ".tmp" file into the destination file accordingly.
7. Clean up the ".tmp" file.

That's it! Now we have extracted the embedded binary file.

Embedding foreign scripts inside your Batch file script

Often times, it is easier to set up a build environment using Batch files prior to executing a Perl, Python, PowerShell or a Jscript script.

The following sub-sections illustrates how to embed those languages in your Batch files. The Batch file script will do any pre-tasks (setting up the environment, etc.), bootstrap the embedded script by calling the appropriate interpreter command and do post-tasks if needed.

Embedding Python code in your Batch file script

It is possible to have a hybrid script that is first executed as a Batch file script, and then as a Python script. To achieve this, we rely on two tricks.

The first trick is to rely on Python's "-x" command line switch which allows the Python interpreter to ignore the first line. On the first line, which will be ignored, we will turn off the command echo.

The second trick relies on using the **REM** keyword on the second line to create a multi-line Python comment (**HEREDOC** style). Inside the Python comment, which will be ignored, the Batch file script will set up the environment (if needed) and then invoke Python.

Here's the *batch-python.bat* script:

```
@echo off ①
rem = """ ②
:: Anything Batch file goes here but will be ignored by Python
python -x "%~f0" %* ③
exit /b %errorlevel% ④
:: End of batch file commands
""" ②
⑤
# Anything here is interpreted by Python
import platform
import sys

print("Hello world from Python %s!\n" % platform.python_version())
print("The passed arguments are: %s" % sys.argv[1:])
```

Let me explained how the annotated Batch file script code above works:

1. Turn the command echo off. Because we will be launching Python with the "-x" switch (at marker ③), we don't need to worry if this first line contains an invalid Python syntax.
2. Use the **REM** keyword to create a Batch file script comment.
3. This line invokes the Python interpreter with the "-x" switch while passing the fully qualified Batch file script path (using *%~f0*) as the input script along with all the passed arguments (using "*%**").
4. Use the "**EXIT /B**" command to exit the Batch file script with the same exit error code (denoted in the *ERRORLEVEL* pseudo-environment variable) returned by the Python script. If you don't care about the exit error code, you may equally use "**GOTO :EOF**" to exit the Batch file.

Note that at marker ③, we assume that the Python interpreter is in the *PATH* environment variable. If Python was not in the *PATH* environment variable, then you can use the following syntax to attempt to find the default installation path of the Python interpreter:

```
for /l %%n in (24,1,31) do if exist c:\python%%n\python.exe (
c:\python%%n\ python -x "%~f0" %*)
```

Because the code at marker ③ invoked the Python interpreter, the input file will be interpreted as Python syntax. Let me now explain the code markers once more, when the script is executed as a Python script:

At marker ①, the line is skipped because Python was launched with the "-x" switch.

At marker ②, we define the variable "*rem*" to be equal to all the lines following the initial three quotes until their occurrence again a few lines later. All the lines inside the triple quotes are part of the "*rem*" variable and do not do anything meaningful in Python. Please refer to the **HEREDOC** syntax in the Python language. With this variable assignment trick, we discarded all the Batch file commands that would have caused syntax errors if they were interpreted by Python.

From marker ⑤ and onwards, the code is solely Python syntax. Let's execute the script with some arguments and observe the output:

```
C:\BatchProgramming>batch-python.bat arg1 arg2 arg3
Hello world from Python 3.4.2!

The passed arguments are: ['arg1', 'arg2', 'arg3']
```

Notice how Python picked up all the parameters that were passed to the Batch file script as if they were passed directly to the Python script itself!

Embedding JScript code in your Batch file script

Jscript is Microsoft's implementation of ECMAScript. The Jscript interpreter engine can be invoked and used using the Windows Script Host (**WScript.exe** or **CScript.exe**) from the command line.

To embed the Jscript in the Batch file, we rely on Jscript's conditional compilation syntax. The conditional compilation concept is similar to that of the C language's conditional preprocessor directives (the **#ifdef** and **#endif**).

Jscript's conditional compilation syntax is as follows:

```
@if CONDITION …
…
@elif CONDITION
…
@else
…
@end
```

<u>Note:</u> the "@elif" and "@else" are optional.

It so happens that in the Batch files scripting language, the "@" sign is used to turn off the command echo. Similarly, the **IF** keyword is valid in both languages. Voila! That's all we need to write a polyglot script.

Let's illustrate how to write such a polyglot script (*batch-jscript.bat*):

```
@if (1 == 0) @end /* ①
@echo off ②
cscript.exe /E:jscript /nologo "%~f0" %* ③
goto :eof */ ④
⑤
WScript.Echo("Hello world from Windows Scripting Host!");

for (var i=0, c=WScript.Arguments.length;i<c;i++)
{
      WScript.Echo("Arg:" + WScript.Arguments(i));
}
```

Here's the explanation of the annotated code:

1. Use the conditional compilation with a condition that is never satisfied. This line is a valid syntax in both languages. We cut the conditional compilation condition short by ending it on the same line with the "*@end*" keyword. On the same line, we also start a multi-line comment using Jscript's syntax. The multi-line comment starts with "/*" and ends with "*/" (just like in the C language).
2. From the Batch file script's perspective, this line and all the subsequent lines until the end of the multi-line comment (at marker ④) are going to be executed. However, from Jscript's perspective, all the lines inside the multi-line comment (from the end of the line at marker ① until marker ④) are ignored.
3. Invoke "cscript.exe" and specify the Jscript engine with the "/E" switch. Also pass the fully qualified Batch file script path along with all the passed arguments.
4. Exit the Batch file script.

When marker ③ invokes "**cscript.exe**", the Jscript interpreter will skip over marker ① which is a conditional compilation statement that does nothing and will also skip over the multi-line Jscript comment that ends at marker ④. From marker ⑤ and onwards, all the code is interpreted as a Jscript syntax.

Embedding Perl code in your Batch file script

In this recipe, I will illustrate how to embed Perl code inside your Batch file script. We also rely on the "-x" switch from the Perl's command line interpreter which is similar to Python's "-x" switch but with slight difference: it will let Perl ignore all lines until it reaches a line starting with "#!" and containing the word "Perl".

Here's the script (*batch-perl.bat*):

```
@echo off ①
perl -x "%~f0" %* ②
goto :eof ③

#!perl ④
print "Hello world from Perl!\n";

my $i = 1;
foreach my $arg(@ARGV) {
        print "Argument #$i: $arg\n";
        $i++;
}
```

Here's the explanation of the annotated code:

1. This line and all subsequent lines until marker ④ will be skipped due to launching the Perl interpreter with the "-x" at marker ②.
2. Launch the Perl interpreter with the "-x" switch and pass the fully qualified path name of this Batch file script, also pass all the arguments (with "%*").
3. Terminate the Batch file script. At this point, you may optionally exit the Batch file script with the same error code returned by the interpreter using the "**EXIT** /B %ERRORLEVEL%" command.
4. This is the special marker that tells the Perl interpreter that the Perl code is to be found in the subsequent lines.

Another simple variation of the script above is to put the Perl script immediately after the first line, and then use the *__END__* token to mark the logical script end as follows (*batch-perl-end.bat*):

```
@goto runperl
#!perl
print "Hello world from Perl!\n";

my $i = 1;
foreach my $arg(@ARGV) {
        print "Argument #$i: $arg\n";
        $i++;
}
```

```
__END__
:runperl
@perl -x "%~f0" %*
```

Embedding PowerShell code in your Batch file script

PowerShell is a powerful scripting language used for automating administrative tasks among other things. Additionally, it has access to the .NET Framework, the WMI and COM.

To run a PowerShell script, we need to ensure that the execution policy is properly set, otherwise you won't be able to run PS scripts:

```
C:\Windows\system32>powershell
Windows PowerShell
Copyright (C) 2015 Microsoft Corporation. All rights reserved.

PS C:\Windows\system32>Set-ExecutionPolicy Unrestricted
```

Once the policy is set, you can run PowerShell scripts. I will be presenting two methods on how to embed PowerShell scripts inside Batch file scripts.

Method 1 – Using "findstr" and piped input

The premise of this method is that we can launch PowerShell and have its input script piped from another command's output.

Here's a simple demonstration:

```
c:\>echo Write-Host Hello from PowerShell | powershell -
Hello from PowerShell
```

> *Note: Notice the trailing dash character ("-"). This tells PowerShell to read the script from the standard input.*

All we did in the code snippet above is pipping the **`Write-Host`** PowerShell command using the **`ECHO`** keyword to the PowerShell interpreter.

Now to generalize this method, we need to pipe a complete script to PowerShell minus all the Batch file commands.

To make things simple, we will prefix all the Batch file script lines with the "@" symbol (which omits the command echo) and the only Batch file command we will use is the invocation of the

"**FINDSTR**" command with the proper regular expression to filter out the Batch file script lines (*batch-powershell-1.bat*):

```
@findstr /v "^@findstr.*&" "%~f0" | powershell - & goto:eof

Write-Host Hello from PowerShell!
```

By invoking the **FINDSTR** command with the "/v" switch, we are telling it to print all lines except those that match the provided regular expression. The regular expression in question means: "find all lines that start with '@findstr', followed by any other characters and containing the ampersand character thereafter". Therefore, since we print all the lines except for the Batch file script lines, then only the PowerShell lines are piped to the PowerShell interpreter.

After all the output from **FINDSTR** is piped to PowerShell, it will consume that output as input and then terminate. When PowerShell terminates, we are back to Batch files scripting syntax. The script then issues the "**GOTO :eof**" statement to terminate the Batch file script before it has a chance to fall-through and attempt to execute the subsequent lines (which are PowerShell lines).

One shortcoming of this method is that we cannot pass command line arguments to it.

Method 2 – Using PowerShell itself to filter out the Batch files syntax

This method has the same logic as the previous method, however it allows you to pass arguments and relies on PowerShell alone. I found it in an MSDN blog post by Jay Bazuzi here:

> *http://blogs.msdn.com/b/jaybaz_ms/archive/2007/04/26/powershell-polyglot.aspx*

The *batch-powershell.bat* script illustrates how to have an embedded PowerShell script inside of it:

```
@@setlocal
@@set POWERSHELL_BAT_ARGS=%* ①
@@if defined POWERSHELL_BAT_ARGS set
POWERSHELL_BAT_ARGS=%POWERSHELL_BAT_ARGS:"=\"% ②
@@PowerShell -Command Invoke-Expression $('$args=@(^&{$args}
%POWERSHELL_BAT_ARGS%);'+[String]::Join(';',$((Get-Content '%~f0') -
notmatch '^^@@'))) & goto :EOF ③

# Anything from this line and on is PowerShell
Write-Host Hello from PowerShell!
Write-Host The passed arguments are: $args
```

Let me explain how this script works:

1. Take all the arguments and store them in an environment variable.
2. Escape the quotes with a backslash using the string substitution syntax.
3. Run PowerShell and use **`Invoke-Expression`** to start an expression:
    a. First, the expression creates an array (called *$args*) containing all the arguments passed to the Batch file script.
    b. The second expression reads the contents of the input Batch file ("%0") while filtering out all lines that begin with "@@". Since the "@" character means do not echo the command, we can safely use them to mark any number of Batch file script lines we need in our script logic.
    c. Because of the latter, all the other lines (not beginning with "@@") will be passed to PowerShell.

Let's try the script:

```
C:\BatchProgramming>batch-powershell.bat hello world
Hello from PowerShell!
The passed arguments are: hello world
```

Embedding any other script in your Batch file

Let us conclude this recipe by explaining how to embed just any other script in the Batch file itself and have the appropriate interpreter consume the embedded script. This generic method should work even if the interpreter in question does not have any means (like Python's or Perl's "-x" switch) to facilitate such tasks.

The general premise of the approach is to extract the embedded input script to a temporary file, pass it to the program that can interpret it and then delete the temporary file. For this recipe, we will use a simplified logic from the previous recipe entitled "Extracting embedded text files", however we will put the embedded script at the end of the script and only use the begin marker.

This is how the Batch file script logic along with the embedded foreign script would look like:

```
@echo off
Batch File Script code:
  Extract embedded file to temp
  Run associated interpreter against the temp file
  Clean up temp file
EmbeddedFileMarker-Begin
Embedded script
...
END OF FILE
```

In the following recipe, I will embed a simple "Hello World" *COMPEL* script in the *batch-compel.bat* Batch file script.

> *Note: COMPEL is a less known open-source interpreter language that is designed to be taught to anyone with no or little programming background. You can find more about it here:*
>
> *http://lallouslab.net/2014/08/29/introducing-compel-a-command-based-interpreter-and-programming-language/*

Here's the script source code:

```
@echo off

setlocal enabledelayedexpansion

set LINENO=-1
FOR /f "useback tokens=1 delims=: " %%a in (`findstr /N
/C:"$$EMBEDDEDSCRIPT$$" "%~f0"`) DO SET /A LINENO=%%a ①

if "%LINENO%"=="-1" ( ②
      echo Error: No embedded script found!
      exit /b -1
)

set TEMPFN=%TEMP%\%~0%RANDOM%.compel ③
(
      FOR /F "useback skip=%LINENO% delims=" %%a in ("%~f0") DO (
            echo %%a
      )
) >%TEMPFN% ④

ccompel %TEMPFN% ⑤

if exist %TEMPFN% del %TEMPFN% ⑥

goto :EOF

$$EMBEDDEDSCRIPT$$ ⑦
var $msg "Hello world from COMPEL!"
echo "$msg"
```

The annotated code is explained as follows:

1. Find the embedded script marker. Usually it is after the Batch file code's end (at marker ⑦).
2. If no marker was found, then exit with error.
3. Generate a temporary file name and remember it in the *TEMPFN* variable.
4. Open the currently executing Batch file (*%~f0*), skip *LINENO* lines and start displaying each line. Since the output is grouped, it will all be emitted at once to the *TEMPFN* script file (using the output redirection syntax).
5. Run the interpreter "*ccompel*" on the newly generated temp file that contains the embedded script.
6. Delete the temporary embedded script file that was saved into *TEMPFN*.
7. This is where we put the embedded script marker. Prior to the marker, all the lines were Batch file script syntax, and following that marker all the syntax is a COMPEL syntax.

Embedding an FTP script

It is very common to embed FTP scripts in your Batch file. Let us modify the script above starting from marker ⑤ and onwards, like this (*batch-ftp.bat*):

```
ftp -s:"%TEMPFN%" ftp.microsoft.com ⑤'

if exist %TEMPFN% del %TEMPFN% ⑥'

goto :EOF

$$EMBEDDEDSCRIPT$$ ⑦'
anonymous
ebooks@passingtheknowledge.net
cd Products/mspress/library
ls
quit
```

The new marker ⑤ executes the built-in command **`FTP.exe`** while passing the "-s" script that designates the FTP script to execute after connecting to the host. The first two lines following marker ⑦ are the username and password used to login, and then they are followed by a series of commands and finally the "quit" command to disconnect from the FTP server and terminate the **`FTP.exe`** program and return back to the Batch file script.

Let us execute the script, *batch-ftp.bat*, and observe the output:

```
C:\BatchProgramming>batch-ftp
Connected to ftp.microsoft.akadns.net.
220 Microsoft FTP Service
200 OPTS UTF8 command successful - UTF8 encoding now ON.
User (ftp.microsoft.akadns.net:(none)):
331 Anonymous access allowed, send identity (e-mail name) as password.

230-Welcome to FTP.MICROSOFT.COM. Also visit
http://www.microsoft.com/downloads.
230 User logged in.
ftp> cd Products/mspress/library
250 CWD command successful.
ftp> ls
200 PORT command successful.
125 Data connection already open; Transfer starting.
ANIMAT.ZIP
index.txt
MEMLOG.ZIP
MFCANIM.ZIP
NAVDEMO.EXE
rkhelp.exe
rktools.exe
SHOWPAL.ZIP
splitter.zip
226 Transfer complete.
ftp: 116 bytes received in 0.01Seconds 12.89Kbytes/sec.
ftp> quit
221 Thank you for using Microsoft products.

C:\BatchProgramming>
```

This concludes the recipes about embedding other script files inside Batch file scripts.

Getting files information

In this section, I will be showing a few recipes that show you how to retrieve file information using: the arguments and **FOR** keyword variables modifiers, the **FORFILES** command, and tokenizing the output of other commands.

Please refer to the "Command line arguments and FOR loop variables modifiers" in Chapter 1.

Getting file's last modification time

File time can be retrieved with the "**%~tN**" modifier (where *N* is the argument number).

The *get-ftime.bat* script illustrates how to achieve that:

```
@echo off

setlocal

       if "!%1"=="" (
              echo Please pass a file name
              goto :eof
       )

       call :get-file-ftime %1 ftime
       echo file time is = %ftime%

       goto :eof


:get-file-ftime <1=filename> <2=result-var>
       set %~2=%~t1
       exit /b 0
```

In order to get the file's last modification time including the seconds, you can use the **FORFILES** command. The script *get-ftime-secs.bat* illustrates this:

```
@echo off

setlocal
       if "!%1"=="" (
              echo Please pass a file name
              goto :eof
       )

       call :get-file-ftime %1 ftime
       echo file time is = %ftime%

       goto :eof


:get-file-ftime <1=filename> <2=result-var>
       setlocal
       set P=%~dp1 ①
       set P=%P:~0,-1% ②
       for /f "usebackq tokens=* delims=" %%a in ( ③
```

```
    `forfiles /P "%P%" /M "%~nx1" /c "cmd /c echo @ftime"`) DO ( ④
                endlocal
                set %~2=%%a
    )
    exit /b 0
```

At marker ①, we use an intermediate environment variable (called *P*, short for path) to store the drive and path parts of the passed file name (using both the modifiers "d" and "p"). Note that the "p" modifier (of the "%~dp1" modifier) always returns the path including the trailing backslash ("\").

The **FORFILES** will fail when the value passed to its "/P" switch contains a trailing backslash. Therefore, the code at marker ② removes the trailing backslash using the substring syntax.

In the "FORFILES command" section of Chapter 2, I already mentioned that you should use the "cmd /c" prefix along with some form of output tokenization in order to pass information between **FORFILES** and its caller. This is precisely what the code at markers ③ and ④ are doing.

Getting file's attributes

A file's attributes can be retrieved with the "**%~aN**" modifier. The *get-fattr.bat* script shows how to achieve that:

```
@echo off

setlocal

    if "!%1"=="" (
        echo Please pass a file name
        goto :eof
    )

    call :get-file-attr %1 attr
    echo file attributes are: %attr%

    goto :eof


:get-file-attr <1=filename> <2=result-var>
    set %~2=%~a1
    exit /b 0
```

Getting a file's size

To return the size of a file using a Batch file script, we can use the "**%~zN**" modifier. The *get-fsize.bat* script illustrates how to achieve that:

```
@echo off

setlocal

      if "!%1"=="" (
            echo Please pass a file name
            goto :eof
      )

      call :get-file-size %1
      echo file size = %errorlevel%

      goto :eof


:get-file-size <1=filename>
      exit /b %~z1
```

I use the "**EXIT /B** ExitCodeValue" keyword to directly return the size in the exit code. The caller picks it up from the **%ERRORLEVEL%** pseudo-environment variable.

Triggering a command when files are modified in a directory

This is a useful recipe if you want to monitor file system changes in a given directory and then when any change takes place, then a Batch file script will be invoked. Common actions to take when file system changes are detected are:

- Invoking the compiler to re-compile the sources automatically.
- Launching automatic backups.
- Running a deployment script.
- Etc.

The following steps best describe the logic behind writing this script:

1. On the script's start, take account of all the files information into a state file. This is our baseline file that we want to use to compare against a freshly computed state file. The captured file information includes the following attributes: file size, last modification date, file name.

2. Enter a loop and wait for a few seconds on each iteration and then repeat the following steps:
    a. Take account of all the files information into a state file.
    b. Compare the baseline state with the current state file from the previous step.
    c. If we detect any differences between those two state files, then that means file system changes took place → trigger the desired command.
    d. Replace the baseline state with the actual state that was computed in the step above.
    e. Loop again.

Let's first write a function that captures the files state information in a given directory (and optionally its sub-directories):

```
:Get-State <1=WatchPath> <2=OutStatFileName> <3=ExtraSwitches>
        setlocal
        set P=%~dp1 ①
        set P=%P:~0,-1% ①
        ②
        forfiles /p "%P%" /m *.* %~3 /c "cmd /c echo @relpath @ftime
@fdate @fsize @isdir" >%~2

        endlocal
        goto :eof
```

The *Get-State* function takes three parameters: the directory to watch, the output file name to hold the files state information and the third argument contains a free-style value that will be passed to the **FORFILES** command.

At code markers ①, we get rid of the trailing backslash from the passed path and at marker ② we invoke the **FORFILES** command. We pass the "cmd /c" as the command to execute and then echo enough information that we want to include in the state file. Most importantly, we output the "*@ftime*" which, unlike the **FOR** variable modifier "*%~tN*", it also includes the seconds and not just the hour and minute of the file modification time.

The second part of the script is the actual directory watch loop. The *Watch-Loop* function will keep looping while waiting for file system changes:

```
:Watch-Loop <1=WatchDir>
        call :Get-State "%~1" "%BASEFILE%" %Watch-Recursive% ①

        :: Make a choice that times out.
        choice /t %WatchInterval% /c:qc /d c >nul ②
        if !errorlevel!==1 goto :eof ③
```

```
call :Get-State "%~1" "%CURFILE%" %Watch-Recursive% ④

:: Compare
fc "%BASEFILE%" "%CURFILE%" >nul ⑤
if "%errorlevel%"=="1" ( ⑤
   echo Changes detected on %DATE% %TIME%
   if exist "%~dp1trigger.bat" call "%~dp1trigger.bat" ⑥
   )

:: Set baseline to be the current state
move "%CURFILE%" "%BASEFILE%" >nul ⑦
goto Watch-Loop ⑧
```

The *Watch-Loop* function takes one explicit argument which is the directory path to watch. However, it expects other environment variables to be set a priori by the caller:

- *BASEFILE* → Contains the temp file name that holds the baseline state information.
- *CURFILE* → Contains the actual state information (it is computed per iteration).
- *WatchInterval* → User controlled watch interval in seconds. When the interval elapses, the loop wakes up, checks for modification and then sleeps again.
- *Watch-Recursive* → A switch specifying whether to watch recursively or not.

At marker ①, the function starts by capturing the baseline state. At marker ②, we use the **CHOICE** command to wait for the 'Q' key press with a timeout and default choice. If the user presses the 'Q' key, then it returns from the script and thus stopping the watch loop (marker ③). If, on the other hand, the **CHOICE** command times out, then the loop continues normally.

At marker ④, after the interval has elapsed, we compute the state once more into the *CURFILE* state file.

At this point we have two states: *BASEFILE* state (taken before the time interval has elapsed) and the *CURFILE* state (taken afterwards). We assume that in between this time interval the watched directory's contents might have changed.

At marker ⑤, we use the **FC** command to compare the two state files. The **FC** command returns an *ERRORLEVEL* value of 0 if no difference is found and returns 1 otherwise. That's why, if the *ERRORLEVEL* is 1, then at marker ⑥ we call the *trigger.bat* script which resides in the watched directory. The *trigger.bat* script may contain any user code that shall be executed whenever file system changes are detected.

At marker ⑦, we update the baseline state file by replacing it with the last state we computed. Finally, at marker ⑧, the watch loop starts all over again.

Now that we have all the prerequisite core functions, the only thing that is left is the driver function that parses the command line arguments and kicks off the logic:

```
        setlocal enabledelayedexpansion

:main
        if "%1"=="" goto Usage ①
        if "%2"=="" goto Usage ①

        :: Copy the watch interval
        set /A WatchInterval=%~2 ①

        :: Set default interval to 5 seconds
        if WatchInterval==0 set WatchInterval=5 ①

        :: Set the recursive switch
        if /i "%3"=="/S" set Watch-Recursive=" /S " ①

        :: Generate temp files
        set BASEFILE=%TEMP%\B%RANDOM%_%RANDOM%.txt ②
        set CURFILE=%TEMP%\C%RANDOM%_%RANDOM%.txt ②

        set /p "=Watching the directory %1 every %2 second(s) " <nul
        if DEFINED Watch-Recursive echo ^(recursively^)
        echo.
        echo Press 'Q' to quit at any time.

        call :Watch-Loop "%~1" %~2 ③

        :: Cleanup
        del %BASEFILE% /q >nul 2>&1 ④
        del %CURFILE% /q >nul 2>&1 ④
        goto :eof
```

The main function simply parses the arguments (markers ①), prepares two temporary file names (marker ②), enters the watch loop (marker ③) and cleans up before quitting (marker ④).

Let's test this script:

```
C:\BatchProgramming>watch-dir c:\temp\sync-dir 5 /s
Watching the directory c:\temp\sync-dir every 5 second(s) (recursively)

Press 'Q' to quit at any time.
Changes detected on Mon 04/17/2017 12:17:58.07

C:\BatchProgramming>
```

While the script was running, I went ahead and modified one of the files inside the watched directory. The script has successfully detected the changes as you can see from the output. To conclude my test, I then pressed "Q" to abort the script and return back to the command line prompt.

Can you modify the script so it emits the file names that were modified, deleted or added?

Get the version string of MS Windows

You can use the **VER** command to get the version of Windows like this:

```
C:\BatchProgramming>ver

Microsoft Windows [Version 10.0.10240]

C:\BatchProgramming>
```

However, to get the version string and not the version number, you can use the "**NET CONFIG WORKSTATION**" command like this:

```
C:\>net config workstation
Computer name                        \\PC01
Full Computer name                   PC01
User name                            user1

Workstation active on
        NetBT_Tcpip_{11107838-8111-1111-1111-111111111111} (000C11811111)

Software version                     Windows 10 Pro

Workstation domain                   DOMNAME
Logon domain                         PC01

COM Open Timeout (sec)               0
COM Send Count (byte)                16
```

```
COM Send Timeout (msec)                 250
The command completed successfully.
```

The command above outputs a lot of information, however we are only interested in the "Software version" line. It is a simple matter of calling this command again combined with the **FINDSTR** command like this:

```
C:\>net config workstation | findstr /C:"Software version"
Software version                         Windows 10 Pro

C:\>
```

And finally, to get the software version value alone, we can use the **FOR** keyword to tokenize the output.

Let's write a small script, *get-win-ver.bat*, to illustrate the whole process:

```
@echo off
setlocal

      call :get-ver vername

      echo Windows version is: "%vername%"
      goto :eof


:get-ver -> %result-var%
      for /f "usebackq tokens=3*" %%a in (`net config workstation ^|
findstr /c:"Software version"`) DO (
            set %~1=%%a %%b
      )
      goto :eof
```

Creating a compressed archive containing all your version controlled source files

In this recipe, let's assume that *Git* is the source control versioning system that you are using. Now let's assume that you want to compress all the tracked files into a single archive and then backup the archive file, how can you do that?

Git offers such a functionality natively (check the "**GIT ARCHIVE**" command reference) however, it limits your choices of the archivers that can be used: it only supports the *zip* or *tar* file formats.

What if you want to use the *Rar* file archiver (http://www.rarlabs.com) and password protect your archive for example? What if you want to do some pre-processing on the file list before archiving them? What if instead of compressing the files, you want to copy them to some other location (say a Dropbox folder for cloud syncing)? Etc.

This recipe serves as a model script that will give you some ideas on how to achieve this goal or solve other similar problems.

To begin with, we have to ask *Git* to give us a list of tracked files:

```
C:\BatchProgramming>git ls-files
.gitignore
Script.bat
File1.bat
...
```

The output of this command returns all the tracked files. We can then capture that list into a text file and then use that file as a response file and pass it to the *Rar* archiver:

```
C:\BatchProgramming>rar.exe a archive.rar @response.txt
```

The syntax above uses the "a" command to create an archive, followed by the archive file name, then the "@" symbol to specify the response file (a file containing a list of files to be archived).

> *Note: You can also pass the "-p" switch to the RAR archiver to specify a password for your archive.*

The *pack-tracked.bat* script illustrates how to do this:

```
@echo off

setlocal enabledelayedexpansion

set L=rarlst.lst
set A=archive.rar

if exist %A% del %A%
git ls-files >%L%

"c:\Program Files\WinRAR\rar.exe" a %A% @%L%

if exist %L% del %L%
```

If you need to exclude some tracked files from being compressed, then you can pipe the "git ls-files" output to the "FINDSTR /V" command before redirecting the output to the response file.

Parsing INI files

If you are an administrator, you may want to write a Batch file script that is driven by a configuration file. A simple and powerful configuration file format is the MS Windows INI file.

An INI file is a text file that has the following format:

```
; Comment
[Section Name]
Key1=Value
Key2=Value
; Comment
[AnotherSection]
Key3=Value
Key4=Value
```

All comment lines start with a semicolon character. Sections are enclosed between the open and closed square brackets ("[" and "]"). Inside each section, there is a set of key/value pairs separated by the equal sign ('=").

> *Note: refer to the Wikipedia entry here: https://en.wikipedia.org/wiki/INI_file for more information about the INI file format.*

There are various ways to read INI files using a Batch file script however, I will use a longer and easy to understand logic in order to exercise your Batch file scripting skills.

First, let me explain the logical steps that will be used to write the script:

1. Open the file and start reading it line by line. If a line starts with a semicolon, then skip that line
2. If a line starts with the open square bracket ("["), then:
    a. Tokenize that line with "[" and "]" as delimiters. This allows us to retrieve the section name.
    b. Compare the section name against the section we are looking for. If we find that section, then set a flag to remember that we are now inside the body of section in question.

3. If we encounter the open square bracket ("[") while still inside a previous section, the function should stop parsing and return a failure. This means we are entering a new section and have reached the end of the current section without finding the key in question.
4. If we are inside an INI section already (we can tell that by using a flag variable), then start parsing all the key/value pairs:
    a. Tokenize each line using the "=" as a delimiter.
    b. Compare the first token (the key) against the desired key.
    c. If we find the right key, then return the value back to the caller and exit the function.
5. The function keeps looking for a matching section and key name. If the file end is reached without meeting this condition, then the function fails and returns an empty result.

The following script below is one way to implement the algorithm we just described (*parse-ini.bat*):

```
:get-ini <arg1=filename> <arg2=section> <arg3=key> <arg4=result>
       set %~4=
       setlocal
       set insection=

       for /f "usebackq eol=; tokens=*" %%a in ("%~1") do ( ①
              set line=%%a ②

              rem We are inside a section, look for the right key
              if defined insection ( ③
               rem Let's look for the right key
               for /f "tokens=1,* delims==" %%b in ("!line!") do ( ④
                          if /i "%%b"=="%3" ( ⑤
                                 endlocal ⑥
                                 set %~4=%%c ⑦
                                 goto :eof ⑧
                          )
                    )
              )

              rem Is this a section?
              if "!line:~0,1!"=="[" ( ⑨
                    for /f "delims=[]" %%b in ("!line!") do ( ⑩
                          rem Is this the right section?
                          if /i "%%b"=="%2" ( ⑪
                                 set insection=1 ⑫
                          ) else (
```

```
                                   endlocal
                                   if defined insection goto :eof ⑬
                              )
                         )
                    )
          )
endlocal
```

Now, let me explain the annotated code from the script above:

1. Open the INI file, grab all tokens and skip comment lines. Use the "eol" option to easily skip the comment lines.
2. Take the line and store it in an environment variable so we can use the substring functionality to check if the line starts with an open square bracket. This helps us to determine whether the line marks an INI section beginning or not.
3. If we are in a section already, then start looking for the right key.
4. Parse the "key=value" lines.
5. Check (case insensitive equality) if we matched the right key.
6. Restore the environment block with **`ENDLOCAL`**. This gets rids of our temporary work variables.
7. Pass the parsed value to the caller.
8. Return to the caller.
9. Use sub-string and check if this is a section beginning.
10. Extract the section name by tokenizing the section line.
11. Is this the section in question?
12. Set a flag to signal that we are now inside the section in question.
13. If we were previously in the right section, then no need to continue parsing the file when we encounter another section, just return to caller.

Let us use the *settings.ini* INI file as a test file:

```
; the display settings
[display]
width=400
height=400

; recent files
[files]
file0=c:\temp\test.txt
file1=c:\temp\prog.pas
file3=c:\temp\duqu.asm

; general settings
[settings]
autosave=true
lastsaved=04/17/2015
```

To test our script, we can use the following:

```
@echo off

:main
      setlocal enabledelayedexpansion

      call :get-ini settings.ini display height result

      echo r=%result%

      call :get-ini settings.ini settings lastsaved result
      echo r=%result%

      goto :eof
```

When we run the script, we observe the following output:

```
C:\BatchProgramming>parse-ini
r=400
r=04/17/2015
```

> *Note: the parse function and the driver program all reside in the same file. You may use the technique used in the section entitled "Building, testing and using a utility Batch file script library" from Chapter 3 to learn how to extract the function into a reusable library.*

One last thing to mention before concluding this recipe is that you can improve this code by using the **FINDSTR** utility with the "/L /B /N" switches to quickly locate the beginning of the INI file section, and then start the **FOR** loop with the "SKIP=StartOfIniSection" option to start parsing directly from that section's beginning.

Please see the previous recipe called "Extracting embedded text files" in this chapter for more information on how to use this technique.

Interactive Batch file scripts

Interactive Batch file scripts come in handy when your script does not know about all the needed input and requires to interact with the user. Interactivity may also come in handy when your script has multiple functionality and you want your user to select which functionality to carry.

In essence, the interactivity comes from the fact that we can display a prompt text and then wait for input from the users. That's all there is to it.

To make interactive Batch file scripts more user friendly and more maintainable, programmers spend time thinking about how to best design the code and how to present the prompts to the user on the screen.

Questions such as the following may arise:

1. How many menu items should the script present?
2. Should there be nested menu screens or just a single long menu list?
3. Should colors be used to decorate the prompt screens?
4. Should the menu choices be hardcoded in the Batch file script itself or read from an external configuration or menu file?
5. Etc.

There is no single answer to all those questions above: programming is a matter of experience and presentation is a matter of taste. For this reason, I will simply show you a couple of programming practices and design choices and leave it up to you to adopt or create any style you may see fit.

Before we begin, let me quickly recap some of the commands that I will use to achieve interactivity:

- **CHOICE** → This command allows the script to ask the user to press a key and make a choice. The prompt will not go away unless the user breaks the script (with Ctrl-C) or enters a valid choice.

- **TITLE** → This command is used to change the title of the command prompt. It is nice to change the console window title to display the progress of your script as it runs.
- **SET /P** → This is used, as you have seen before, to prompt for a text from the standard input.
- **CLS** → This is used to clear the screen. It is nice to clear the screen when switching from a menu screen to another.
- **COLOR** → Allows you to change the console window colors.
- **MODE** → This command can be used to adjust the console window dimensions.

Simple menus

Let's get started by illustrating how to build a very simple menu. The idea is to display the choices text, wait for the input from the user, execute the selected choice and starts over again. Keep repeating all the previous steps until the user chooses to quit.

The code to display the menu, prompt the user and then dispatch the chosen command looks like this:

```
:: Draw the menu
:Show-menu
      ①
      echo.
      echo ---------------------------
      echo Interactive Batch file v1.0
      echo ---------------------------
      echo.
      echo 1. Display processes
      echo 2. Kill processes
      echo 3. Other
      echo Q. Quit
      echo.
      ②
      choice /C:123Q /M "Please choose an action: " ③
      echo.

      if %errorlevel%==1 call :Display-processes ④
      if %errorlevel%==2 call :kill-processes ④
      if %errorlevel%==3 call :Other ⑤

      if %errorlevel%==4 goto Quit ⑥

      goto Show-menu ⑦
```

All the code lines between marker ① and marker ② simply display the choices text. By convention, the first letter of the choice text is the menu/choice key. The code at marker ③ invokes the **CHOICE** command with the "/C" switch followed by all the letters in the menu. The "/M" is used to display the prompt text.

> *Note: It is very common in interactive Batch file scripts to clear the screen with the **CLS** command each time the menu screen is displayed (markers ①).*

After the **CHOICE** command is executed, the *ERRORLEVEL* pseudo-environment variable is updated with the choice key index. By "index" I mean the position of the choice key in the "/C:" choice list.

For instance, if we launched the **CHOICE** command with the "/C:HKGT" switch, then the *ERRORLEVEL* with value 1 corresponds to the choice "H", the *ERRORLEVEL* with value 2 corresponds to the choice "K", etc.

At the code markers ④ and ⑤, we check each *ERRORLEVEL* value and then **CALL** the proper handler label. We could equally use the **GOTO** keyword as long as the destination label jumps back to the *Show-Menu* label.

At marker ⑥, we use the **GOTO** keyword to go to the *Quit* label which will terminate the script instead of looping again as does the code at marker ⑦.

The following are the menu handlers which are called from the code at marker ④:

```
:: Display all the processes that match a criteria
:Display-processes
      setlocal
      set /p m=Enter process name (with extension):
      tasklist /FI "IMAGENAME EQ %m%"
      endlocal
      echo.
      pause
      goto Show-menu

:: Kill processes
:Kill-Processes
      setlocal
      set /p m=Enter process partial name (extension not needed):
      choice /C:YN /M:"All processes matching %m%* will be terminated.
Are you sure?"
      if %errorlevel%==1 (
            taskkill /im * /f /fi "imagename eq %m%*"
            pause
```

```
    )
    endlocal
    echo.
    exit /b 0
```

Unlike the two previous handlers, the code handler for the label *Other* (called from marker ⑤) displays a sub-menu. That would be a nice example to show you that it is possible to have an unlimited level of menus and sub-menus:

```
:: Sub menu
:Other
    echo -------
    echo Options
    echo -------
    echo (C) Change console color
    echo (D) Change console window dimensions
    echo (R) Run administrative prompt
    echo.
    echo (B) ^<-- Go back
    choice /c:CDRB /m "Please choose an option:"

    if %errorlevel%==1 call :Change-Color
    if %errorlevel%==2 call :Change-Dimensions
    if %errorlevel%==3 (
        start "" runas /user:Administrator cmd.exe
    )

    exit /b 0


:Display-Colors-Numbers
    for /l %%a in (0, 1, 7) do (
        color /? | findstr /C:"%%a = "
    )
    exit /b 0

:Change-Dimensions
    setlocal
    set /p lines=Enter desired number of lines:
    set /p cols=Enter desired number of columns:
    mode con: cols=%cols% lines=%lines%

    endlocal
    exit /b 0

:Change-Color
    call :Display-Colors-Numbers
```

```
        setlocal
        set /P bg=Select background color number:
        set /P fg=Select foreground color number:
        :: Just take a single digit
        set bg=%bg:~0,1%
        set fg=%fg:~0,1%

        color %bg%%fg%
        endlocal
        exit /b 0
```

In this sub-menu, we applied the same logic as the main menu: display the menu, prompt for a choice, dispatch and repeat.

At marker ⑥, we handle the quit script case. The *Quit* label simply waits 5 seconds and then terminates the script:

```
::
:: Quit menu
:Quit
        echo Thanks for using the Interactive Batch file^!
        echo.
        set /p "=This script will terminate in 5 seconds"<nul
        for /l %%a in (1, 1, 5) do (
                set /p "=." <nul ①
                timeout /t 1 >nul ②
        )
        exit /b 0 ③
```

Note: At marker ①, we use a trick to display a dot without also emitting a new line. At marker ② we wait one second. When ① and ② are repeated 5 times, we get 5 dots displayed on the same line each displayed one second apart. That's a nice visual progress indicator that you can use elsewhere in your scripts.

Please note that even though the *Quit* label ends with an "**`EXIT /B`**" (at marker ③), it will not return to the caller because it was never called (see marker ⑦).

You can find this script's complete source code in the *menu-simple.bat* file.

Dynamic menus

In the example above, we illustrated a very simple and basic way to build an interactive Batch file script.

Adding, moving and updating menus (menu display text, menu labels and choice letters) is a tedious task especially if you have a lot of menu items. Luckily, there's a nice and elegant way to manage and maintain menus as I shall show you in this recipe.

The idea behind this concept is to be able to figure out what are the menu items directly from the Batch file script itself, render the menu dynamically, prompt the user for an action, dispatch the action and go back to the menu screen.

To achieve this, we need a method to encode the menu information inside the Batch file directly. Therefore, we can achieve that goal if we follow a convention. I chose to describe each menu item using a label that has a unique name prefix, followed by a dash and the choice letter, then by the menu display text.

It will be easier to understand what I mean if I showed you an example:

```
:MyMainMenu-A Show app store apps ①
      tasklist /apps
      echo.
      pause
      exit /b 0

:MyMainMenu-D Display date/time ②
      echo %DATE% %TIME%
      echo.
      pause
      exit /b 0

:MyMainMenu-B Launch web browser ③
      start http://www.passingtheknowledge.net/
      exit /b 0

:MyMainMenu-Q Quit ④
      echo Thanks for using this script!
      echo.
      pause
      call :TermScript 2>nul
```

The unique label prefix is "*MyMainMenu*", the choice letters are "A", "D", "B", and "Q" for markers ① to ④ respectively. Because the space character can never be part of the label name, anything after the label name is a free-style text. Remember, we previously used this convention throughout the book to create comments or to describe function "prototypes".

We now have defined the three most important aspects that constitute a menu:

1. The menu text
2. The menu choice letter
3. The menu handler label

Let's construct a function that parses the Batch file script looking for the three needed pieces in order to build the menus accordingly:

```
:: Build the menu
:Build-Menu <1=Menu-Prefix> <2=MenuVar-Out>
        set nmenu=1 ①
        for /F "tokens=1*" %%a in ('findstr /c:":%~1-" /b "%~f0"') do ( ②
                set Menu-%~2-N[!nmenu!]=%%a ③
                set Menu-%~2-Text[!nmenu!]=%%b ④

                set /A nmenu+=1 ⑤
        )

        set /a Menu%~2=%nmenu%-1 ⑥
        set nmenu=

        :: Return the number of menu items built
        exit /b %nmenu%
```

The *Build-Menu* function takes two arguments: the menu prefix and an output variable name that will hold the necessary parsed menu information. Additionally, it uses data structure concepts already explained earlier in this book (in the "Basic data structures" section in Chapter 2) therefore, I won't be explaining those concepts again here.

To begin with, the function uses the *nmenu* variable as a menu items counter (marker ①). Then at marker ②, the script looks for all the lines that denote a label that matches the label prefix value passed by the caller. It uses the **FINDSTR** syntax, please see the "Extracting embedded text files" recipe.

The code at marker ③ creates a 0-based array of the form "*Menu-XXX-N[]*" that holds the target label.

The code at marker ④ creates another 0-based array of the form *"Menu-XXX-Text[]"* that holds the menu's text. Before the loop iterates again at marker ⑤, the *nmenu* counter is incremented once.

Lastly, at marker ⑥, the function stores the 0-based total count of the parsed menu items in a variable of the form *"MenuXXX"*. It is stored as 0-based because the count value will be used with the "**FOR /L**" syntax which includes the upper bound value in its counting.

Now that we are done with parsing the menu, let us test this function:

```
:: Build the menu one time
call :Build-Menu "MyMainMenu" MainMenu
```

These will be the newly created environment variables that hold the necessary parsed menu information:

```
Menu-MainMenu-N[1]=:MyMainMenu-A
Menu-MainMenu-N[2]=:MyMainMenu-D
Menu-MainMenu-N[3]=:MyMainMenu-B
Menu-MainMenu-N[4]=:MyMainMenu-Q
Menu-MainMenu-Text[1]=Show app store apps
Menu-MainMenu-Text[2]=Display date/time
Menu-MainMenu-Text[3]=Launch web browser
Menu-MainMenu-Text[4]=Quit
MenuMainMenu=4
```

Now the next step is to render that menu on the screen and display the proper choice prompt. The function *Display-Menu* will handle that:

```
:: Show a menu
:Display-Menu <1=MenuVar-In> <2=Prompt-Text> <3=Dispatch-Label-Out>
      setlocal
      set choices= ①
      for /l %%a in (1, 1, !Menu%~1!) do ( ②
       for /f "tokens=2 delims=-" %%b in ("!Menu-%~1-N[%%a]!") do ( ③
                   set choice=%%b ④
                   set choices=!choices!!choice! ⑤
            )
            echo ^!choice!^) !Menu-%~1-Text[%%a]! ⑥
      )
      choice /C:%choices% /M "%~2" ⑦
      (
            endlocal
            set %~3=!Menu-%~1-N[%errorlevel%]! ⑧
            exit /b 0
      )
```

The *Display-Menu* function takes three arguments: the menu variable name that was created using the *Build-Menu* function, the prompt text that will be passed to the **CHOICE** command with the "/M" switch and the last argument which is an output argument that will hold the target label associated with the choice the user picked.

This function uses the *choices* variable (defined at marker ①) to hold all the choice letters encountered so far while it displays the menu text.

The code at ②, starts a zero based **FOR** loop to iterate through all the menu items using both of the arrays: *Menu-XXX-N* and *Menu-XXX-Text*.

At marker ③, we tokenize the items from the *Menu-XXX-N* array in order to extract the choice letter and at marker ④, we remember the choice letter in the *choice* variable. We then append it to the *choices* variable at marker ⑤.

At marker ⑥, we display the menu choice letter followed by the actual menu text. After the loop finishes and all the menu items have been displayed, the code at marker ⑦ displays the choices with the **CHOICE** command and passes the appropriate choice letters (contained in the *choices* variable) and the choice prompt text (the second argument).

After the user makes the choice selection, the code at marker ⑧ uses the *ERRORLEVEL* pseudo-environment variable value as an index and retrieves the actual label target form the *Menu-XXX-N* array.

Let me now illustrate how to use the two functions (*Build-Menu* and *ShowMainMenu*) together:

```
:Main
       :: Build the menu one time
       call :Build-Menu "MyMainMenu" MainMenu

:ShowMainMenu
       echo.
       echo ------------------
       echo Dynamic menus app
       echo ------------------
       echo.
       call :Display-Menu MainMenu "Please make a selection" R1

       call %R1%

       goto ShowMainMenu
```

And the output would look something like this:

```
C:\BatchProgramming>menu-dynamic

------------------
Dynamic menus app
------------------

A) Show app store apps
D) Display date/time
B) Launch web browser
Q) Quit
Please make a selection [A,D,B,Q]?
```

In conclusion, as I said before, building an interactive Batch file script is a matter of style and choice (pun intended). I hope that the two techniques illustrated above will help you in writing your own interactive Batch file scripts. You may find the source code used in this recipe in the *menu-dynamic.bat* script file.

Time for fun - Let's play hangman!

What is better than concluding this book by designing and implementing a game?

If you have not played the Hangman game before, let me quote this explanation from Wikipedia:

> *The word to guess is represented by a row of dashes, representing each letter of the word. In most variants, proper nouns, such as names, places, and brands, are not allowed. If the guessing player suggests a letter which occurs in the word, the other player writes it in all its correct positions. If the suggested letter or number does not occur in the word, the other player draws one element of a hanged man stick figure as a tally mark.*

Let me break down all the needed logical steps we need in order to build the game code:

1. We need to be able to pick a word from a given words list file at random. Each time we start a new game, a new random word should be picked. For this, we need a file containing a list of words. The words in the list could all follow a common theme. For instance: one words file can contain the name of all the countries, another could be a list of animal names, and another the name of all the world capitals, etc.

2. We need to be able to draw the hangman stick figure in progression. Each time the player misses a guess, more of the hangman stick should be drawn. When the player has no more tries then all of the stick figure should be drawn, thus signaling the end of the game.
3. We need to be able to prompt the player for letters and if any of the letters exist, then we should reveal all those letters in the word that the player is trying to guess.
4. The final step is to put all the pieces together and write the game loop.

These are all the steps we need to be able to code the game using the Batch files scripting language. I will address each step separately and explain how to write the appropriate Batch file script functions accordingly.

Step 1 – Reading a random word from the list file

Let's assume you have compiled a words list file. In this example, I have compiled a list of the 300 most difficult SAT words. I took the list from https://www.vocabulary.com/lists/191545.

Now we need to figure out how to get a random line from a text file. To achieve that, we need to generate a random number between 1 and the total lines count in the words list file. Since it is tedious and slow to count the lines in the words list file each time we run the game, let us agree to put a special marker character at the end of the words file.

Here's the partial listing of the words list file (*words-sat300.txt*) that I will use for this game:

```
abject
aberration
…
utilitarian
…
zephyr
wily
tirade
#
```

Please note the "#" at the end of the file. With the presence of this marker, we can easily use **FINDSTR** with the "/N" switch to get the last line number:

```
C:\BatchProgramming>findstr /N /B "#" words-sat300.txt
301:#
C:\BatchProgramming>
```

We can then tokenize the output and parse the first token to get the total lines count.

Finally, we can use the *%RANDOM%* pseudo-environment variable with the **SET /A** syntax to do a modular arithmetic and retrieve a random number between 1 and the total lines count. If *MAXLINES* was the variable containing the maximum lines count (including the "#" marker), then the formula would be:

```
SET /A RANDLINE="1 + (%RANDOM% %% (MAXLINES-1))"
```

Now that we have a random line number, we can use the **FOR /F** syntax with the "SKIP" option to go to the desired line and return it.

However, there are two catches we need to be mindful of:

1. The formula above always adds 1 to the *RANDLINE* variable and therefore forcing us to always skip one line. This means we will never get the first line in the words list file.
2. We cannot use the option "SKIP=0" because it is a syntax error.

To address those two issues, we will conditionally omit the "SKIP" option if the *RANDLINE* variable was 0, and we will no longer add 1 to the *RANDLINE* calculation. Hence, we will now generate numbers from 0 to *MAXLINES-1* (exclusive).

Here's the whole function that retrieves a random line from a given file:

```
:get-random-line <1=filename> <2=result-var>
        setlocal enabledelayedexpansion
        set MAXLINES=-1
for /f "useback tokens=1 delims=:" %%a in (`findstr /N /B /C:"#" "%~1"`)
DO (
set MAXLINES=%%a
)

        if %MAXLINES% EQU -1 (
        echo Error: the words list file %1 does not end with the "#"
marker!
                call :TermScript 2>nul
        )

        :: Draw the random line a few times to increase randomness
        set /a i=0
        :get-random-line-rnd
                SET /A RANDLINE="(%RANDOM% %% (MAXLINES-1))"
                set /a i+=1
                if %i% NEQ 3 goto get-random-line-rnd

        if %RANDLINE% EQU 0 (SET SKIPSTX=) ELSE (
              SET SKIPSTX=skip=%RANDLINE%
        )
```

```
        :: Skip some lines and return a single line (a word)
        for /f "usebackq %SKIPSTX% delims=" %%w in ("%~1") DO (
                endlocal
                set %~2=%%w
                exit /b 0
        )
:TermScript
if
```

That was the first step! Let us now write the function that draws the stick figure in progression.

Step 2 - Drawing the hangman stick figure

This part is really easy, it is like doing ASCII art. Let's assume we will allow the player at most 5 tries before ending the game, therefore we need 5 individual drawings for each number of tries exhausted so far. We also need an additional step that draws no stick figure at all; that will be used at the beginning of the game.

Depending on the number of tries used so far, we draw one of the 5 following stick figures:

```
:draw-hangman <1=steps>

        if "%~1" EQU "0" (
                echo.
                echo.
                echo.
                echo.
                echo.
        )

        if "%~1" EQU "1" (
                echo       (o.o^)
                echo.
                echo.
                echo.
                echo.
        )

        if "%~1" EQU "2" (
                echo       (o.o^)
                echo.        ^|
                echo.     ___^|
                echo.
                echo.
        )
```

```
if "%~1" EQU "3" (
        echo        (o.o^)
        echo.         ^|
        echo.      ___^|___
        echo.
        echo.
)

if "%~1" EQU "4" (
        echo        (o.o^)
        echo.         ^|
        echo.      ___^|___
        echo.         ^|
        echo.        /
)

if "%~1" EQU "5" (
        echo        (o.o^)
        echo.         ^|
        echo.      ___^|___
        echo.         ^|
        echo.        / \
)

exit /b 0
```

Depending on the number of steps passed to the function, then the corresponding stick figure will be drawn. When we pass the number 5, then the whole stick figure is drawn and this is when we signal to the player that the game is over!

> *Note: We had to escape the closing parenthesis ")" and the pipe characters "|".*

Step 3 – Prompt and reveal

In this final step, we need to prompt for a letter, then reveal all the matching letters contained in the random word.

For example, if the random word was: "hello". When the game starts, nothing is revealed, and thus we display: "_____". If we prompt the player and we get the letter "L" then we reveal that letter and display: "__ll_". If we get the "h" in a subsequent prompt, we reveal the following: "h_ll_". We keep doing this process until either the number of wrong guesses is exhausted or there are no more letters to reveal (in that case the player has won).

To keep the implementation of such logic simple, I will keep another word of the same length containing either 0 or 1 that denote whether the character is revealed or not at a given letter position in the word.

For example:

```
batch ← the word
00000 ← the bits indicating the revealed letters
_____ ← text to display: nothing is revealed
```

Now, let's reveal the letter "b":

```
batch ← the word
10000 ← the bits indicating the revealed letters
b____ ← text to display: the letters revealed so far
```

Now, let's reveal the letters "t" and "h":

```
batch ← the word
10101 ← the bits indicating the revealed letters
b_t_h ← text to display: the letters revealed so far
```

Etc.

The first function we need to create is the *init-word-bits* function that creates a bit string with equal length of the word that we want to gradually reveal. We will make use of the *str-len* function that we covered in an earlier chapter.

```
::
:: Initialize the word bits. Create the corresponding empty bits
::
:init-word-bits <1=word> <2=wordbits-var>
      setlocal enabledelayedexpansion
      set Word=%~1
      set WordBits=

      call :strlen "%Word%"
      set /a len=%errorlevel%-1
      for /L %%i in (0, 1, %len%) DO (
            set Word_I=!Word:~%%i,1!
            if "!Word_I!"==" " (set Bit_I=1) else (set Bit_I=0) ①
            set WordBits=!WordBits!!Bit_I! ②
```

```
    )
    ( ③
            endlocal
            set %~2=%WordBits%
            exit /b 0
    )
```

A few things to note at the annotated code:

1. After computing the string's length, scan each character in the string and automatically mark as revealed (with the bit value of "1") all the space characters. Mark as hidden all the other characters (with the bit value of "0").
2. Concatenate the corresponding reveal bit value to the *WordBits* variable.
3. End the localization in a compound statement and return to the caller the corresponding *WordBits*.

Now let us create the actual *reveal-letters* functions:

```
::
:: Reveal letters in a word
::
:reveal-letters
:: Args:
::      <1=Word-Val>                The value of the word
::      <2=WordBits-Var-InOut>      WordBit variable name
::      <3=Letter-Val>              The letter to reveal
::      <4=NewWord-Var-Out>         Variable to hold the revealed word
::  Returns:
::      Number of newly revealed letters

      setlocal enabledelayedexpansion

      :: Get the input string length
      set Word=%~1
      call :strlen "%Word%"
      set /A WordLen=%errorlevel%-1

      :: Get the current revelation bits
      set Bits=!%~2!

      :: Reset internal variables
      ①
      set NewBits=
      set NewWord=
      set /A NbReveal=0

      :: Scan and reveal
```

```
    for /L %%i in (0, 1, %WordLen%) DO ( ②

        :: Take the revealed letter
        set Word_I=!Word:~%%i,1! ③

        :: Take the current revelation bit
        set Bit_I=!Bits:~%%i,1! ③

        :: Not previously revealed?
        if !Bit_I! EQU 0 ( ④
            :: Check whether to reveal
            if /I "%~3"=="!Word_I!" ( ④
                set Bit_I=1 ⑤
                set /A NbReveal += 1
            ) ELSE (
                set Word_I=_ ⑥
            )
        )
        :: Form new revelation bits and word
        set NewBits=!NewBits!!Bit_I! ⑦
        set NewWord=!NewWord!!Word_I! ⑦
    )
    (
        endlocal
        set %~4=%NewWord% ⑧
        set %~2=%NewBits% ⑧

        exit /b %NbReveal%
    )
```

I tried to do my best to keep the logic easy to understand (but not necessarily the most optimal).

Here's the explanation of the annotated code:

1. Use the *NewBits* and *NewWord* variables to hold the values of the revealed bits and word respectively.
2. Loop for each character in the string. Use the 0-based loop because the string substring operation uses 0-based indexes. This explains why I stored the string length minus one into the *WordLen* variable.
3. For convenience, take a copy of both the letter and the bit at the position of the index *i*.
4. Check if the letter has already been previously revealed. We do that by checking if the bit at the index *i* is zero. If it was not, then we compare the player's passed letter with the letter at the current index *i*.

5. If the letter matches, then we should mark the bit position at the index *i* with the value "1" so it gets revealed. We also increment the *NbReveal* count as well.
6. If the letter to be revealed did not match the current letter in the word at index *i*, then we should not reveal the real letter, but instead we should reveal the underscore ("_") character.
7. Keep forming (using the concatenation syntax) the new word bits and the new word at each iteration.
8. After the loop is over, return the new bits and the revealed word to the user.

Let's test this function along with the *init-word-bits* function and see how they behave:

```
::
:: Test letter revelation functions
::
:test-reveal-letters
     setlocal
     set word=hello Elias
     echo The word is: '%word%'
     call :init-word-bits "%word%" bits ①
     echo InitBits=%bits%

     call :reveal-letters "%word%" bits _ rev ②
     echo Reveal nothing = %rev%

     call :reveal-letters "%word%" bits l rev ③
     echo Reveal 'l' = %rev%

     call :reveal-letters "%word%" bits e rev ④
     echo Reveal 'e' = %rev%

     call :reveal-letters "%word%" bits h rev ⑤
     echo Reveal 'h' = %rev%
```

We use this simple test function to exercise the *init-word-bits* function once and the *reveal-letters* a few times to reveal the letters in progression.

At marker ①, we initialize the word bits for the string "hello Elias". We receive the "*bits*" variable as a return value. It should be a string composed of 11 zero bits.

At marker ②, we pass the underscore letter to be revealed. This will not match in the input word and therefore we will get nothing revealed in the *rev* variable! That's a good way to display the initial guess prompt.

At markers ③, ④ and ⑤ we reveal the letters "l", "e", and "h" respectively.

Let's observe the output below. I have used the same annotations for the output as I did for the code above to help you directly link the source code and its corresponding output:

```
The word is: 'hello Elias'
InitBits=00000100000 ①
Reveal nothing = _____ _____ ②
Reveal 'l' = __ll_ _l___ ③
Reveal 'e' = _ell_ El___ ④
Reveal 'h' = hell_ El___ ⑤
```

Step 4 – Putting it all together

This is the final and most rewarding step because we will see the game in action. Without all the prerequisite steps from before, we would not be able to glue those functions together and write the main game driver code.

The game starts by picking a random word from the words file. It then enters a loop and prompts the player for characters to reveal. The loop will keep repeating as long as you are guessing correctly or you have exhausted the number of tries:

```
:PlayGame
      :PlayGame-Again
      call :get-random-line words-sat300.txt word ①

      call :Game %Word% ②
      choice /c:yn /m "Do you want to play more?" ③
      if "%ERRORLEVEL%" EQU "1" goto PlayGame-Again ④

      goto :eof
```

To keep it simple, I broke the logic in two parts. The above code is solely responsible for picking the random word (marker ①), calling the *Game* function (marker ②) and then asking the player (marker ③) whether to play again or not (marker ④).

The code below deals with the actual game logic. It takes a single argument which is the word to guess in the form of the hangman game:

```
:Game <1=WordToGuess>
      setlocal enabledelayedexpansion

      :: Reset the retries counter
      set /a MAX_TRIES=5
      set /a NbTries=0 ①
```

```
:: Initialize the word
set Word=%~1

:: Initialize the word bits
call :init-word-bits "%Word%" WordBits ②

:: Reveal nothing
call :reveal-letters "%Word%" WordBits _ RevealedWord ③

:Game-Letter-Loop
       cls ④
       call :draw-hangman %NbTries% ⑤

       :: Did we exhaust all the tries?
       if !NbTries! EQU !MAX_TRIES! ( ⑥
              echo.
              echo Game over^^! The word was: '%Word%'^^!
              echo.
              exit /b 0
       )

       ECHO Guess: %RevealedWord%

       :: Did we reveal all the letters?
       if /I "!Word!"=="!RevealedWord!" goto Game-Finished ⑦

       :: Take a single letter
       SET /P Letter="Enter a letter: " ⑧
       SET Letter=!Letter:~0,1! ⑧

       set OldBits=!WordBits!
 call :reveal-letters "%Word%" WordBits !Letter! RevealedWord ⑨

 :: If nothing was revealed then decrease the number of tries
       if !OldBits!==!WordBits! SET /A NbTries+=1 ⑩

       :: Repeat
       goto :Game-Letter-Loop ⑪
```

We start the game loop by initializing the number of tries, *NbTries*, to 0 at marker ①. We then create the word bits as the *WordBits* variable (marker ②).

At marker ③, we compute the initial string to reveal into the *RevealWord* variable. The initial reveal word is entirely consisted of the "_" letters. Afterwards, we will enter the game loop.

Marker ④ designates the start of the *Game-Letter-Loop* label. In the loop, during each iteration, we clear the screen (with **CLS**) each time we prompt for a character in order to give the impression that the stick figure is getting updated rather than being totally re-drawn. At marker ⑤, we draw the stick figure using the *draw-hangman* function based on the number of tries exhausted so far.

At marker ⑥, we quit the game and tell the player that s/he lost the game if the number of tries are equal to or exceed 5. While on the other hand, at marker ⑦, we check if the revealed word matches the word to be revealed. If both the revealed word (*RevealWord*) and the picked random word (*Word*) match, then that means that the player guessed the word correctly and has won this round.

At marker ⑧, we prompt for a string but then only take the first letter. At marker ⑨, we try to see if the letter exists in the word and then reveal the letters using the *reveal-letter* function accordingly. Marker ⑩ checks the result of the function call to determine if any new letter has been revealed or not and then increments the number of failed tries accordingly.

Finally, at marker ⑪, we loop again and repeat the process all over again starting at marker ④.

Here's how the game output looks like after 4 wrong tries and 4 correctly revealed letters:

```
     (o.o)
       |
    ___|___
       |
      /
Guess: p_o_l____y
Enter a letter:
```

Eventually, I lost game and failed to guess the word properly after 5 tries:

```
     (o.o)
       |
    ___|___
       |
      / \

Game over! The word was: 'proclivity'!

Do you want to play more? [Y,N]?
```

Let's run the game and win this time:

```
    (o.o)
      |
   ___|___


Guess: prurient

Good job!

Do you want to play more? [Y,N]?
```

I won! Well...not really: I cheated using *GodMode* actually. I'll leave it to you to read the source code of the script and figure out how to enable that cheating mode!

Conclusion

That's it! You have reached the end of this book but not the end of the learning journey. You can now officially call yourself a Batchographer!

We covered a great deal of Batch files scripting topics. Here's brief recap of all what was covered in this book:

- In Chapters 1 and 2, I explained the Batch files scripting language features, syntax, its basic and advanced uses. Topics such as conditional statements, repetition control structures, standard input/output redirection and pipes, string manipulation and data structures were covered.
- In Chapter 3, I covered more theoretical and high-level concepts. I also showed important tips and tricks such as coding conventions, writing Batch file scripts libraries, testing Batch file scripts and how to debug and troubleshoot your scripts.
- Chapter 4 concludes this book by putting everything you learned so far together in the form of scripts or recipes. Each recipe had two goals: to show you how to solve a technical problem and to further enhance your understanding of the language.

It is my hope that you now feel confident about the Batch files scripting language and can solve day to day technical problems by easily putting a script together.

The Batch files scripting language is not fully documented and users will keep discovering new tricks that can be used in this language. If enough people read this book, show interest and send me feedback, then I will keep this book up to date so it always remains a comprehensive reference.

Finally, I hope you enjoyed reading this book as much I enjoyed writing it. Please feel free to reach out and share your comments and suggestions at the PassingTheKnowledge.net website or via email at ebooks@passingtheknowledge.net.